The
Surrealist Mind

THE
SURREALIST MIND

J. H. Matthews

Selinsgrove: Susquehanna University Press
London and Toronto: Associated University Presses

Associated University Presses
440 Forsgate Drive
Cranbury, NJ 08512

Associated University Presses
25 Sicilian Avenue
London WC1A 2QH, England

Associated University Presses
P.O. Box 39, Clarkson Pstl. Stn.
Mississauga, Ontario
Canada L5J 3X9

The paper used in this publication meets the requirements
of the American National Standard for Permanence of Paper
for Printed Library Materials Z39.48-1984.

Library of Congress Cataloging-in-Publication Data

Matthews, J. H.
    The surrealist mind / J. H. Matthews
        p.   cm.
    Includes bibliographical references.
    ISBN 0-945636-06-7 (alk. paper)
    1. Surrealism.   2. Arts, Modern—20th century.   I. Title.
NX456.5.S8M38   1991
700'.9'04—dc20   88-43398
                                                            CIP

For Stephen Robeson Miller

For his loyal friendship

Contents

Foreword: John H. Matthews and Surrealism   9
Acknowledgments   12

1 A Surrealist Mind?   15
2 The Automatic Principle: Why Write?   31
3 The Critical Reception: What Is Poetry?   58
4 Surrealist Poetry in Writing and Painting   81
5 Painting in the Surrealist Mind   99
6 Creativity and Criticism   119
7 The Critical Example: André Breton on Painting   146
8 Perspectives on the Avant-Garde   164
9 "A Certain Point of the Mind"   186
Conclusion   207

Notes   222
Bibliography   228
Index   231

Foreword: John H. Matthews and Surrealism

John H. Matthews has been one of the most prodigious of critical writers in the American university community in the quarter century since the appearance of his first work on surrealism, *An Introduction to Surrealism*. His successive publications added up to eighteen books on surrealism alone at the time of his death. They won him world-wide recognition. He left two more manuscripts behind him, which have become his legacy to the readership of his longtime odyssey into the multidirectional domain of this major artistic, literary, and ideological movement. Two months before Matthews died an accidental death—trying to pull his car out of a snow bank in the Lake Placid area where he had his home—he had invited me to lecture on his campus at Syracuse University. As we sat there after the lecture in his office, with a wall-to-wall array of surrealist books as a background, we compared notes and reminisced on his outwardly quiet life and his turbulent, unrelenting quest for ever more insights into the surrealist movement which, as we both believed, had made every other modern trend pale in contrast. I wondered how this self-motivated, self-disciplined, vigorous man, many years my junior, combining scholarly qualities with an artistic temperament, had achieved such a monumental corpus, and I speculated on how much more he was likely to contribute in this inexhaustible field, to which he and I were so dedicated and that many presumably learned twentieth-century specialists chose to ignore.

If the power of the pen can make the work survive after its creator has been felled, J. H. Matthews's writings will long and uninterruptedly grace our libraries and hold their place on our bookshelves, sparking the minds of new readers in whom he will, generation after generation, arouse an unquenchable thirst to know more and more about the spectacular surrealists who stirred their own generation out of intellectual torpor, but who have been minimized in most American college curricula.

Curiously, had J. H. Matthews never written a single line on surrealism but conformed to the more popular choices of

9

literary studies of his time, he would have had enough of a
scholarly production to become an esteemed academic for his
extensive and original work on Maupassant, Zola, Céline, and
other realist and naturalist novelists. For these accomplishments
he would have received at his retirement a well-deserved fest-
schrift from his colleagues as the standard academic recognition.

Instead, he moved into a totally different area with his writings
on surrealism in literature, art, and the cinema. To be able to
encompass such a wide range, and keep in balance so many
literary and artistic differences within the broader similarities,
was a veritable *tour de force*. He was a formidable intellect
and at the same time possessed an exhuberant empathy with
the writers and artists who provided him with the desire and
incentive to be so productive. His own energy and vigilance
matched the spirit of surrealism and reflected the dynamic character of the vast body of literature he knew from every angle.
His commentary, thoroughly documented and in every case
comprehensive, traced the surrealist impact in every genre: the
novel, theater, cinema, photography, philosophy as well as the
principal one of poetry.

Not only did he write more extensively on surrealism than
any other critic of our era, he made surrealist writing accessible
to the general public in well selected and readable form. I am
thinking of his two anthologies that constitute the mainstay
of initiation into surrealist studies. One covers the classic poetry
of surrealism; the other, a prose collection called *The Custom
House of Desire*, is a treasure trove the like of which is not
yet available in the original French that he so painstakingly
translated. These judiciously chosen materials resulted from his
assiduous search into unknown editions and publications out
of print. The interest these lost works command shows how
worthwhile their retrieval has been. This anthology will be increasingly appreciated, as the sampling of the lost work included
leads the reader into further discoveries. Moreover, his choice
of texts manages to avoid the kind of idiosyncracies that so
often mar such anthologies.

In his comprehensive study of surrealism, Matthews brings
to light many of the neglected surrealists such as Benjamin Péret,
of whose colorful life he gives a striking picture, Jean Mayoux,
who was both an artist and a poet, and the Egyptian Anglo-
French Joyce Mansour. For these and others he plays the media-
tory role in helping them reach a public they might otherwise

never have known in the academic world and in the circles of the new American poets.

Of his two posthumous works, one is in an area most appropriate for current reception: a long line of photographers who performed as surrealist artists through the medium of film, used along the same lines as canvas—as a locus of provocative mediation between the artist's inner models and the noncommital world outside. The other, the current publication, most befittingly entitled *The Surrealist Mind*, shows how after having probed the gamut of the surrealist galaxy John H. Matthews reached its quintessence.

For the twenty-first century, Matthews's work of patient, expert scholarship, personal contacts with many of the people he wrote about, and an impelling power of communication will be a link with an upheaval in the arts resulting from a new way of perceiving the life experience that he will have kept alive and distinct among the miscellany of books of a century that has written too much.

The reason for Matthews's total and sometimes lonely involvement in this unique research and critical writing is inherent in *An Introduction to Surrealism*. We should be reminded of his initial statement about surrealism as we read his ultimate work: "Man must seek and find his freedom now; he must establish a sense of discovery, revelation and conquest, which Surrealism claims can come only from within man himself." If we substitute the name of Matthews for the word "Surrealism" in the quotation we have the perfect statement of this writer's credo which he incorporated in his own work. The secret is that he possessed the wherewithal to live by that credo: his total love for his wife, Jeanne, the courage of independent thinking, and close touch with nature on the shores of Lake Placid.

No better epitaph could be found for John H. Matthews than the one he chose in his dedication of his book on Benjamin Péret to surrealist E. F. Granell:

"A bon entendeur salut."

ANNA BALAKIAN

Acknowledgments

There are many whom my husband would wish to acknowledge for the help given to him when he was writing this book,
however, I am not fortunate enough to have those names. I
can therefore only offer thanks and appreciation to those who
have helped and encouraged me to pursue my goals to get this,
one of the two last manuscripts that J. H. Matthews wrote before his tragic death in February of 1987, into print. I am indebted to the following for their support and encouragement:
Anna Balakian, Jon Graham, Stephen Robeson Miller, Les Starks,
David Wiley of the Susquehanna University Press, and Mareille
Rainbow-Vigourt. Without these people, this book would proba-
bly have never been published. Thank you.

JEANNE BROOKS MATTHEWS

The
Surrealist Mind

1
A Surrealist Mind?

By and large, the critics have treated surrealism in a manner fluctuating between condescension and hostility, open or veiled. Evidently an affirmation by the French surrealists' principal spokesman, André Breton—that criticism is a form of love—has failed to elicit an echo in most commentary dealing with surrealism. Antagonism has proved to be a remarkably consistent reaction, as though anything short of severity were not merely indicative of undue sympathy but already proof of submissiveness, surrender of critical faculties, and hence inexcusable capitulation to surrealist demands.

Listening to objections impugning the integrity of surrealism, one very soon realizes that, to many observers, even postulating the existence of a surrealist mind is tantamount to betraying unwarranted tolerance, not to say incipient conversion to surrealist beliefs. Such a judgment harks back to the early days of surrealist militancy in the 1920s, when it seemed to critics, watching what the surrealists were doing in Paris, reading the texts they wrote, and looking at their paintings, that the only responsible reaction was protest against apparently haphazard violations, in surrealism's name, of moral, ethical, and aesthetic codes consecrated by Western art, culture, and literature.

Does anything less than condemnation of surrealism mark failure by the critics to fill their role, to do what we are entitled to expect of them? Surrealism's noteworthy tenacity, its survival for half a century and more, demonstrates the absurdity of such a question. Many people have been and continue to be willing to grant that surrealism deserves better than dismissal as impertinent, as an unwelcome hiatus in the aesthetic and cultural evolution of the twentieth century. Yet in these same people, caution or residual mistrust often breeds reluctance to credit the surrealists with a program unified enough to incite one to speak of a surrealist mind, worth examining with some care. To these individuals the very idea of discussing the surrealist

mind appears debatable, since it entails looking for serious and
coherent motives behind theoretical positions and expressive
modes they can neither take seriously nor credit with coherence.
No doubt, most would agree that it is an exaggeration to say
that probing the surrealist mind brings one up against mindless-
ness. Even so, the surrealists' reputation for being adamant opponents of reason does predispose many to resist the thought that
a mental posture distinctive of surrealism merits consideration.
    The hypothesis that one may learn to understand surrealism
better when approaching it by way of an examination of characteristics of the surrealist mind surely will not go unchallenged
by everyone opening this book. Far from admitting to prejudice,
skeptical readers may feel that their response is amply justified
and the author must pay a price for attempting to develop an
indefensible paradox. Is the idea of a surrealist mind not only
pretentious but actually misplaced? By merely entertaining that
idea is one not conceding more than circumstances warrant,
raising surrealism above the rank to which it belongs? In the
eyes of more than a few observers, certainly, one can safely
(and accurately) refer to a surrealist mind only as a contradiction
in terms, a paradox that must collapse of its own weight, so
bearing out preconceptions regarding the nature and meaning
of surrealism which they see no occasion to dispute.
    Why is so much resistance displayed to the thought of a surre-
alist mind? An answer begins to take shape as soon as one
opens André Breton's first surrealist manifesto of October 1924,
which states, "We are still living under the reign of logic, that,
of course, is what I am getting at. But logical procedures, nowadays, no longer apply to anything but the resolution of problems
of secondary interest."[1] Is it logical that a group of young men
whose principal theoretician attacked rational logic should have
revealed an inclination to reason logically? More to the point,
we may ask, were such men really capable of doing so? Reacting
in this fashion, we grant the surrealists less than full stature.
We should be well advised to read on, in the same paragraph
of Breton's expository text, until we come upon an implied
protest against proscription of "any mode of searching for truth
that does not conform to custom." For such a mode provides
the *Manifeste du surréalisme* with its subject matter. Denying
the possibility that a surrealist mind could have developed out
of the protest voiced by André Breton, one cannot but betray
favoritism toward the custom with which he took issue. In so
doing, one inadvertently lends substance to Breton's claims.

Many times over the years, efforts have been made to discredit surrealism—or at all events to undermine the public's willingness to place confidence in it—through the argument that there is something unacceptably illogical about reasoning logically in favor of illogicality. What divides surrealists and their detractors in this areas is that the former separated from creative activity the language of theory and, in addition, the thinking that dictates use of this language. From the outset, the surrealists drew a distinction between the language of prose (identified in Breton's parlance as "the language of immediate exchange") and the language of poetic communication. The constituent elements of both languages being the same—words of interpretable meaning—the important difference lay in the motivation underlying their disposition on the page: meaning rationally communicable, in the first language; meaning poetically revealed/ discovered, in the second. It was, the surrealists contended, simply a matter of deciding where exactly rationality had its place in the communicative act and to which mode of communication it rightfully belonged. Surrealists never belittled rationality as such. Yet they concurred in regarding the contribution it was capable of making as limited and, furthermore, as extraneous to poetic exchange. The question, then, is not whether they behaved inconsistently when seeking to bypass reason in some situations but not in all. Rather, what counted was the functional role they ascribed to rational language in certain aspects of human relationships and the reasonable exchange they denied in others. While poetry was regarded as central to surrealism, rational communication had only an accessory role to play—but a role nevertheless.

A more subtle objection to positing the existence of a surrealist mind than the one already encountered grows directly out of a statement occurring in the 1924 manifesto: "Imagination alone gives me an account of what *can be*, and this is enough to raise the terrible interdict a little, enough also for me to abandon myself to imagination without fear of being mistaken (as if one could be more mistaken). Where does imagination begin to turn bad and where does the security of the mind come to an end? For the mind, is not the possibility of wandering the contingency of good?" (p. 17). The manner in which Breton conducted his argument—by way of faith in imagination, to mistrust of its supervision by rational thinking, then on to the contention that the security of the mind is assured by imagination alone—seems to support a deduction that many of his readers have found quite equitable: that reason is liable to impede the mind's response to imagination and therefore threatens its security. Are we not to infer, then, that the surrealist mind was simply a mind left free to roam at imagination's whim, hence essentially a directionless mind, surrendering purposeful activity to fanciful play? Are we not in danger of mistreating surrealism, of attempting to reverse an earlier statement on the same page of the original surrealist manifesto–"Among so many disgraces we have inherited, we really must recognize that *the greatest liberty* of mind remains to us. It is up to us not to seriously misuse it"?

If we accept the answers that these questions invite, there is no reason to continue further. In other words, we cannot continue beyond this point unless we call those same questions into service for one purpose only: to clarify that, to the surrealist, thinking and imagining were neither contradictory nor mutually destructive but—as everything that follows below stands to illustrate—complementary expressions of the surrealist mind in fruitful operation.

The inability to take this preliminary step has undermined much of what has been written about surrealism. The consequences have proved confusing. For example, discussing the texts assembled in her *Surrealists on Art*, Lucy R. Lippard asserts, "They are almost the sole contemporary documents on the development, intentions, and preoccupations of Surrealist visual art."[2] This highly debatable statement—at which Lippard arrives, presumably, by pretending that André Breton did not write his *Le surréalisme et la peinture* (from which she does not quote once) and that José Pierre was never even born—is followed by a doleful prediction: "As such, they will prove confusing, unreasonable, and often bewilderingly 'poetic'—qualities that plague many artists' attempts at verbalization but were particularly rampant in the self-consciously liberated atmosphere of Surrealism." Underlying this assertion is a presupposition about surrealism shared by many a critic: that the surrealists liberated themselves into mental confusion. Supposedly, advocates of surrealism found in their devotion to the unconscious an irresistible invitation to jumbled thinking. And what is Lippard's conclusion? That "the official Surrealist movement continued into its senility with the death, in 1964, of André Breton. . . ."[3] So eager is the commentator to be done with surrealism that she moves its leader's death up two years, a feat surpassed only by Sidney D. Braun who, in his *Dictionary of French Literature* (1958), dates Breton's passing from 1954.

Although just as clumsily phrased as Lippard's, Charles Edward Gauss's observation reflects a more appropriate perspective. "The surrealist work of art is a vehicle by which artist and spectator are brought up against the center of the world where thought and things meet."[4] Yet this remark does not prevent Gauss from declaring later, "If a spectator ever feels any kinship with others before a work of art it is insofar as he can rationally interpret that work."[5] A critic like Gauss has no interest in discussing the surrealist mind. Committed to rational interpretation exclusively, he cannot conceive any necessity for such a mind to exist, because he has no inkling of its function.

In *Surrealism: The Road to the Absolute* (1959) Anna Balakian places a chapter called "Breton and the Surrealist Mind—The Influence of Freud and Hegel." Discussing the dissatisfaction with Dada felt by the future surrealists, she uses the word *mind* for the first time when commenting, "It dawned on these young writers and artists that perhaps it was not man's mind that was wanting, or even the utilization of the mind and of the object of its experience."[6] It is clear that, while not really questioning the existence of a surrealist mind, at this stage Balakian is concerned with the surrealists' attitude toward the mind, speaking of the capabilities that the surrealists ascribed to the human mind. Only toward the end of the chapter does she employ the phrase "the surrealist mind," so becoming the first commentator to use it in the sense in which it will appear below. After examining the influence of Freud and Hegel, she writes, "As can be observed by examining these two influences, one of the basic characteristics of the surrealist mind is its uncompromising will to find a foolproof unity in the universe."[7] To Anna Balakian goes the distinction of having first drawn attention to a phenomenon that provides the present study with its point of focus.

Searching for proof of the existence of a mind that may be accurately called surrealist would lead nowhere unless that mind could be shown to evidence sufficient constancy of purpose to come to terms with the world around us or a scale broad enough to command attention and even respect. This book rests on the hypothesis that such a mind existed. It will argue that, distinctive in the attitudes it expressed and the demands it made, this mind generated ideas and creative practices cohesive enough to warrant identifying its activity by an adjective, *surrealist*, familiar to many but a source of confusion to some and of suspicion to others.

To the suspicious it may appear that one can speak of a surrealist mind only after prejudging evidence of as yet unproven reliability. Referring to a surrealist mind presupposes its existence, the dubious might contend, and therefore requires us to disregard a few basic questions which objectivity demands that we face. Can one discuss the characteristics of a phenomenon that, despite a single sentence by Anna Balakian, remains only hypothetical and even—the skeptical would point out—questionable? Are we about to embark on an inquiry demanding an attitude of detachment, yet to which we find ourselves bringing a complicity that must intervene between us and unbiased judgment? To these questions the following response may be made.

This book has not grown out of prejudgments, at all events beyond the conviction that the topic it treats is of some interest. Its author did not begin with presuppositions he was determined to validate. When he started, his title, like that of the present chapter, ended in a question mark. In its final form his study testifies that, between its inception and completion, he came to the conclusion that the question mark could and should be removed. In other words, *The Surrealist Mind* tests a hypothesis instead of proving a theory. If it has an implicit thesis, it is one the writer is far from reluctant to summarize: surrealism still receives less respect than it deserves because it is still less well understood than its prominent place in twentieth-century art entitles it to be.

Attempting an exhaustive examination of the surrealist mind would be an exhausting undertaking. It would require exploration of a variety of fields, from ethics to sociology. One or two aspects of the topic have already been treated competently—by Ferdinand Alquié, for example, in his *Philosophie du surréalisme*—or tentatively, as in Victor Crastre's study of the French surrealists' early involvement in politics, *Le drame du surréalisme*. The present essay does not represent an effort to add to such studies. Instead, it is offered as a consideration of the surrealist mind in one of its most significant and revealing functions. Designed to show how the surrealists envisaged, reacted to, and practiced art as a creative activity, it concentrates on painting and poetry. Limiting our area of inquiry permits us to witness the operation of the surrealist mind within a frame of reference where we may examine how theory relates to practice and how their interrelationship becomes enlightening.

Skimming the chapters below, the reader will notice how frequently the name André Breton appears. Breton's prominence among the surrealists and, more to the point, his gift for lucid exposition and capacity for drawing pertinent inferences from surrealist principles make it essential to give his writings special attention. These writings shed light not only on an individual case but also on the mentality that Breton shared with his fellow surrealists. The question is, do we need to consider only Breton's writings if we are striving to understand that mind?

Repeatedly, reflecting on the surrealist mind brings us back to consideration of Breton's ideas and the outlook that fostered them. The danger here is that we will limit our field of vision, concentrating so much on what Breton thought, and why, that we conclude that the surrealist mind was nothing other and no more than André Breton's mind. From here it is but a short step to the inference that the surrealist mind was so closely identifiable with Breton's that, when discussing its distinctive traits, we are really only examining the quirks and peculiarities of just one man. The net result is that we will incline to the belief that one can dispose of the influence of the surrealist mind by the simple expedient of ignoring André Breton. Doing this is as unfair as arguing that the surrealist mind was a phenomenon that owed nothing to the example Breton set his followers.

However, the relationship of the surrealist mind to Breton's is a source of possible confusion. Breton's well-known intransigence—easily interpreted by many, especially those who had quarreled with him, as a sign of inflexibility—seems to lend weight to the contention that the surrealist mind was unbending, oppressive in its demands, stifling in its effects on anyone seeking independence from surrealist orthodoxy. Yet how many of those who parted company with Breton and with surrealism would have been willing to admit in the end, with Roger Caillois, "Facing this man who has been so readily taxed with dogmatism and accused of having wantonly multiplied excommunications, I must acknowledge that, all in all, I am the one, though, who has received so much from him . . . , who showed himself to be intolerant"?[8]

Another, and related, thing. The authoritative tone that was Breton's—perhaps even more noticeable in his second surrealist manifesto, originally published in 1929, than in the first—leaves readers with the impression that his theoretical statements were, and were intended to be considered, definitive. His prose style contributed much to fostering that impression, to persuading many of his readers that his definition of surrealism, for instance, could never come under review, expansion, or modification. This was so far from being true that one might well begin examining the surrealist mind by first examining the hypothesis that surrealism flourished and broadened its horizons to the extent that its defenders enlarged upon and refined the premises laid down in Breton's manifestoes. Moreover, in fairness to the author of those tests, we should recognize that from the beginning he refused to imprison within a rigid system the means appropriate to surrealist investigation. Breton declined to assert that surrealism's point of departure must inevitably limit its goals and prescribe, once and for all, the route by which those goals should be pursued. Two statements in the first manifesto are particularly informative in this connection: "I do not believe in the early establishment of a surrealist stereotype" (p. 56); "Surrealist means would need, by the way, to be expanded" (p. 57).

André Breton's attitude was typical, not unique. The surrealists kept their faith alive by continually reviewing past achievements and speculating on means for bringing about further progress. Thus Breton's preference for the designation "surrealist movement" underscored their need to avoid stagnation brought about either by complacency or by inertia. Perceiving surrealism as offering potentially limitless advance, Breton and his associates reproved any accommodation betraying contentment with past accomplishments or resignation, any acceptance of the thought that no additional progress might be possible. The optimism keeping the surrealist mind alert drew its energy from the concept of the surreal as located tantalizingly on the horizon, withdrawing before the advancing surrealist, encouraging his forward motion as it did so. The surrealist mind would not have attained its full dimensions had surrealists failed to recognize and acknowledge, openly and gladly, that the surreal appeared inexhaustible, its enlightening possibilities unlimited. Those possibilities would have seemed unduly restricted if the surrealist mind had theorized too closely and defined its ambitions too narrowly, restricting creative techniques accordingly. Surely, the vagueness present in Breton's Légitime Défense of 1926 is proof not of indecisiveness but of openmindedness:

"Once again, all we have is that we are endowed to a certain degree with the word and that, by it, something great and obscure tends imperiously to find expression through us, that each of us has been chosen and designated to himself from among a thousand to formulate that which, in our lifetime, has to be formulated." Interviewed by Guy Dumur for *Le nouvel observateur* nearly forty years later, on 10 December 1964,[9] Breton would describe surrealist behavior as taking strength from the need to *go further*, finding in that need a vigor which, he predicted, would outlive the group he himself headed.

The surrealist mind derived energy from its self-consciousness. The central discovery of the automatic principle described in Breton's first manifesto, and the sympathy all surrealists felt for spontaneity in artistic creation might suggest that theirs would have been a *laisser aller* mentality. In fact, they displayed a penchant for self-analysis and self-evaluation that quite contradicts this preconception of how the surrealist mind ought to have functioned, once the 1924 *Manifeste* had laid the groundwork for a program. But even as we notice this, we should note also that the program surrealists devoted themselves to promoting did not anticipate creative practice in every precise detail. It left room for innovation and inventiveness. Also it assured freedom to evaluate innovations in ways making possible the assessment of the benefits of novel approaches, not simply relating to past investigation but also shedding new light on surrealism, even expanding its scope.

It is not overstating the case nor is it a criticism to say that the surrealist mind was self-obsessed. The operation of that mind was concentrated primarily on understanding itself better, on sharpening its perceptions and pushing back its horizons. The surrealist mind devoted itself to verifying its own capabilities with greater precision. This is why it held in contempt all thought processes conflicting with its own, meanwhile responding with curiosity and sympathy to any that paralleled its ambitions, confirming its capacities, promising to expand them.

To whom or to what did the surrealist mind address itself when engaged in theoretical exposition? The tone of surrealist theoretical texts is never placatory, often aggressive, belligerent. Hence the product of the surrealist mind, operating in theoretical mode, is unlikely to earn new recruits from among old enemies. It is just as unlikely to induce opponents of surrealist beliefs to show more tolerance. A surrealist text citing the surrealists' differences from their detractors generally rehearses these differences without adding much to our understanding of or sympathy for them. More often than not, reading surrealist theoretical writings lets us see the surrealist mind communing with itself instead of seeking converts. The surrealist mind's goals were less to enlighten the uninformed than to reaffirm its own prerogative. As it expounded theory, its distinguishing features were self-absorption, refusal to be diverted from its aims, eagerness to observe where those aims were leading, and delight in discoveries made along the way.

An apparently paradoxical characteristic of the surrealist mind is that it was self-reflexive while nevertheless seeking to devise and implement extra- or anti-reflexive creative methods. Could a mind so completely devoted to satisfying its needs meet those needs while yet applying techniques that released the creative-exploratory gesture from dependence on conscious control? To the surrealist this question would have seemed false, misleading in its premise that stating theoretical positions must demand the very same sort of mental activity as the mind demonstrates while creating. In other words, our impression of the activity of the surrealist mind will continue to be distortive until we acknowledge that mind's duality.

More than one commentator has noticed an apparent discrepancy between the way surrealists talked about surrealism and the way they wrote creatively. The inference is that the theory of surrealism was not quite consistent with surrealist practice, that language, at all events, was used differently by the surrealists for theoretical formulation and for their theory's application. If this were the only conclusion drawn there would be no excuse to quarrel with it. However, not satisfied with observing indisputable differences, many a critic has challenged the content of surrealist creative writing, treating it as inauthentic. The assumption is that nobody who reasons as surrealists did could have functioned creatively the way surrealists did. Hence, we are urged to conclude that once their theories had been promulgated in general terms and the time came to put ideas into practice, eschewing reasonable language and the thought processes reflected in reasonable language must have committed the surrealists to posing, to contrivance. It is as though they had to pretend now that they could no longer do something they had been doing efficiently enough before: retain adequate command of rational expression.

Could we argue in good conscience that the surrealists were

their own worst enemies, that having publicly ridiculed and sought to discredit reason, they fell victim to inconsistency when undertaking to defend their position in the language of reason? A simplified deduction, this one has its appeal, especially for anybody skeptical about surrealism. But we cannot subscribe to it without choosing to disregard the following. The text that earned notoriety as the *Manifeste du surréalisme* bore, in manuscript, the far more modest heading of preface. André Breton began writing it as an introduction to a succession of his own experiments with verbal automatism called *Poisson soluble* (Soluble fish), which antedated composition of the preface. Once the latter had turned into a manifesto, *Poisson soluble* ceased to be the focal point of attention, and no one could be blamed for looking upon those automatic texts as an appendix, offered in illustration of the theory they followed. Breton obviously saw no inconsistency in employing one kind of language "the language of immediate exchange") when presenting material which experience had taught him, excitingly, could be produced only in another language, the antirational language of surrealist poetry. From the moment surrealism came before the public at large, therefore, it presented itself concurrently, and without inner contradiction, as two functions of the surrealist mind.

In a group where new recruits joined old ones, replaced some, and then in many cases were replaced in turn, proclaiming the deficiencies of reason never deterred participants from using rational language whenever they chose to discuss their attitudes. Incoherence was never for a moment among the surrealists' ambitions. Approaching art as a viable expression of their aspirations, without needing to discuss the matter they acknowledged that the function of theory is to provide a bridge to practice. And they appreciated all along that no outsider could be expected to consider stepping out onto a bridge where he felt unsure of his footing. All the same, however broad the bridge erected with rational materials, and however reassuringly stable it might appear, it could not limit the possibilities for surrealist creative effort. Nor could it confine the mystery of surrealist creativity, which was no less an expression of the surrealist mind than the theory going by the name of surrealism.

The singular talent possessed by the surrealist mind to reason its theoretical positions while adopting as a consequence antireasonable working methods encourages in some commentators the impression that the surrealists were well-nigh schizophrenic. A disadvantage of this interpretation is that it spreads doubt regarding surrealism by implying that the surrealist was two persons in one who did not realize the fact. It ignores an interesting aspect of the surrealists' outlook: that they reasoned about their antirationalism and deliberately elected to deny reason. Indeed, willingness to avail themselves of rational discourse for the purposes of communicating their theories underlined their conviction that those means are irrelevant to the purposes of poetry. If reason is incompatible with poetry, they reasoned, then suppression of reason's demands is an essential precondition of poetic communication. All in all, it is an error to suppose that the surrealist mind, which in the moment of creation divested itself of reason's controls, had to forfeit the right and ability to borrow the language of reasonable exchange when reviewing its own creative practices and the significance these had for surrealism. Equally erroneous is the supposition that because rational discourse cannot be simulated, the surrealists' demonstrated gift for expressing themselves reasonably warns us to be suspicious of any departures from rational language, to regard these as proof of inauthenticity, of pretense. One can entertain this hypothesis only at the cost of ignoring the efforts surrealists made—and, more particularly, the significance of these efforts—to release their thinking and imaginative play from the burden of restrictive reason.

The surrealists established an enlightening correlation between the rational and something they termed the irrational, more accurately definable as the antirational. The latter designation helps us grasp the nature of the correlation in question. If there had been no traceable explanation for its appeal to the surrealist mind, the antirational would have lacked a norm for the evaluation of its contribution. It would have been, in fact, very close to irrationality, a state of mental imbalance to which one is reduced when ties with the rational have parted under stress of some kind or other.

The surrealist mind's preoccupation with the antirational bespoke deliberate choice, consciously acted upon. Among surrealists, interest in the antirational took root in the firm conviction that it is capable of bringing revelations beyond the scope of the rational. At the same time, reason permitted the surrealists to measure how far beyond reasonable anticipation such revelations can carry the imagination. Thus the surrealist mind's investigation of the antirational was never involuntary, and its fruits were always subject to careful appraisal. In short, the surrealists knowingly violated certain communicative norms and, in order to derive fullest benefit from doing so, needed to be aware that profitable violation had taken place. Here then is just one aspect of the duality of the surrealist mind contributing to the vigor of surrealist experimentation in a variety of creative media. Duality was indeed the seminal influence upon surrealist creative investigation, removing surrealist art, in all its forms, from aimlessnes and the haphazard.

The first experiments with verbal automatism undertaken in conjunction by André Breton and Philippe Soupault grew out of a dissatisfaction with inherited poetic practices and norms. They were not prompted by a theory but by curiosity to see whether the poetic coefficient of the verbal image could be raised by the expedient of suppressing conscious control. When starting out, Breton and Soupault shared no theoretical objection to reason's domination of thought. Rather—and the original surrealist manifesto stated this five years later—Breton's decision to obtain from himself what Sigmund Freud had obtained from his patients by having them engage in free association ("spoken thought," in Breton's phrase) led the two future surrealists to investigate the poetic possibilities of automatic writing. True, *Les pas perdus*, published eight months before the *Manifeste*, did not describe the experiment in quite the same terms. There Breton remarked that he and Soupault had "thought to reproduce voluntarily" in themselves the state of half-sleep in which phrases marked by "poetic elements of the first order" are formed.[10] Yet there is one element underlying both reminiscences. The original surrealist manifesto does not modify the evaluation offered in *Les pas perdus*, where the texts written in collaboration by Breton and Soupault in 1919 and published the following year as *Les champs magnétiques* (The magnetic fields) are described as "only the first application of this discovery" (p. 150). Nowhere did Breton speak of applying a theory in his early attempts at automatic writing. Nor was Soupault to speak of having done so, when recalling many years later:

> At that period, while André Breton and myself had not yet baptised ourselves surrealists, we wanted at first to give ourselves up to experimentation. It led us to consider poetry as a liberation, as the possibility (perhaps the sole possibility) of granting the mind a liberty we had known only in our dreams and of delivering us from the apparatus of logic.

In the course of our inquiry we had discovered indeed that the
mind released from all critical pressures and from academic habits
offered images and not logical propositions and that, if we agreed
to adopt what the psychiatrist Pierre Janet called automatic writing,
we noted down texts in which we discovered a "universe" unex-
plored up to then.[11]

The early surrealists' experience with verbal automatism typifies the role of the surrealist mind. Originally, Breton and
Soupault undertook to empty their minds of thoughts and intentions, to bring about a mental condition they considered receptive to unforeseeable word images. Eventually, after a period
of reflection extending over half a decade, Breton drew some
conclusion about that experiment. Theory was not meant to
contaminate in any way what had been central to the experiment—suppression of the reflective evaluative principle. Surrealist theory derived from it lessons reflectively formulated and
presented in a format that now changed the basis of communication with readers. Thus two communicative modes were employed: the poetic, attained at the cost of reasoned discourse;
and the theoretical, reached only after antirational illumination
had been achieved. The writer finally reverted to the medium
of exchange for which the vehicle was rational language. It
would remain a distinguishing feature of surrealism that the
distinction never ceased to be made by its defenders between
poetry as an investigative procedure of which unprecedented
discoveries could be expected and, on the other hand, prosaic
formulas in which deductions were made, conclusions were
reached, and theory took shape.

When one sets Les pas perdus beside the Manifeste du surréalisme a noteworthy change comes to light all the same. In the
former, suppression of reason's supervision over the shaping
of poetic images is said to have been practiced experimentally.
In the latter, reason is already a villain to be resisted and ultimately defeated. Thus theory has overtaken practice, advancing
a step beyond and now requiring future practice to reflect the
new position, which has become a major article of surrealist
doctrine. It would be equally unjust to omit to note that the
evolution in thinking from Les pas perdus to the first manifesto
indicates André Breton's special aptitude for facilitating the
progress of surrealist ideas. His capacity for giving theory impetus from practice illustrates the activity of the surrealist mind.
It forewarns us against imagining that mind to have existed,

fully formed in all its attitudes, before surrealist works ever came into being.

One ends up with an incorrect impression of surrealism by assuming that either the surrealists theorized first and afterward sought to apply theory to practice or that their practice invariably engendered theoretical justification. The vitality of the surrealist mind owed much to the interdependence of theory and practice, to the way practice at moments gave momentum to theory while at other times taking impetus from it. The suppleness of that mind is sometimes hidden from sight behind ideas and positions, the brutality with which the surrealists stated their opposition to attitudes they condemned. A major lesson learned by those surrealists (Breton and Soupault among them) who previously had participated for a while in Dada was that dogmatism is stultifying in the long run, even though it may appear both necessary and rewarding at first. However violently opposed they may have been to individuals and attitudes they judged to be hostile, members of the surrealist movement always remained receptive to new concepts that impressed them as opening closed doors or locating doors where before they had been aware of none.

The supervisory role of the surrealist mind was demonstrated in the productive balance struck between control (evidenced, for example, in Breton's admonition that surrealists prevent the public from "entering") and receptivity, reflected in the surrealists' willingness to accept into their ranks anyone they deemed capable of contributing positively. A measure of the vigor of the surrealist mind was its openness to new concepts. It was the ability to bring together ideas and their consequences on the plane of creative action, not so that the ideas justified their consequences but to illustrate the interdependence of surrealist thought and creative expression.

Examining the surrealist mind widens our knowledge of the coherence of surrealist thought. It is no occasion, though, to impose rigorous systematization on that thought. Surrealism could not have survived for so long had its advocates failed to respond to innovation while remaining dedicated to defending principles that gave all forms of creative expression the only value they could be seen to possess when viewed from surrealist perspective.

The duality of the surrealist mind rested on the belief that artists should be at liberty to assess what they have done without

however letting the evaluative principle inhibit the creative gesture. As for the coherence of surrealist thought, it is a sign
that the surrealist mind was a mind in quest, in pursuit of
goals defined clearly enough to give creative activity of various
kinds impetus, direction, and discernible purpose, yet not so
narrow as to discourage boldness or rule out originality. For
the surrealist mind was a self-regulating organism, admitting
obligations to nothing but the idea of surrealism that it entertained and kept alive. Thus the infamous excommunications
and exclusions from the surrealist group in France were not
so much the result of personal differences as confirmation of
a few individuals' inability to live up to the demands of the
surrealist mind. If there is any meaning at all to the comment—
usually made in disparagement of surrealism—that one individual or another had fallen from grace, it lies in his demonstrated
failure to keep faith with the surrealist mind. It was not for
nothing that, taking Salvador Dali as an example of its evil
consequences, André Breton warned against the dangers of a
criminal act of which no surrealist must ever be guilty: "self-
kleptomania."

Ultimately, examining the surrealist mind enables us to face
a potentially confusing question with confidence: how to distinguish the authentic from the false, how to separate surrealist
from surrealistic. It does not merely allow us to understand
better what surrealism was. It takes us to the core of the matter
by helping us comprehend why surrealism came into existence
and what it existed to accomplish.

2

The Automatic Principle: Why Write?

In his *Les pas perdus* André Breton recalls an inquiry, "Why Do You Write?" opened in the pages of the magazine *Littérature*, which he cofounded with Louis Aragon and Philippe Soupault. He reports that the answers received from "some of the so-called outstanding names of the literary world" were less "satisfactory" than a response culled from Knud Hamsun's novel *Pan*. There one of the characters formulated the reply, "I write to shorten time." Commenting in *Les pas perdus*, Breton remarks that the jotting from Lt. Glahn's notebook is the only answer to which he can still subscribe, "with this reservation that I believe I also write to lengthen time." In any case, he adds, his intention is to "act upon it" (p. 13).

At the moment when "Pourquoi écrivez-vous?" appeared in *Littérature*, in November 1919, André Breton was still a long way from the mental position in which he drafted his 15 October 1924 *Manifeste du surréalisme*. He still had not quite reached that position when he wrote the essay "La confession dédaigneuse" for *Les pas perdus* in February 1923. Yet one thing was clear enough. He already had pinpointed a question to which he would return repeatedly after bringing out the first surrealist manifesto. Occasionally, he would face that question openly—as when writing *Nadja*, completed and published in 1928. However, even when he did not ask himself in front of readers, so to speak, what justification one could have for being a writer, that question underlay everything he published as a surrealist.

A cursory reading of "La confession dédaigneuse" may leave the impression that, although not yet the acknowledged leader of a group identified in the original manifesto as having given proof of "ABSOLUTE SURREALISM," Breton was furnishing evidence consistent with an admission made later, in his 1929 *Second manifeste du surréalisme*, that surrealism was the "tail"—at best a prehensile tail—of nineteenth-century romanticism. But only hastiness could induce us to confuse the attitude

31

he expressed in 1923 with the romantic's posture of ennui,
of world-weariness acute enough to transform the act of writing
into a paradoxical gesture for which the sole excuse really must
have been vanity.

André Breton was above vanity, or at least he was untouched
by that form of it which demands vindication of posterity while
exulting in rejection by contemporary society. He had no time
or inclination to seek approval from the world about him or
even from those coming after. Consecration by history, in which
Stendhal had placed his trust, was something for which Breton
saw no point in striving. His allusion in Les pas perdus to
"quelques-unes des prétendues notabilités du monde littéraire"
("some of the self-styled notables of the literary world") fixed
his current position fairly precisely. He had started out as an
adolescent aspirant poet, respectful of the accomplishments of
Stéphane Mallarmé, Jean Royère, and Francis Viélé-Griffin, def-
erential to literary figures of the day like Paul Valéry and André
Gide. Already before "Pourquoi écrivez-vous?" the standards
by which success is measured in literary circles had ceased
to mean anything to André Breton. By 1919, then, the ambiguity
of Guillaume Apollinaire's outlook—his craving for recognition
and attachment to tradition never quite ousted by his ambition
to reinvent poetry—had forfeited Breton's enthusiasm, unable
to withstand the icy blast of Jacques Vaché's skepticism regarding Apollinairian achievement and aspirations. At most, public
recognition looked suspect to André Breton. Literary success
marked a failure, more or less ill-concealed, which invited condemnation when judged by criteria taking definition, in his
mind, in opposition to tradition and convention.

An observant critic has demonstrated quite thoroughly that
Breton erected "La confession dédaigneuse" on the principle
of negation.[1] Her phrase, "un véritable cogito négateur," neatly
captures Breton's state of mind in 1923. At that time, Bretonian
thought progressed under negative impulses toward a position
of strength. The latter was not merely defensible but, in Breton's
estimation, impregnable. From it he was soon ready to launch
an attack in the name of a new positive program, called surrealism.

Described in such terms, however, the advance Breton needed
to make before being ready to compose the 1924 surrealist manifesto is subjected to distorting simplification. Our impression
is that, multiplied often enough a wrong must give a right,
that systematic denial of standards in the past considered ap-

plicable to writing will eventually yield new criteria for the future. The impression appears to be reinforced when we turn from "La Confession dédaigneuse" to the *Manifeste du surréalisme*. In the later text the essential discovery of "the poetic surrealism" (Breton's declared subject) is identified as a communicative method, termed automatic writing. As described in the first manifesto, automatic writing is too far removed—quite deliberately—from conscious intent to persuade every reader that it merits attention as a serious response to the question of why one should write. In fact, Breton's conduct looks distinctly self-contradictory. After spending so much time, since his adolescence, wondering how writing is to be validated, when drafting his surrealist manifesto André Breton proposed a technique the first consequence of which looks to be the following. It releases the writer, supposedly, from any obligation toward his readership, presumably releasing him from any sense of responsibility to the public.

Why write? Fundamental to Breton's development from imitative neophyte poet to writer in revolt against tradition, at the end of 1924 this question seems to have been pushed into the background by another: How to write? It is as though, in fact, the latter had invalidated the former, technique having replaced intention as the focal point of Breton's concerns. Had he reviewed his goals, then, now finding it profitable or even necessary to change them? Examination of the principle of automatism, as set forth in the *Manifeste du surréalisme*, shows how far astray we shall wander, imagining the two questions mentioned above to have been in conflict or incompatible. A major contribution made by André Breton's text lay in superimposing *How to write?* on *Why write?* with the result that they became, for surrealists, one and the same question.

Even this description can sound misleading. It encourages the belief that solving a purely technical problem disposes concurrently of motivational difficulties, in so doing setting aside—even eliminating—moral issues to which "La confession dédaigneuse" gave prominence. A dangerous inference is that, once a writer had borrowed or adapted, devised for himself, or just happened upon a method of writing he deems acceptable, no considerations other than methodological ones need concern him or indeed will detain him any longer. He will have become the practitioner, so it would appear, of a surefire method. At best, this turns him into an amanuensis. At worst it reduces him to the status of a machine, unthinking and—not that it matters any more—incapable of thought.

It is all the more important to challenge this erroneous deduction because André Breton sounds as though he himself is authorizing us to make it when he alludes in his manifesto to surrealists as "the deaf receptacles of so many echoes" and calls them "modest *recording instruments*" (p. 42). Is the only message he wishes to share with readers, in the end, that he and his fellow surrealists have reduced themselves voluntarily to the level at which effort on the writer's part has become altogether superfluous? Such a conclusion takes shape and takes hold easily enough, if one misreads the adjective *automatic* and interprets it as synonymous with *mechanical*, thus failing to appreciate why Breton gladly placed faith in automatism.

The essential difference is the one separating an apparatus operating mechanically from an instrument attuned to a particular function, better yet, an instrument capable of attuning itself to that function, which it modestly intends (and not is intended) to fulfill. Here lies the significant feature of automatism as practiced in the name of surrealist poetic investigation. Automatism represents conscious choice, not mere necessity. More than this, it is deliberately selected for a purpose. The suspension of one faculty (in the case of verbal automatism, we are talking of the reflective process of thought, founded on rationalism) electively closes off one avenue of poetic inquiry to the advantage of another, to which access is facilitated by recourse to automatism.

No machine is capable of making a choice on the basis of poetic aspiration. Hence the distinction is clearly drawn, in surrealism, between writing as a meaningless mechanical exercise and writing as the chosen medium of an individual who willingly accepts the role of "recording instrument," modestly, not arrogantly, played. In the practice of automatic writing intentionality was a major factor, even though not permitted to influence the manner in which automatism divested reasoned discourse of its prerogatives. In other words, the decision reached by the surrealist when electing to avail himself of the automatic method (or the step he took when writing automatically without prior discussion or reflection) responded to the challenge *Why write?* subsumed in an answer to the question *How to write?*

In surrealist verbal automatism, technique did not dispose the question of justifiable motivation. Instead, automatic writing was seen by those who used it as having a justification rooted less in methodological considerations than ideological ones. The latter extended beyond aesthetics into an area for which the designation "poetry" appeared viable so long as the poetic was defined in light of surrealist principles. Thus, if up to this point, the pendulum apparently has swung toward the technical (How to write?), surrealist ideological aspirations now cause it to swing back toward the motivational (Why write?).

Really, though, in the productive tension to which surrealists ascribed poetic effect by way of automatic writing, technique and motivation balanced one another. Methodology did not enjoy priority, thus enabling the writer to entrust himself unthinkingly to automatism as a (mechanical) working technique, sure to bring results. Nor could conscious aspirations be allowed to dominate, to subject the how of writing to close supervision by its why. Everything giving meaning to verbal automatism was located in the unpredictable interplay between methodology and ambition. There the benefits of technique were valuable to the degree that they could not be estimated, in advance of the writing process, by reference to clearly foreseeable goals. Simplifying in the interest of shedding light on the mental adventure on which the surrealist automatist was launched, one may say the following: A truly accurate answer to the question, Why write? eluded the honest practitioner of automatism so long as experimentation still lay ahead. Only after he had engaged in automatic writing could the surrealist reply to the question of why he did so. The answer at which he finally arrived lay beyond projection, in a zone where—if his technique indeed had proved its worth—realization had outstripped anticipation.

Projected aims held no significance if achievement had patently fallen short of reaching them. What had looked initially like assurance of success (not to say its foolproof guarantee)—not merely an excuse for writing, but its unassailable justification—eventually turned out to be nothing of the kind. In short, asking one question, How to write? did not coincidentally offer a solution to another, Why write? Neither question provided a full answer to the other. Nevertheless, the two were interrelated.

André Breton would have been the first to acknowledge one thing and treat it as a source of pride. If, in advance of trying verbal automatism, a surrealist had been able to predict what automatic writing would bring, he would have seen no profit in giving himself over to that activity. Similarly, had he been capable of projecting with some measure of confidence the answer to *why* he wrote, then his motive for doing so would have deserted him. In such circumstances, automatism would have become an unpardonably dull mechanical procedure. Thus no justificatory explanation could have added enough meaning to validate, in the surrealists' eyes, a gesture perpetually threatened by the stigma of vanity.

Now comes to light another factor which no surrealist worthy of the name would have dared ignore. Responsibility to one's audience meant, in surrealism, accepting obligations under which vanity would have been incapable of concealing itself in the guise of altruism. Nobody, they acknowledged, can write for himself without writing for others also. Yet this truism is not sufficient on its own to warrant the gesture of verbal communication, to lend value to an activity that appears open to question. In the interplay between *Why write?* and *How to write?* lay a perpetual exchange vitally important to every surrealist employing verbal automatism: each question to which the other referred the writer sent him back to the preceding one. When its turn came, the latter directed him forward again to the other, without inducing stagnation, however. Each question posed served usefully to bring the writer up against the necessity to face the other and then to try to respond to it. As a result, he was denied a lulling, complacent sense of full accomplishment. To be more accurate, he was spared it. At every turn, he was confronted by the necessity to review his progress so far, to face the need to examine it from changed perspective, as *how* replaced *why* and then became *why* once again.

Most likely, an observer who anticipates simply frustrating results betrays an assumption inimical to surrealist poetic practice. In any event, the surrealists would have contended that he is in error. They would have traced his mistake back to its point of departure in the supposition that creativity expresses conscious intent, the realization of ends designated in advance and pursued with some degree of skill as well as with tenacity. Surrealist theory located the virtues of verbal automatism in the unpredictable, the unforeseeable. Thus those virtues could be traced right back to automatism's principal attraction for the surrealist mind: its ability to lead the artist past expectation and outside the anticipated. Here a stage was attained at which justifying the act of writing furnished answers of special import to every surrealist. Apparently taken for granted in the question

Why write? the conventional presuppositions of intentionality now collapsed. They gave way before the perceptible benefits of a creative effort that had carried the writer further than aspirations, knowingly entertained, into a region where revelations were to be made.

Naturally, automatism permitted the surrealist to make discoveries he regarded as revelatory only so far as the automatic method allowed access to things his principles incited him to invest with significance. This meant that the fundamental contribution of automatism to surrealist doctrine, and practice too, went beyond committing surrealists to a single technical device, routinely applied. It turned their attention in a markedly different direction from the one that, traditionally, has given focus to creative aspirations associated with literary convention in Western culture. Consequently, in surrealism optimism about the *how* of writing was generated and sustained by the hope with which surrealist ambitions invested the *why.* That hopes eludes definition while we, seeking to estimate its scope, apply literary criteria in the belief that from the first the surrealists were attempting to blaze a new trail to familiar goals.

Not knowing ahead of time where verbal automatism would lead placed the surrealist automatist in a situation most writers would regard as unacceptable. He would have found it impossible to reply to *Why write?* with the assurance that many another would consider a prerequisite to setting pen to paper. Yet while most would hesitate (that is the least one can say), he looked forward to learning from an approach having distinctive rules laid down by his own response to *How to write?* Those rules challenged customary literary practices in which reflective thought, taste, aesthetic values, and so on have their part to play. Instead, unsupervised thought was permitted, even encouraged, to run free, by implementation of a technique sure to eliminate safeguards without which literary tradition has taught that it is unproductive, unwise, or even foolhardy to undertake literary endeavor.

Why write? did not elicit from the surrealist automatist the answer that some new forms of literature must be pursued and achieved. Meanwhile, in his view, *How to write?* had nothing to do with producing literature by novel means, so in some fashion "revitalizing" it. As they collaborated on *Les champs magnétiques,* the excitement released in Breton and Philippe Soupault would have been less acute had the texts they produced come merely as proof that a new literary method had fallen into their hands. The benefits of automatic writing became visible at a time when both Breton and Soupault were thoroughly disenchanted with literature as practiced by their elders. The two of them were increasingly mistrustful of the methods applied by the older generation. As for automatism, it brought to light word images of a kind that literary methodology had furnished readily and which the authors of *Les champs magnétiques* considered it absurd to judge by the standards of literature.

What, then, accounted for the delay between the writing of *Les champs magnétiques* in 1919 and the composition of the 1924 surrealist manifesto, where Breton made verbal automatism the cornerstone of surrealist theory and its application? Investigating that question, we are struck by one fact above all. Breton, Soupault, and their associates did not attempt to capitalize immediately on the discoveries of 1919. Before we can explain the hesitancy shared by individuals who would not publicly call themselves surrealists, for several more years, we have to appreciate one thing. At the start, the negative significance of automatic writing was the most impressive aspect to the future surrealists. Automatism made its impact initially as a tool for breaking down barriers within which literary activity was restricted. The positive value of automatism—as a means for renewing poetic expression, for facilitating poetic communication between writer and reader, was to be acknowledged increasingly with the passage of time. But this would never obscure or push aside the advantage of automatic writing as a method for shattering the confining mold of literature.

Their methodology and its motivation placed the surrealist automatists beyond the confines of literature. Yet theirs was not the unenviable situation of the outcast, peering in and regretting his isolation. On the contrary, they looked off in a direction that only incomprehension—as Breton sought to make clear—could confuse with the one where men of letters seek and count on the fulfillment of their aspirations. In the context of surrealism, the *how* and *why* of automatic writing assumed radically revolutionary significance, when the results they precipitated were judged next to those commonly identified as productive expressions of literary ambition. A complete reversal of the poet's traditional role—at least in some of its supposedly characteristic aspects—is implied in the automatic method by which *how* invests *why* with new meaning. Instead of boasting of having freely chosen his pathway to poetry, for example, the surrealist automatist would have been able to claim, with André Breton and Jean Schuster, "This pathway has chosen me freely."[2] Vanity over what one has accomplished was replaced by pride in what one had been the occasion for bringing to expression.

Automatism could not have nourished and sustained vanity in the surrealist the way that literary practices satisfy the vanity of the *littérateur*. But this was no disadvantage to André Breton even in 1919. In fact, dating from 1916, his acquaintance with some of the ideas of Sigmund Freud made him particularly responsive to automatic writing as a method whereby the creative act could be prolonged beyond satisfaction of the ego, to put the practitioner in illuminating contact with the superego, as images welled up unbidden from levels within over which reason exerts no control. In the circumstances, our best approach to the answer to *Why write?* underlying the use of verbal automatism is to recognize that the surrealist practiced automatic writing in the hope of achieving some success (manifest in unprecedented images) in areas where the goals consecrated in literature by tradition and convention do not belong and have no influence.

While writing automatically, the surrealist voluntarily surrendered the benefits of established and proven literary techniques. He did not sacrifice them so much as rule them out and free himself of their effects. Employing automatism, he jettisoned the burdensome weight of literary impedimenta. Thus, traveling lighter, he was able to push forward beyond literary effect. The method utilized brought back, captured in words and images as edifying to the writer himself as to those capable of reading what he had written without succumbing to the prejudices for which literature is responsible in collaboration with rational discourse.

In the situation in which the surrealist placed himself gladly, the *how* corresponded to a *why* taking its full dimensions only after the event, when the writing was done and came under review for the revelatory images it yielded. Assessment ceased to be the obligation of an author striving with all the control he could muster to make the most of what he had to say. It had become instead the privilege shared with his audience by the writer, rereading himself, curious to see what his technique (so distant from a method of composition) had placed before him. And so, for the verbal automatist, acting responsibly meant the very opposite of contrivance, of calculated effect. It demanded the fullest possible respect for material that Breton had no hesitation in calling the subliminal message. It required concentration on keeping open lines of communication along which that message passes without the contamination the surrealist felt sure must attend preoccupation, during the act of writing, with the question, *What does this mean?*

In surrealism evaluation applied as a brake on the free flow of words was viewed as injurious to the subliminal message. Hence the practice of automatic writing presupposed suspending critical supervision of verbal expression by the reasoning mind. Convinced that the purity of the image can be judged in relation to its resistance to rational explanation, the surrealists looked upon reason as a contaminant. This is why, in his first manifesto Breton spoke of beautiful images as those released in a rarefied atmosphere, one from which surveillance by reason has been withdrawn. Surrealists declined to hold the poet answerable to reason. They went further, to assert that poetic purity could follow solely upon the application of means precluding reason's intervention in the production of images (in their production, we notice, not their careful elaboration). The *how* became important now because the *why* directed the poet's attention to sanctions, instructed him on what his images must not be. This was the surrealist's way of clearing a path for what would follow upon his success in liberating himself from restraints which had been accepted, in the past, as the sine qua non of poetic communication.

In surrealist automatic writing, motivation and technique took impetus first of all from rejection. Both signalled profound dissatisfaction with literary custom and convention for having engendered results the surrealists dismissed as being of questionable poetic value. Expressing confidence in the future, both directed the writer to break with the past. But neither reflected an effort to prejudge what the future should bring. This is to say that the vital characteristic of automatic writing was that it remained investigative, an exploratory experiment with language. Locating poetry beyond rational projection, surrealists looked to verbal automatism to bring poetry within reach, to record in language something they believed that reasonable use of words cannot encompass.

A noteworthy feature of verbal automatism was the reversal of the relationship between mind and image to which literature has accustomed us. Basic to the theory lending automatism its prestige was the surrealists' willing surrender of conscious control over the image recorded in language. To supervision by reflective thought surrealists preferred the unrestrained outpouring of images for which no explanation could be furnished by the reasoning mind. Bringing about such a departure from familiar practice was not difficult, once the surrealists had accepted without reluctance the principle of automatism. Implementation of the method of writing automatically would have held little value, however, if it were not for the benefits it brought in an area over which rational projection exercises no control and therefore can impose no limitations. In other words, the surrealists were convinced that measurement of poetic effect begins with the shock administered to reasonable thought, when it comes into contact with the imagery released through automatic writing.

So far as the surrealists were concerned, the superiority of images produced automatically over imagery created conventionally was not a matter of blind faith. It was a demonstrable fact, predicated on the technique from which the automatic image resulted. In verbal automatism the mind does not progress toward the definitive image, gradually fashioned by reflective thought. Instead, the image leads the mind to the extent that, as Breton puts it in his first manifesto, it becomes "convinced" little by little of the "supreme reality" of images born of automatic writing, which are a pure expression of surreality. Under these conditions, poetic communication will not be complete until, in the mind of the reader and of the author himself, the surprise provoked by the image has given way to acceptance, the mind being stimulated to advance farther than reason has the power to take it.

Implicit here is a notion that rationalism would vigorously contest: that departing from the pathway patrolled by reason marks progress, not losing one's way in confusion or chaos. Crucial to our understanding of the place automatic writing occupied in surrealist doctrine is awareness of the conviction, widespread among surrealists in France, that automatism expands the capacity of the mind by effectively removing some of the restraints exerting a retarding influence, from which surrealism demanded release. If verbal automatism were no more than a trustworthy device for facilitating writing—to make more of us able to write better—then the surrealists would have questioned its usefulness very seriously. Only because it grants poets the ability to cast off restraint and, by so doing, to expand their power to stimulate the imagination did automatic writing

earn itself high ranking among the creative techniques promoted
in the name of surrealism.

In his 1924 manifesto, André Breton stressed the apparent
arbitrariness of the automatic image. This is to say that, pointing
to images that defied the logic of rational thinking, he contended
that they merely appeared arbitrary. Acceptance of the image
as viable comes most quickly, surrealists would have claimed,
when the reader is not held up by an impression of arbitrariness
but goes on to acknowledge the supreme reality of the automatic
image. Thus the metaphor employed in the *Manifeste du surréalisme* to convey the effect of the image—that of the spark it
sets off—is consistent with the role of surrealist imagery as
an illuminating phenomenon. However it may seem at first
glance, the purpose of automatic writing is enlightenment, not
obfuscation. So if first contact leaves the reader puzzled or even
infuriated, his reaction indicates how far he still has to travel
before he can hope to intrude with the surrealists into "the
enchanters' domain."[3]

All we learn about automatism when reading the first surrealist manifesto begins to fall into place when we hear André
Breton contend that logical processes apply only to the resolution of problems of secondary interest. Implied here, and made
explicit in his remarks about automatic writing, is another idea:
antilogical procedures are the only kind that can resolve problems of primary concern. This takes us to the very core of
surrealist theory as it relates to surrealist practice.

The surrealists seemed to be in pursuit of means of avoiding
the literary, of circumventing it. This was because they regarded
literature as evasive, as shirking issues to which they attached
most importance. Among those issues that of self-knowledge
through self-discovery was paramount. Hence their detestation
of literature as an exercise in the careful application of acquired
techniques, knowingly utilized with a view to certain attainment
of foreseeable results. Hence, too, their rejection of aesthetic
considerations as being sure to divert attention from essentials
and directing it, instead, to concerns holding significance for
the surrealist imagination. For literature as pastime, or even
as alibi, surrealism aimed to substitute poetry as revelation,
as a process of discovery in which meeting literary criteria had
no positive contribution. Thus with the elimination of retarding
influences originating in literary aspirations went, in automatic
writing, something the surrealists valued far more highly: libera-

tion, through spontaneously generated images, of imaginative stimuli corresponding to a poetic experience they deemed revolutionary. Therefore, verbal automatism filled a dual function. It short-circuited literary pretensions, conducting the current valued by the surrealists as poetic all the more efficiently because automatic writing removed inhibitions ranging from the rational to the moral. Evident here is the influence of Freudian free association, with which André Breton had had the opportunity to experiment during his wartime service in a French neuropsychological hospital. No less important is the belief underlying the 1924 manifesto that free association is a tool lending itself to poetic purposes, not merely therapeutic ones.

The surrealist writer never turned to automatic writing in hope of getting better. His ambition was to see better. The imagery liberated through automatism was by no means exclusively visual in nature, of course. All the same, the examples one remembers most vividly frequently owe their effect (taking us by surprise) to their ability to make us see something not seen before, independently of presuppositions born of past experience and outside assumptions fostered by reason. The jolt given the mind by the automatic image was proof to the surrealists that the latter emits the vital spark they regarded as its extraliterary virtue.

According to surrealist theory, such a spark cannot be struck when one confines oneself to employing procedures consecrated by literature. Hence we may question the surrealists' argument without managing to curtail its far-reaching consequences for surrealist writing. There is no way, for instance, to invalidate the surrealists' inference that, as a mode of writing, verbal automatism is without a competitor at providing the rarefied atmosphere in which, the *Manifeste du surréalisme* emphasized, the spark of the image is transmitted best. One may retain the distinct impression that André Breton and his companions reasoned in circles, without for all that being able to contest the vitality of surrealist thought in promoting verbal automatism to a position unassailable within the framework of surrealist doctrine. From whichever direction it is approached, the surrealists' answer to *Why write?* favors automatism, attributing it a degree of purity to be judged only on surrealist terms.

If by surrealism's standards literature evidenced contamination, then automatic writing was poetry purified of literary taint. Therefore nothing short of infidelity to surrealism's edicts could have led any surrealist to condone evaluation of the fruits of verbal automatism by criteria established in the name of literary merit. The energy, not to say violence, with which from the very first the surrealists affirmed their independence of and opposition to literature was generated by the conviction that defense of surrealism and affirmation of its principles required a firm line to be drawn between the surrealist poet and the *littérateur*. As much during the lifetime of the surrealist movement as since its demise, the widespread custom of examining surrealist writing in the narrow perspective of literature is proof enough of one important fact. The surrealists were never elitist, preaching a doctrine of literary refinement so as to prove themselves better writers than those they condemned and even reviled. All the same, Breton's second manifesto inadvertently explained the causes of the misunderstanding to which surrealism had fallen victim from the outset.

We should begin by noting a reaffirmation of surrealist aspirations consigned to the *Second manifeste:* "the idea of surrealism tends simply to the total recuperation of our psychic strength by a means which is none other than vertiginous descent into ourselves, systematic illumination of the hidden places and progressive obscuration of the other places, a perpetual walk in the forbidden zone" (pp. 167–68). Following this remark came another, referring to the general problem which surrealism had taken upon itself to raise, *"that of human expression in all its forms"* (p. 183). As Breton observed, "Whoever says expression says, to begin with, language." This is why "you must not be surprised to see surrealism place itself first of all almost exclusively on the plane of language. . . ." (p. 183).

It was all very well for Breton to pour scorn on "the little idiot towns of literature." It was all well and good for him to assert that "the logical mechanism of the sentence is showing itself on its own to be more and more powerless, in man, to set off the emotive jolt which really gives some value to his life" (pp. 183–84). The clarity with which the surrealist position was stated in the *Second manifeste du surréalisme* of 1929 has never protected it from attack by critics expressing the common viewpoint, when identifying creative language with literature and its emotive use with logic.

An approach different from the surrealists' accounts for the reception according surrealism by well-intentioned commentators whose inclination to treat it as literature has led them into confusion. There is an additional reason why automatic writing has suffered, like other expressions of surrealism, at the hands of critics in whom incomprehension of surrealist goals has proved capable of generating insensitivity and even hostility.

To set things in perspective we have to take André Breton at his word, to appreciate how honest he was when explaining in the first manifesto, "Surrealism rests on a belief in the superior reality of certain forms of association neglected heretofore" (p. 40). After all, he could affirm in good conscience that surrealism "tends to ruin definitively all other psychic mechanisms and to substitute itself for them in resolving the main problems of life" He did so neither by right nor by general agreement, but on the basis of faith alone. There was no way for its adherents to prove surrealism to be exactly as Breton had defined it, "pure psychic automatism" suited to expressing "the real functioning of thought." Indeed, considering quite objectively the adjectives *pure* and *real*, figuring in the Bretonian definition could not be more questionable. They must even appear suspect to anybody who, not sharing Breton's beliefs, remains unconvinced that it can provide a solid foundation for the argument erected in the *Manifeste*, the *Second manifeste*, and other theoretical texts of surrealist provenance. Nevertheless the surrealists themselves were quite sure of what they meant when characterizing psychic automatism as pure. Similarly, they were confident that practicing automatism made them witnesses to thought functioning in a real manner. However, if not for the ability and willingness to share their faith, lending credence to their interpretation of purity and reality calls at least for a willingness to concede them the right to take belief as their starting point for formulating a theory. If we examine, for instance, the phrase "the real functioning of thought," we notice it makes indisputable sense so far as its author and those prepared to listen without objecting agree in their expectations of thought, so long as it is understood to allude to what they all concur in considering the function of thought to be. Breton's phrase reflects a certain concept of reality while denying another, dismissed as impertinent. This is not because, as the higher form of reality that is surreality, the first is demonstrably superior to the second, but because the first enjoyed his confidence whereas the second never could. Therefore it would be absurd to submit those illustrations of the functioning of thought claimed as real, in surrealism, to assessment in light of values inspired by the sense of reality opposed by surrealism.

Like their mistrust of anyone presuming to evaluate their

achievement from outside their group, the surrealists' apparently well-deserved reputation for arrogance had its origins here. The basis for disagreement with their critics was not unforgivable conceit, however. Nor was it the conviction that the best way to escape being condemned for failure was to pretend that, whatever critics might say, surrealists could not fail. As described in the 1924 manifesto, surrealism proposed psychic automatism as a means for expressing the real functioning of thought. Automatism was to be a method whereby the practitioner elected to perform "at the dictation of thought, in the absence of any control exercised by reason" (p. 40). Implied at that point was the following idea: the real functioning of thought is inhibited or thwarted as soon as reason is permitted to intervene, either in the thinking process itself or in its transcription, during the stages by which it is communicated to an audience. Also implicit was the idea that communication presupposes in the automatist's audience the capacity to respond extrarationally, to receive the poetic image on the wavelength used for its emission. However successful the automatist has managed to be, when working at thought's dictation, his success in transmitting poetic images will depend on his public's ability to tune in precisely, without attempting to listen while distracted by static produced by reason's intrusive pretensions.

In Breton's definition of surrealism there was a feature well worth noting. When alluding to "the dictation of thought," it drew a distinction between thought and thinker to which most people are unaccustomed. Normally taken for granted, the proprietory relationship linking man to his thought was rejected in Breton's text. Moreover, this was not a passing fancy with Breton, who reversed the order of priority, describing man as "soluble in his own thought." Born under the sign of Pisces, he gave the automatic texts appended to his first surrealist manifesto the title *Poisson soluble* (soluble fish). Viewed as Breton regarded it, thought cannot be encompassed within the mind of man. Instead, it exists autonomously. Man's obligation—at the same time his privilege—is to record whatever he can of thought, seen as functioning outside human supervision and thus retaining its purity.

Since man no longer controls thought, the surrealists maintained, he should aim to let himself be possessed by it, taken over by a force to which he can respond most freely while practicing automatism. Premeditation may be described as an effort to break in upon thought, instead of tapping it, as automatism has the virtue of permitting the poet to do. And that, Breton suggested, is a futile attempt, destined to fail because it cannot bring results comparable with those achieved when a poet placed himself at the disposal of thought, writing at its dictation. Certainly, in surrealism premeditation was judged incapable of presenting the writer who availed himself of it with the opportunity to test a fundamental article of surrealist faith: that language can assume a cognitive function.

The nonreflective use of language seems likely to commit a writer to chaos. Yet the surrealists were persuaded that it permits him to bring a new order to light. It was a major article of their faith that removal of contaminating rational reflection has neither a crippling nor an inhibiting effect. Instead, they argued, with release from restraints imposed by reason comes revelation, to cast the writer in a role to which surrealist doctrine ascribed special significance.

Among the surrealists practitioners of verbal automatism gave up control over what they consigned to paper in the expectation of seeing this sacrifice prove beneficial. The benefits anticipated were expected to combine to open up a new perspective on the world, bringing new perceptions of it. Whatever automatic writing rendered visible had nothing to do with studied, calculated effect and everything to do with unpredictable discovery. Consequently, discovery beyond the anticipated, beyond the projected, would be unfettered by the reasoning mind. More than this, it would lie outside the limits of the hoped for. Thus automatism offered surrealists the unrivalled prospect of finding more than they could seek consciously, of learning more than they could knowingly want to know. Experimenting with automatism launched the writer on an adventure that released him from the confines over which reason exercises tutelage.

Central in all this is the fact that automatic writing does not betray loss of control but its deliberate surrender. Hence it is possible for the writer when reviewing his text to marvel over the revelations it places before him. Far from being imprisoned in a mental universe from which he cannot escape (as would be the case, sadly, with someone of unbalanced mind), the practitioner remains at liberty to stand back afterward from what he has written. Thus rereading seems to coincidence with resumption of the critical posture reason makes possible and indeed imposes on the evaluative mind. All the same, as reference to evaluation helps us understand, things are not quite as simple

as they sound. We sense why when, in the *Manifeste du surréalisme*, we come across Breton's frank admission, more of a boast,
really, "I am in no hurry to understand myself" (p. 48). Only
a few pages later we are told that reason will confine itself
to "noting" and "appreciating" the automatic image (p. 53).

One can accept that reason will consent to take note of the
existence of the image in question. Even so, without supposing
reason predisposed to approve, one cannot feel confident that
it will go on to appreciate "the luminous phenomenon" that
Breton called the image. This would mean condoning something
that would not exist at all, had not reasonable objections to
its formulation been forestalled by a technique to which the
writer is indebted for the images he prizes. Does not the inconsistency here appear insurmountable?

In the writing procedure outlined in the first surrealist manifesto reason is treated as a factor to be excluded from the tran-
scriptive process only to be called back into service once that
process is complete (or, to be more exact, suspended). Summoned to examine the fruits of automatic writing, reason is
assumed to be capable of responding sympathetically to imagery
that has come into existence thanks to the writer's implementation of a technique utilized precisely because it bypasses reasonable resistance to the blossoming image. Of course, André Breton
specified that reason should be pressed into evaluative service
only if needed. But when doing this he begged one question
at least. Who or what was to decide when reason's evaluative
services were needed? One thing is clear, all the same. Reason
was to be allowed to intervene only where it would offer confirmation that the automatist had been justified in writing in total
disregard of reason.

On the surface, Breton's manner of conducting his argument
in the *Manifeste du surréalisme* and the presuppositions underlying that argument appear flawed, even quite erratic. He posited
a submissiveness that can only seem questionable to rational-
ists. The objection appears well founded that he neither played
fair nor even tried to do so. Actually, though, this objection
does not take full account of what Breton looked to verbal automatism to provide. Calling reason into service after the event,
he was not taking for granted its voluntary surrender of prerogatives, confident that it would join in celebrating its own defeat.
Approval from reason was more than he expected, more, he
would have acknowledged, than could possibly be expected.
Still, however antagonistic reason might prove to be, with re-

spect to the automatic image, it could provide a valuable service all the same.

At the time the automatist reread what he had written, reason supplied a yardstick for measuring the distance traveled by the imagination liberated from reason's surveillance. When Breton declared that surprise must be sought for itself "unconditionally," he was laying down a condition of his own: that the creative act be undertaken subject to circumstances that could induce surprise, a reaction left for the reasoning mind to register. Inviting reason to admit surprise was very far from requesting its approval and just as far from seeking reconciliation with it. Indeed, the less likelihood there was of reconciliation, the more convincing the surrealists would have considered evidence in image form of automatism's success in playing its part as an agent of imaginative release. Thus the role reserved for reason was not to encourage or condemn, but to bear witness to the capacity resident in a nonreflective technique to precipitate images of a kind that reason itself could not inspire.

It was not Breton's hope to make reason an accomplice in its own defeat. All the same, he left place for it in the review process by which the usefulness of automatism was to be judged. Excluded during the creative act of writing, reason was readmitted at the evaluative stage for which rereading provided the direction of imaginative liberation. Hence its contribution was far from negligible. In fact, reason emerged as important when the moment arrived to ask why the practice of verbal automatism had been appropriate to promoting surrealism's aims. Because automatism spared those who used it the necessity for exercising conscious control over what they wrote, one thing was patently essential. After their material had been recorded on paper, they had to present it for scrutiny, probing enough to obviate the criticism that automatic writing was nothing, really, but a feeble excuse for self-indulgence. At that point, the hostility with which reason could be relied upon to greet the automatic image yielded proof enough that verbal automatism had vindicated itself.

Now we can grasp the meaning of Breton's celebrated dictum, "surrealism is what *will be*." Far from constituting an unsubstantiated claim relying on succinct formulation to lend it a measure of persuasiveness, that dictum drew strength from the surrealist practice of automatism. The surrealist automatic text presents as already existing things that reason flatly denies or tries to bring into question. It records poetic intuition. It communicates a perception that does not need reason's support before it can command attention and inspire confidence. The surrealists prized poetic intuition as evidence of prescience. They saw it as now attaining—in the case of automatic writing, through recorded verbal imagery—something that, over reason's objections, will manifest itself in our daily lives at some later date.

The distinction between the products of reason (as well as things enjoying reason's confidence), on the one hand, and the products of automatic writing, on the other, is brought out in a metaphor from Breton's *Anthologie de l'humour noir*, where Tristan Corbière is credited with having introduced verbal automatism into French poetry with his *Amours jaunes* (1873). Breton refers to Corbière as having been the first to let himself be borne along by "the wave of words" in opposition to which most people set up "the dyke of immediate sense."[4] Immediate sense is to be understood as meaning identified and endorsed by reason. If the wave of words is permitted to gather sufficient force, we infer, it is capable of breaching the dyke and hence carrying the poet on to a sense not immediately perceptible because reason cannot embrace it. At the moment when the automatic text comes under examination, the value of reason is neither to reject nor to cavil. Reason provides, rather, an opportunity for the poet to estimate how far automatism has carried him beyond the point at which reason would have interfered to curb the imagination. It is summoned as a hostile witness, delivering its testimony by withholding approval of the automatic image. Thus to surrealists reason's objections continually confirm that automatism is a practical means for arriving at viable images. The latter are "luminous," to borrow André Breton's adjective, in that they shine with a light emanating from sources over which reason is forced to confess it exercises no influence. Reason, then, is not summoned to review the material provided by automatism in the hope that approval will follow. Instead, reason's unwillingness (inability) to approve authenticates the automatic method, confirming its validity. From this we learn that surrealists for whom the *how* of verbal automatism answered the *why* of writing practiced automatism because to do so was, in their estimation, the best means of circumventing certain obstacles.

It was André Breton who observed that the obstacles facing man are of two kinds, those inside him and those outside. Verbal automatism was valuable in supplying a means for man to cast down obstacles rising within him. Erected and kept in repair mainly by reason, its demands, and interdictions, these inner obstacles subjected thoughts and images to confinement within the rational field. They were, therefore, obstacles that could be toppled only if one succeeded in discrediting reason as the unquestioned arbiter overseeing image-making activities. Release from reason's tutelage, surrealists did not doubt, guaranteed right of entry to poetry. Now automatism furnished the writer with a safe conduct into a zone where poetic revelations would come his way without his having to seek them, even though—given the conditions under which he wrote automatically—it was not in his power to choose or reject them. The magic of automatic writing was that it made possible informative reconnaissance into the poetic domain. Moreover, it did this with enough success to deepen the surrealists' respect for poetry. Hence in their eyes, it justified reserving the adjective *poetic* for imagery that the criteria of literature were inadequate to assess.

A fascinating thing about automatic writing was that it seemed to invest those practicing it with special powers. More fascinating still was the fact that engaging in automatic writing convinced the surrealists of automatism's capacity to bring them into contact with a power that then spoke through them. Automatism did not appear to open up a source of images on which they might draw at will. Instead, it made them excitingly available to that source, which now transformed their writings into vehicles for imagery of a richness they found quite astonishing.

At this point we gain a clearer perception of the significance, in the first manifesto, of Breton's reference to thought's dictation. With the role of verbal automatist went privileges rewarding enough to explain the surrealists' enthusiasm over automatism. With it went also the necessity to accept an obligation without which the writer would play his designated role inadequately. His first and only duty, we understand, was to place himself at the disposal of the power-generating images such as he was unable to produce with the aid of reflection, within an aesthetic frame of reference. The purity of the subliminal message had to be protected from debasement of the kind that surrealists argued would result from interference by reason. This is why Breton proposed deciding, in advance of a session of automatic writing, upon a letter of the alphabet with which the writer would resume his text, should it be interrupted at any time.

The arbitrary choice of that letter would help protect the automatist from the temptation to prolong what he had already written,
whether associatively or logically.

In what the surrealist manifesto has to tell about the technique
of automatic writing everything encourages us to look upon
thought as autonomous and upon man as permitted, through
automatism, to serve as witness to thought. In 1924 Breton's
excitement over the revelations of verbal automatism was great
enough to induce him to require poets to write solely at
thought's dictation. The danger was one that it took surrealists
a little time to perceive and acknowledge.

Described the way it was in the *Manifeste du surréalisme*,
automatism extended equal opportunity to all who practiced
it. Breton did nothing to refine the idea that eluding reason's
supervision is sure to bring the writer luminous images in pleas-
ing profusion. Thus he skirted a question of capital importance.
Why do automatic texts by a variety of writers display images
of palpably varying richness, distributed in uneven density?

Looking back to André Breton's remarks about the impression automatic writing made upon him in 1919, we see they
all reflect amazement at automatism's capacity to release images he found admirable. The circumstances under which *Les
champs magnétiques* was written did not provide a sampling
broad enough to force Breton to consider how narrow his conclusions actually were. In attributing all that was exciting about
verbal automatism to the release effected by automatism, he
was already on the way to making a deduction from which
his later definition of surrealism would grow—that automatism
permits individuals writing at thought's dictation to become
modest recording instruments. Despite his acquaintance with
the teachings of Freud, when drafting his manifesto Breton failed
to stress that in reality the automatist writes at the dictation
of his own thought. As a result, no one reading *Poisson soluble*
is likely to mistake this text for the work of a lifelong surrealist
automatist, Benjamin Péret.

Breton was concerned with demonstrating in his original surrealist manifesto that automatism was a precious technique for
bringing writers into contact with poetic surrealism. Hence he
risked giving his audience the impresson that poetry was, and
had to be, a quite monotonously uniform blessing. It was left
to an associate, Louis Aragon, to point out—his tone rather sharp
in *Traité du style* (1928)—that inanities resulting from applica-

tion of the automatic method are no less inane than those produced by any other method. The purity with which surrealist
theory credited the products of automatism, as writing was withdrawn from reason's influence, should not be thought to have
placed the automatic text above criticism of any kind. Surrealists
were too sensitive to the quality of images—graded according
to their intensity (in Breton's metaphor, by the length of the
poetic spark)—to refrain from judgment, to grant every automatist equal success, every time.

Again, though, it is important to avoid confusing evaluation
with the judgment for which one looks to reason. Here Breton's
metaphor of the illuminating spark is instructive. One does not
need reason's assistance when estimating the length of an elec-
tric spark traversing a vacuum. Indeed, Breton's faith in automatic writing as efficiently producing a vacuum (the absence
of reflective thought) for the spark's passage complements another belief: that while one may produce a spark by bringing
into proximity two conductors of differing potential one cannot
plan an image of the kind surrealists admired by delibertely
trying to bring "two distant realities" together. The deductive
process that is reason's prerogative is dismissed as irrelevant.
In Breton's judgment the two terms constituting the image—
where two unrelated realities meet in surreality (the higher sense
of reality to which Herbert Read correctly alluded when translat-
ing surréalisme as "superrealism")—cannot be assembled "with
a view to the spark to be produced." They are, instead, the
simultaneous products of the activity called surrealist in the
Manifeste du surréalisme.

The first surrealist manifesto characterizes images as guiding
man in the headlong galop of automatic writing. "The mind,"
we are told, "is convinced little by little of the supreme reality
of these images" (p. 53). Reason has dropped back, now, even
though Breton persists in mentioning it, in drawing it into the
game, so to speak. The mind that lets itself be convinced of
the supreme reality of automatic images has ceased to submit
them to reason for appraisal. This mind is described as "borne
along by those images which delight it, which scarcely leave
it time to blow on the fire of its fingers." Not surprisingly, a
mind that has fingers to blow on has left reason far behind.
It is to this mind that the "strongest" images, after Breton's
classification, offer their appeal. For we are facing images "which
one takes the longest time to translate into practical language,"
into the language of rational exchange.

During the cognitive process of image making through automatic writing, the knowledge gained comes from outside reason's jurisdiction. Thus it may be prized—will be prized, Breton thought—even though (especially because) reason is reluctant to learn anything from the revelatory image and is patently incapable of doing so. Cognition, therefore, benefits the mind unfettered by reason. This mind will perceive the beauty of the image-spark, not aesthetically but on a plane where illumination owes least to rational comprehension. In the circumstances, the strongest images, in Breton's view, were the ones presenting "the greatest degree of arbitrariness."

Just when it seems that reason has been eliminated, after all, from the automatic image, it is summoned to play a role. For what else but reason will classify a given image as arbitrary? What is the arbitrary, if not a challenge reason has been unable to meet? Favorable reaction to the arbitrary image calls for acknowledgment that rational associations have been rendered inoperative, that the mind is therefore at liberty to admire things reason can neither help us glimpse nor prevent us from seeing. Whether the surrealist alluded to the quality of the automatic image or to its intensity, the scale of values invoked was one to which reason is powerless to refer. Reason's inadequacy is thus proportionate to the image's success, the *Manifeste du surréalisme* implies, when, for instance, Breton cites images carrying "an enormous dose of apparent contradiction" (pp. 53–54). Two deductions suggest themselves at this point. First the contradiction flagrantly perceptible to reason being no more than apparent, it must be treated as a delusion by which one may judge the inability of reason to come to terms with the image fruitfully. Second, beneath apparent contradictions the mind that has dispensed with reason manages to perceive as consistent elements in a given image that appear arbitrary only on the surface, the level at which reason operates.

The latter deduction is critical to fuller understanding of the value surrealists attached to verbal automatism. The purpose in writing automatically was not to discomfort reason. Nor was it, even, to aggravate men and women of rational bent. To the surrealists, reason was not the last enemy that shall be destroyed but a hindrance. Setting that hindrance aside facilitated progress along the route by which they expected to advance toward something lying past the obstacle of rationalism. If reason might be said to overlay the surface of the mind, then automatism could be regarded as the means available to writers eager to

penetrate that surface, to reach depths of perception and response where imagination, not rationalist thinking, governs the
mind's reaction to whatever it encounters, conditioning it. Thus
so far as the image is to be seen as an illuminating spark, it
is not unfair to speak of reason as an agent possessed of unwelcome flame retardant properties.

The surrealists developed an original point of view on the
creative act and its interpretation. That it was, coincidentally,
a radically dissident viewpoint may be gauged when, next to
the argument conducted in André Breton's 1924 manifesto, we
place, for example, the one behind Noam Chomsky's question,
"What is the nature of mental representations in the domains
where it is reasonable to postulate them?"[5] Fundamental to
Chomsky's position—which he obviously sees no necessity to
defend—is the supposition that, to be tenable, postulations have
to be reasonable. Underlying Breton's was the conviction that
only antireasonable postulations merit attention, promising illumination. True, when speaking of mental representation, Chomsky does not mean the same thing at all as Breton meant when,
for instance, reporting in his first manifesto how, in a moment
of drowsiness, he became aware of a sentence of untraceable
origin, "There is a man cut in two by the window," passing
through his mind to the accompaniment of "a weak visual representation" (p. 35). All the same, the contrast is inescapable
between what Breton wanted his readers to accept and what
Chomsky, placing himself within a tradition against which surrealism was in revolt, assumes his audience will agree with
him in accepting without question.

Surrealists departed from the tradition that informs Chomsky's thinking when they challenged the idea that the basis of
acceptability for mental representation must be reasonableness.
We notice how, formulating his position, Chomsky relies on
reason to defend reason. Without hesitation, he employs an adjective ("reasonable") that, surrealists would have countered,
is unexceptionable only on the surface where rational values
meet no objection. Not content with raising objections, the surrealists firmly rejected those values. They were convinced that
mental representations deserving of attention gather strength
in proportion as reason proves insufficient to measure their
full impact.

In the *Manifeste du surréalisme* weaknesses ascribed to reason
are given precedence over the strengths it is commonly said
to possess. At the same time, some of these strengths are inter-

preted as grave weaknesses. In 1924 and subsequently, André Breton's intent evidently was to demonstrate reason's inadequacy in dealing with questions that, so surrealists contended, remain the province of poetry. Bringing reason's weaknesses before his readers, he demanded attention in a manner consistent with his desire to illustrate one of the principal virtues surrealists detected in poetry: its ability to address us on a level where reason can do no more than demonstrate insufficiencies and display failings.

With a persistence masked perhaps, initially, by the meandering progress of its central theme, the original surrealist manifesto drew a clear and unwavering distinction. On the one side it placed reason. It placed poetry on the other side, where it would not come under the jurisdiction of reason's court. Thus Breton's presentation was consonant with surrealist practice. For surrealists sought to evade the controls so confidently imposed by reason. More than this, they aimed to show that where poetry exerts its rights, reason's controls are patently inapplicable, swept aside by demands with which the rational mind is out of sympathy because it cannot comprehend them or project fruitful consequences for them. And so submitting automatic writing to reason for authentication would have been entirely inappropriate. In addition, it would have had to be acknowledged as an unacceptable betrayal of the spirit of unrestricted inquiry leading the surrealists to put a premium on automatism.

It was not merely the resounding crash of reason's falling barriers that brought the surrealists pleasure as they wrote automatically. Much more excitingly, the practice of verbal automatism extended them the privilege of discovering that, removed without leaving a trace, those barriers no longer existed for them. Whether or not the surrealists were correct in claiming that what they then witnessed was "the real functioning of thought" is less pertinent by far than one undeniable advantage of automatic writing. Its practice saved Breton and his associates from succumbing to a paradox. They were spared the ridiculous (and at the same time quite dangerous) necessity of trying to reason their way out of dependence on reason. The fascination of automatism—and this would be as true for the surrealist painter as for the word poet—was in seeing it provide tangible evidence of a power operating in defiance of reason to take the artist over, making him creative in ways reason could neither anticipate nor regulate. No wonder the surrealists in Paris, infected with enthusiasm for verbal automatism, were soon eagerly responsive to the appeal of mediumistic trance, to which they were introduced by one of their number, René Crevel. Spiritualism held no meaning for those men and women who were without faith in an afterlife. Yet they felt irresistibly attracted to the thought of being possessed by a force capable of speaking through individuals in whom no opposition from reason would stem its power.

When they engaged in automatic writing and experimented with self-hypnosis, the surrealists were delighted to find evidence convincing them, from two directions at once, of something they considered deeply important. Breton would remember this when declaring later, in his *Ajours* (completed in May 1947), "The act of love, on the same score as the painting or poem, is disqualified if, on the part of the person giving himself over to it, it does not presuppose *entry into a trance*."[6] Surrealists would never cease to maintain that the state of trance, among other functions, serves to reverse the regressive condition they equated with rationalism. They saw it as returning anyone who entered it to the enviable condition of wonderment which André Breton recalled nostalgically from childhood.

That was a distinguishing feature of automatism. A liberative agent, it proved to be a source of creativity. By it the practitioner was blessed with revelations all the more exciting because they allowed him not a moment's hesitation in admitting one thing: he saw automatism as revelatory because it presented him with discoveries he knew no other way to approach. With release from respect for aesthetic regulations and from the moral and ethical demands framed by society came a sense of enlarged capability.

The one rule to follow made but a single demand, that the automatist heed none of the sanctions consecrated by tradition, reason, social and moral obligations. The wonder to which respect for that sole rule earned him access had a clearly definable origin: learning over and over again that neglect of tradition's rules did not cast him adrift in chaos, but guided him from illumination to illumination through a world lit by the effulgence of images.

3
The Critical Reception: What Is Poetry?

It is a truism that the creative artist and critics writing about his work do not always see eye to eye, especially at the time when that work first attracts public attention. Whether critical response reflects mere skepticism or alarm, however, it is common to find some modification in the critics' attitude once the artist's position has taken on clearer definition and his motivation and its consequences appear more tolerable as they are better understood. Eventually the most recalcitrant artists can expect to meet with approval, it seems, and even enjoy consecration, in many instances.

If there is a signal contradiction to an apparently general rule, it is offered in the relationship maintained by critical judgment vis-à-vis surrealism. Where acceptance conditioned evaluation, it afforded surrealism's artists no satisfaction. Indeed, the fact that limited approval elicited more protest than pleasure from within the surrealist group indicates something noteworthy. Assessing achievement in the field of surrealist endeavor gives rise to special problems, which critics still have not managed to resolve in ways the surrealists would have deemed appropriate.

No more is gained by condemning critics as in the wrong than comes from attributing the fault entirely to the surrealists' side. Meanwhile we do not progress far at all by simply taking note of the surrealists' displeasure with conventional literary criticism or again by reviewing, among the remarks of the majority of critics, evidence of misgivings about or disappointment with surrealist works. Instead, we need to ask what may be learned about surrealism from dissatisfaction among its proponents with the treatment they received at the hands of critics and from the surrealists' response to appraisals of what they did, which originated outside their closed circle. The keys to the questions one must ask about the value of surrealist creative action do not lie in mistrust and antagonism but are found in the reasons why, in the surrealists, this mistrust deepened to the point where antagonism, more than simple misunderstanding, appeared to explain the critics' motivation. And as we proceed we should remember that the situation has not improved since organized surrealist activities lost momentum not very long after the death of André Breton.

Most commentators have concluded that the surrealists deserved castigation rather than approval for persisting in what they did the way they did. Was everything the result of misapprehension? It would simplify matters if one could respond with an unqualified yes, and if one were dealing with literary considerations only.

Dedication to meeting the demands imposed upon them made participants in the surrealist movement impatient with anybody who, looking in from outside, presumed to assess their accomplishments from a position other than their own. To surrealists the alternatives were unambiguously clear: one was either for surrealism or one was against it. Hence reference to any code— moral, ethical, aesthetic—that surrealism did not sanction or condone seemed to be proof enough. Suspicion on the surrealists' part was not merely permissible; it was mandatory. A critic who did not identify wholeheartedly with surrealism must be up to no good and easily could do harm.

How could the surrealists have developed such a negative attitude and defend it so vigorously? What grounds did they have for withholding trust, sometimes even before they were confronted with samples of critical commentary? Were these men and women merely bandits, best ignored? Examination of the evidence accessible to us shows their situation to have been more complex and deserving of attention than their isolationism would suggest.

To some extent in any case, surrealism's writers were victims of their situation. Had their principal spokesmen not been, at the start, aspirant poets in the conventional sense of the term, then their later ambition to write poetry according to new anti-literary criteria might not have seemed paradoxical at best and at worst a sign of an impulse to shirk responsibility. If each of them had called himself by a name other than "poet," then all might have had a better chance to escape hearing their work judged according to standards that literary commentators are accustomed to apply to poetic achievement. After all, the progress Breton succeeded in making, out of disenchantment with poetry and into renewed confidence in it, was indicative of

the surrealist posture: if the creative artist could no longer believe in poetry, he was not obligated to steer his way back
to confidence. Instead, it was incumbent on poetry—evidently
Breton, for one—to change in nature sufficiently to earn his
trust. And this could come about only if poetry were to lend
itself to redefinition according to a procedure giving it new
direction and purpose. The surrealists' refusal to be bound by
conventions and regulations with which they saw no reason
to comply lent itself to interpretation as arrogance. And this
interpretation was no more exaggerated than their condemnation
of their detractors as incompetent, insensitive, and unintelli-
gently tradition-bound. Surrealism could not but appear suspect
when its advocates adopted a literary designation for their writings while yet denying that their poems were literature.

There is another factor to be considered also. In part, the
confusion surrounding the function distinctive of surrealism's
writers may be traced to one source. In certain respects, their
conduct seemed to place them at the end of a long poetic tradition. Their dedication to the proposition that poets should and
must play a sacerdotal role gave them the appearance of wishing
to pursue an eminently respectable goal. Yet their interpretation
of that goal and of the requirements they saw it making on
the poet seemed to drain their efforts of respectability.

The birth of the surrealist movement owed much—almost
everything, some would claim—to André Breton's early disappointment with poetry in its inherited forms and to his effort
to give poetic endeavor new direction. Even so, we need to
maintain a balanced view of the origins of surrealism. Specifically, it is important to bear in mind that the individuals with
whom Breton shared surrealist ambitions had shared, too, his
commitment to Dada, had left the Dada ranks just as he had
done, and were, like him, young men who aspired to be poets.
All along, their approach to poetry was no less traditionalist
than his, in that each of them wanted to *write* poems. Had
Breton and his first companions not begun as writers, and (if
we limit attention to the list of names presented in his 1924
Manifeste du surréalisme) had they not continued to pursue
their surrealist goals in the medium of writing, then it would
have been easier to justify their demands that their aims and
accomplishments be judged outside literature.

Here arise hidden questions, which no surrealist ever displayed the least inclination to entertain, let alone answer. In
characterizing their purpose as extraliterary, were the surrealists

actually seeking refuge behind a declaration they really could not defend adequately? Were they not, after all, *littérateurs* who pretended to scorn literature? The answers to these questions lie deeper than in the surrealists' protestations of antiliterary preoccupations. They can be traced to the orientation of texts produced under impetus from surrealist ambitions.

André Breton felt it imperative to discredit the realist attitude. Very early in his first surrealist manifesto he proposed bringing it "to trial." Despite the care he took to pinpoint weaknesses in that attitude—which he condemned as appearing "hostile to all intellectual and mental release" (p. 18), and in spite of his avowed contempt for fiction as an expression of the realist attitude in literature, the *Manifeste* did not make Breton's position entirely clear. From the contempt he expressed for a passage in *Crime and Punishment* readers were free to conclude that he aimed his objections at a literary fashion, roughly dismissed as quite outmoded by 1924. In reality, Breton was protesting against the presumption that, for capturing the real, all one needs is the talent to describe the visible. Behind his attack on Dostoievsky lay the conviction that realism, so called, was a false goal. Breton returns to this theme in his *Second manifeste,* where he sought to draw attention to *"the reverse of the real"* (p. 195). Admittedly, as he himself noted, this last phrase only approximately identified what he had in mind. Still the time had come, he argued in 1929, to put an end to "provoking 'realist' insanities."

Breton's choice of words betokens protest against more than a literary convention. It highlights rejection of the proposition that the real is subject to categorization from the vantage point of objective observation. The degree to which objectivity may be considered a literary convention, and even a delusion, does not enter into the question. What counts most is Breton's unwillingness to countenance the thought that reality is limited to features that surface observation manages to record. His goal was a "general reclassification of lyrical values" (p. 195), which, we are assured, would dispose of "an alibi," whether of a literary kind or any other.

The consequences of Breton's outlook were far-reaching. They began with denial of the hypothesis that realistic description in fiction can represent reality with fidelity. They included adoption of a perspective patently in conflict with the assumptions underlying realistic or naturalistic description and leading to a perception of reality beyond that of realism and naturalism. Rejecting the latter's limitation, Breton opposed the restrictions placed on reality, not only in its fictional rendition but also in our awareness of and grasp upon it. This is why his second manifesto pointed out that in recent years, "the poetic question" had ceased to be raised "from the essential formal angle" (p. 202). Hence facing that question promoted to major importance "the subversive value" of writing by men like—to cite just those named by Breton—Louis Aragon, René Crevel, Paul Eluard, and Benjamin Péret. While Breton saw no need to say as much, he perceived subversion in the writers he mentioned as directed against an antiquated idea of poetry. Subversion took effect by undermining a sense of the real judged woefully incomplete by all surrealists.

From the *Second manifeste du surréalisme* one may infer readily enough that the surrealist mind aimed to broaden poetry by working actively to eliminate restrictions of a formal nature. It is important to notice at the same time that the poetic liberation for which surrealists made their plea did not entail rejection of format considerations simply in order to mark resistance to confinement of poetry within the boundaries of an aesthetic tradition handed down from the nineteenth century to the twentieth. Breaking with that tradition surely was a factor helping encourage in Breton and others scorn for any writer preoccupied with matters of style and form. However, something more was at stake than the issue of aesthetic convention, of course. More significant than the need surrealists felt to depart from literary traditions was their refusal to subscribe to the view—tacitly accepted generally, if not openly defended—that inherited forms can encompass the subject matter of poetry and render it adequately communicable. We lose contact with the surrealist mind if we fail to understand that the surrealists aimed beyond protest against the preservation of traditional modes of literary expression. The central purpose to which they bent their efforts was the liberation of the processes by which the poetic message is transmitted, freeing them from dependence on inherited formal customs. Not content with rearranging and, wherever it might seem necessary, revising literary techniques, the individuals grouped around André Breton shared a mental attitude from which surrealism derived its originality. They all looked upon the preservation of formal conventions as setting inadmissible restraints on verbal expression and, more dangerous by far, on man's perception of reality.

Now many a twentieth-century writer has displayed scant respect for the structures favored in nineteenth-century poetry. More often than not, the poets who have commanded attention since the early 1900s have done so while expressing themselves in forms departing radically from traditionally popular ones. Yet none of them has incurred the critics' displeasure for being formally innovative. Nor has any of them been given cause to complain that, discussing his work, commentators have been guilty of misconstruing its significance, as was the case, surrealists contended, when surrealism came under critical scrutiny. We have to look a little more closely to understand the unique features of the surrealists' position and to appreciate their reasons for affirming that the critics had failed to come to terms with surrealist poetry.

While rejecting formalism of the traditionalist kind, nonsurrealist poets of the twentieth century have tended to develop formalist modes of their own. Feeling comfortable with such modes and seeing their use as productive, those poets have borrowed one or other or several of them, which they perceived as offering a suitable framework within which poems might be cast. In other words, although nonsurrealist modern poets no longer perpetuate nineteenth-century traditions, they agree with the principles dictating those traditions, continuing to treat form both as a disciplinary element and a communicative vehicle worthy of confidence. In this respect, the surrealists saw such poets as keeping alive a myth that according to surrealist theory must be put to rest in order for poetry to be free to serve the cause of affranchisement to which all surrealists devoted their energies.

The surrealists' concept of poetry assigned the writer a task that brought reality under review and subjected it to examination in a manner promoting redefinition of the real. The extent to which that undertaking has been misunderstood, and so misrepresented, is quite easy to estimate.

One has to do no more than notice how frequently the dubious adjective "surrealistic" is used as a designation for the unfamiliar, the fanciful, or the inconceivable to realize how many people imagine surreality exists only in defiance of reality, as a departure from it. Lost from sight is a tenet of surrealist faith—that since it is a heightened sense of the real, surreality denotes a tighter grip on reality and represents an enlarged perception of it. Once surrealists are viewed as having sought to withdraw

from the real world, the purpose of their activity evaporates.
Then surrealism is reduced to the status of an oddity, an aberra-
tion of literature and art. Seen this way, it is entirely dependent
for acceptance on the good will of the public, having no raison
d'être outside the indulgence with which the men and women
who practice it are permitted to attempt to evade reality because
they are judged disinclined to face up to it or simply unable
to do so. By this procedure surrealism is relegated to the rank
of a peripheral activity, liable to amuse or offend, according
to the disposition of the observer. The contrast is plain between
such an estimate of surrealism and the viewpoint of its adherents. The latter saw themselves as dealing with central questions
about the nature of reality and considered themselves betrayed,
when represented as devoting themselves to less serious pur-
suits.

Surrealism did not originate in an attempt to overthrow reality. It was, though, an effort to face up to the real. It did not
demand reducing reality to terms that man can handle without
undue strain but, on the contrary, extending man's response
capabilities. The surrealists declined to confine the real to proportions with which the reasoning human mind finds itself at
ease. Instead, they aimed at expanding man's awareness of reality. They saw understanding of the real as increasing while
presuppositions about it fell away. Thus they linked knowledge
neither with prior acquaintance, rational projection, nor deduction but with imagination, with release from inherited and inculcated inhibitions. They expected that release to follow upon
an imaginative leap beyond the familiar or the predictable into
the never-thought.

The operating principle in which surrealists placed their trust
did not require them to ignore or turn their backs on reality,
least of all to deny its existence. Surrealism demanded that
the aim to communicate increased sensitivity to reality, thereby
invalidating the procedures by which literary realism implicitly
argues for its control when limiting our perspective on what
is real. This is why the surrealists' attitude to the surreal as
an enriched and enriching sense of reality developed along with
their ideas about the relationship between reality and reason.

Imagination became a congitive agent, in surrealism, at the
forefront of knowledge and of primary value to man in his
relations with the world about him. Intuition, prescience, revelations under hypnosis—the surrealist prized all these signs of
extrarational perception. He saw them as intimations of a uni-

verse about which we remain in ignorance so long as the cognitive modes we respect have their basis in reason—so long, for instance, as we give precedence to the idea that reality "makes sense." Thus nonsense, to the surrealist mind, was not close to chaos; it was familiar reality modified and corrected.

Among those who do not comprehend surrealism are people who look upon the real as verifiable, as something to be checked against past experience or observation. These individuals fail to see that for the surrealist the dimensions of the real cannot be gauged by reference to the familiar. So far as the real appears to have limits, they are foisted upon it by the mental, emotional, and imaginative limitations of spectators accustomed to measure the possible by the already known. For this reason, surrealism and many of its contemporary opponents remained inevitably at loggerheads. The one group insisted on estimating the scope of reality by its possibilities. The other condemned the real to be repetitive of what the past had shown them. More than this, they saw of the real only what they had been able to glimpse in the past while using mental, imaginative, and emotional equipment that, the surrealists argued, demonstrably erodes reality. The differences separating the surrealists and their detractors go deeper than literary taste or methodology and center on a fundamental question: What should be the object of the poet's attention (and the painter's too), giving focus to the creative gesture and to its evaluation?

The motivating forces of surrealism elude identification until we grasp one essential point. Even when it first seemed to observers to be no more than a new literary fashion, surrealism already possessed distinctive characteristics it would never lose. It took impetus from two responses at once: dissatisfaction with the present and hope for the future. We shall never understand the tension from which surrealist creative activity originated unless we acknowledge that surrealism grew out of pessimism generated by current circumstances and optimism about a future foretold by art. Succumbing to pessimism, the surrealist artist would have seen the wellspring of his inspiration dry up. Rising above current conditions of life and thought was the reward of art, justifying the latter in ways that traditionalist criticism does not help us better appreciate. Yet this is far from meaning that the surrealists equated art with evasion, with escapism. To the surrealist, art took life only when it surmounted limitations of a mental and emotional nature that condemn us to reliving past experience. Surrealist art was to grant its creator,

as well as those attuned to his work, as sense of release, to
which Benjamin Peret referred when describing poetry as a
"rectification of the universe." We succeed only in entangling
ourselves in misconceptions if we imagine that surrealism represented an effort to distort reality, instead of recognizing that
it existed to set man's perception of reality to rights.

We run a serious risk of missing the point of the undertaking
born in the surrealist mind if we suppose that its purpose was
narrowly focused on discrediting rationalism. Reason was not
the target surrealists wished to destory. The campaign launched
publicly when Breton published his first manifesto mounted
its opening assault on reason with one intention above all. Reason came under attack for reducing the world and man's perception of it to an order the surrealists found unacceptably
confining. Dismissing rationalism, they rejected with it an interpretation of man's relationship to his environment they found
intolerably narrow. Hence resistance to rationalism took Breton
and his friends outside the limits in which it was customary
to judge literature and art as expressions of talent, aesthetic
aspirations, and technical skill.

The surrealists' conflict with reason grew out of their belief
that the rationalist mentality erects barriers that, by shutting
some things in and others out, in their estimation truncate reality. That mentality appeared distortive, seen as forcing restric-
tion on man's perception of the real, on what he took reality
to be. André Breton would not have placed so much faith in
language had he not been persuaded that its principal virtue
is to furnish poets with means for coming to terms with the
world about them. And he would not have preached the affranchisement of language if he had not felt sure that, used
as surrealism directed or permitted, language can broaden and
enrich awareness of reality.

After defining surreality as "absolute reality," the original
manifesto listed the names of several men, singled out as having
given proof of "ABSOLUTE SURREALISM" (p. 40). Breton was
never a negligent writer. So repetition of the same adjective
holds our attention. In the context of Bretonian thinking, repetition testifies to a revealing preoccupation with the absolute.

Surrealists were never to be satisfied with compromise, would
never be content to settle for less than absolute reality. In its
pursuit they remained faithful to Breton's insistence on full
possession of reality as surrealism's primary goal. Positing an

absolute reality and complete confidence in man's ability to
advance to its possession, Breton assured surrealist ideas of
inexhaustible energy. If any of its defenders weakened, their
failure would not reduce the scope of the ambitions they had
fallen short of realizing. The theoretical purity of surrealist aspirations was unsullied by inadequacies in surrealist practice,
bringing surrealism close to a religion that the absence of a
deity failed to deprive of absolutes.

In itself, unswerving fidelity to the search for absolute reality
did not guarantee the surrealist mind total success. Still, it did
supply a yardstick for poetic ambitions and for achievement
in which the desire to progress further was sharpened, not
dulled, by a review of accomplishments already made. Complacency was ruled out as unproductive. It could be no more than
self-delusion in the surrealist or, worse still, marked surrender
of the aspirations animating surrealist art. Conscious of this,
surrealists would not allow themselves to forget that surrealism
militated against what may be termed rationalist prejudices.

To the surrealist mind, rationalist perspectives appeared distortive because they seemed incomplete. And they appeared
incomplete because reason is exclusionary. Thus surrealists saw
reality not as necessarily different from what reason shows us,
but as certainly more than reason enables man to grasp or authorizes him to admit. Thus surrealism was a perception of reality
over which reason was denied the opportunity to exercise confining restrictions. This is why the surrealist mind acknowledged no conflict between real and surreal.

Vratislav Effenberger once declared in the name of surrealism,
"The laws of rational communication are abusive laws which
the reality of communication eludes. They are privative or re-
pressive laws when the regime of works lends them normative
value. It is because it is situated outside the small trade of
information that the word is potentially subversive . . . and
remains capable of undermining the Bastille of formalized rationality by setting up at every moment intersubjective communication in authentic correlations."[1] One thing at least is clear
in Effenberger's statement. Although many surrealists were to
follow André Breton as poets for whom the medium of communication was verbal, none of them would have remained true to
surrealism unless he or she placed language at the disposal
of subversion.

Typically, Vincent Bounoure traced to language surrealism's

opposition to "the present conditions ascribed to the mind."
He spoke of "the certainty that all language is revelatory of
individual structures even when it is made up of the language
of the streets." And he added, that surrealist language stands
out against the "terrorist language"—tending, he said, to impose
itself all around—which he did not hesitate to dub "totalitar-
ian."[2] Bounoure concluded unequivocally with the assertion that
the general objectives of surrealism were to "undermine the
structures of power with which public language coincides at
present," to "return it to its proper function." Those, he affirmed,
were "the terms of surrealist revolution."[3]

The steps through which Effenberger's argument and Bounoure's lead bring us full circle if we now consult a third surrealist, Jean-Louis Bedouin. For the benefit of those who "do not
believe their ears," Bedouin repeated, "we are, we have not
stopped being realists." Nor, he went on, had the surrealists
in the 1970s given up affirming "the all-power of the real,"
to the point of "considering [their] dreams another form of reality."[4] One might add that for surrealists, reality was not an
objective phenomenon but proof of the degree of receptivity
attained by the individual. Thus the limits within which his
sense of reality finds confinement are but the limits under which
the individual responds to reality. Therefore the less reason
is permitted to intrude upon his perception of the real, the
surrealists maintained, the broader will be his awareness of
what reality actually is. The real being potentially boundless
to the surrealist mind, our response to it is restricted only by
the limitations to which we submit—those set up by education,
for example, largely through emphasis on rationalist modes of
perception and evaluation.

The surrealists' aspirations to experience an expanded reality
originated in the firm belief that the world given shape and
purpose by common sense must go on appearing incomplete
and inadequate to man's needs. Identification of poetry with
the removal of commonsensical barriers was to be the initial
step to an increased apperception of the real. Judgment by reason
entailed servitude, the surrealists contended, while poetry was
an affranchisement of potentially limitless scope. Not surprisingly, reproving rationality was consistent with an ambition
to which surrealist ambitions lent meaning: an effort to recover
lost powers of the mind, linked with the characteristic surrealist
endeavor to uncover the previously unknown. For the surrea-

lists looked upon the unknown as presently concealed from us
mainly by the negative influence of rationality.

The surrealists aimed to resolve two questions at one and
the same time, to remedy two weaknesses, each the consequence
of reason's dominance in modern Western man's reaction to
his world. Breton and his associates placed faith in the antirational, used as an instrument for breaking down the barriers
confining man's viewpoint and limiting his outlook. The optimism sustaining the surrealist mind took root in a paradoxical
discovery. Although language, the medium of communication
between men, appears to be a tool reserved for reason's use,
the surrealists concluded that language nevertheless may be
communicative where reason does not govern or restrict its application. In a sense, then, verbal poetry in surrealism turned
language against itself by expanding where rational expression
would retract. The results demonstrated, to the surrealists' pleasure and satisfaction, that reason was no justification for employing language. In fact it could be an obstacle to a revelatory
use of words termed poetry in surrealism.

Looking to poetry to correct our perspective on the real, surrealists separated the creative poetic act from literature. This allowed them to expect the poetic to be weighed on a scale
different from the one used in measuring literary success. So
poetry was not synonymous with avoidance of responsibility
but intimated to the surrealist writer that responsibility lay elsewhere than in meeting literary requirements. By the same token,
being approved by literary critics was neither a consolation
to the surrealist poet nor an excuse for failing to satisfy demands
shaped in the surrealist mind.

Viewed as a technical device, automatic writing was a practical means for increasing sensitivity to the real. Surrealists looked
upon that heightened sensitivity as poetic, in that it transcended
the limits of observed reality and of reality projected within
the boundaries set by rationalist thinking. Very soon, therefore,
automatic writing came to be considered in surrealism as altogether more than a literary method. It exemplifiefd a state of
receptivity from which presuppositions about the nature of the
real had been suppressed. It reflected confidence in reality's
ability to manifest itself beyond the limitations imposed on receptivity by the rational mind. Resistance to those limitations
and denial of the right abrogated by reason to establish them

were fundamental to the surrealist attitude, dictating among other things the following statement in the *Manifest du surréalisme:* "Man proposes and disposes. It rests only with him to belong to himself entirely, that is, to maintain in an anarchic state the gang of his desires, every day more formidable" (p. 31). Allusion to the *bande à Bonnot,* a notorious anarchist gang, underscored Breton's emphasis on leaving human desire in a state of anarchy, in defiance of controls to which reason would subject man.

In his second manifesto, Breton pointed to indications of the annunciatory character of surrealism in its "artistic" expression, placing his adjective in inverted commas. Then he forecast the end of surrealism's preparatory phase, likening to switchmen certain individuals whose arrival he anticipated. Already he was confident of having grounds to be pleased. His 1929 manifesto commended his fellow surrealists for having contributed to demonstrating "the scandalous inanity of what, at our arrival still, *used to be thought*" and for having maintained that "the thought must succumb *at last* before the thinkable" (p. 210).

Breton's remarks bring into focus the surrealist poet's special obligation. Rejection of the already thought distinguishes surrealist poetry from celebration of the familiar. Meanwhile dedication to formulating the thinkable—the not yet thought—required poets to address themselves to the as yet unfamiliar. The basis for communication between poet and public now had to be imaginative projection. This is why the *Second manifeste* called for arresting a "cancer of the mind": thinking that certain things "are," while others—which "could so easily be"—are not (p. 221).

The obstacles to the thinkable raised by reason remind us that the practice of automatism offered the surrealists a method for neutralizing rational thought and so for liberating the rationally unthinkable. It was, above all, a means to embrace what can be in what is, with reality taken to be subjectively grasped, not objectively verifiable. The discovery of verbal automatism led the surrealists to conclude that unmasking something previously not known had to do with recovering powers of the mind lost at a time when respect for rationalist theory was on the upsurge. Once the potentialities of that discovery had been gauged, the surrealist approach to verbal language took on clearer outline and purpose. Thenceforth it could be related to "that generalized temptation to recuperate and restore the 'lost powers' in the face of the gradual dwindling of the human

possible," to which Bounoure and Effenberger referred awk-
wardly,[5] while protesting against "the dominant principles of
so-called western civilization," said to deprive men of the exercise of their "real powers" by prescribing "an increasingly narrow and formalized register of expression."[6]

Behind the surrealist interpretation of the productive use of
language as one of man's lost powers lay the hypothesis that
language as rationalist expression is truly language in decline.
Thus, in the surrealist mind suppression of reason's demands
promoted the rehabilitation of language. Extrarational language
approximated language before the Fall. Reason was cast in the
role of original sin so far as it reflected the hateful intrusion
of society's sanctions on the free use of words, turning language
into the vehicle for utilitarianism instead of poetic communication as surrealists spoke of it. Meanwhile the surrealist judged
society antipoetic in its interests and requirements, seeing it
as equally so in its effects on the purposes to which language
is put. Rejection of Western society and, coincidentally, of Western culture was closely linked with the denial of the social
value of language, which was dismissed as being in radical
conflict with its poetic virtue. From this premise emerged the
postulate that there exists a radical antagonism between poetry
and social exchange of the kind expressed through literature
and other media. Surrealism did not require poetry to be antirational. Still, it did locate poetry beyond range of supervision
by rational thought, where deferring to reason becomes impertinent.

By 1953 Breton had concluded it was time to remind his
readers of something. It was public knowledge, he remarked,
that surrealism as an organized movement had been born of
"a far-reaching operation dealing with language."[7] He took the
opportunity to reaffirm that in its verbal and grapic modes,
automatism owed nothing to aesthetic standards. On the contrary, he now insisted, as soon as vanity allowed such criteria
to take root in any automatist, "the operation was distorted"
while the "'state of grace' which had made it possible was
lost." The loss apeared irreparable because "the state of grace"
had made it easier to deal with "the self-importance of the
elective modes of cognition and intervention" which, according
to Breton, "tempt man during the most recent period of history."[8]
How to replace those unacceptable cognitive modes? The answer
lay in poetic intuition: "It alone provides us with the thread
that sets us back on the path to Gnosis, as cognition of suprasen-

sible Reality, 'invisibly visible in an eternal mystery.'"[9] Another
question takes shape here. How are we to pick up the thread
that will bring us to the pathway of knowledge? The answer
may be traced to the surrealists' concept of the artist's role.

Central to surrealist principles, so far as they affect artistic
endeavor, is the idea of art as mediation. Breton's "Position
politique de l'art d'aujourd'hui" (1935) affirms that art derives
its quality from imagination alone, "independently of the external object that has given it birth" (p. 258). This means that
"everything depends on the liberty with which that imagination
succeeds in bringing itself on stage and in bringing only itself
on stage." Hence surrealism casts the artist in a role best likened
to that of the medium. The surrealist artist did not exist to
formulate a message but to provide the occasion for a message
to reach its audience. While meeting his obligations—essentially
by making himself responsible for communicating a message
faithfully—he was not to be held accountable. Judgment of an
ethical, moral, or aesthetic order was not his to exercise. Nor
did he have to tolerate or submit to being judged on those
terms by anyone encountering his work. His role was to engage
in the communicative process without distorting the message
or reducing its potency.
    One can be tolerant of the theory carried through to surrealist
practice and yet still be puzzled by its application. Indeed, one
continues to be puzzled until the following central question
has received an answer. What message did the surrealist artist-
medium make himself reponsible for communicating? Breton
offered a partial response when explaining, in "Du surréalisme
en ses oeuvres vives": "The whole thing, in surrealism, had
to do with convincing ourselves that we had laid hands on
the 'primary matter' (in the alchemical sense) of language: we
knew, from then on, *where* to find it . . ." (p. 357). Still, he
complained appositely, "There has not been enough emphasis
on the meaning and scope of the operation tending to return
language to its true life." Among surrealists, rejection of critical
evaluation did not denote uncompromising refusal to submit
to assessment by others. It indicated disinclination to look outward while they remained committed to looking inward, attentive to the message they had to share. The artist's only duty
was to the message for which he served as medium. He could
not concern himself about the reception it might receive without
serious risk of modifying that message. Any adjustment to assist
communication in some way would have been a step away

from inspiration toward approval by outsiders. It would have been the first stage in substituting the obligation to meet standards dictated by critical values for another: preservation of the purity of a message prized by the surrealists for its subliminal origins.

The surrealist did not consider himself granted a talent so much as enjoying a special privilege. His attitude precluded vanity. It also designated a role in which his function was limited, but important: to make himself available to the subliminal message. Use of an expressive medium was never to be the exercise of a polished technique or proven skill but the opportunity to reach out to something more than reasoned projection extends *littérateurs* the prospect of attaining thanks to the implementation of reliable, proven techniques.

Scrupulous honesty was required of the surrealist poet, for whom deceiving his public would have precipitated self-deception of a kind that surrealism's demands made it impossible for him to practice voluntarily. Adjustment to the public's expectations entailed self-betrayal and hence invalidation of the surrealist poem. Interruption of contact with the subliminal message could not be remedied by recourse to technical means consciously applied in the hope that they would produce acceptable results. Just as technique guaranteed the surrealist nothing, so it would compensate not at all. For technique was not the highway to art, surrealists felt sure. At best, it might open the door to discovery. Even then, though, it could not lure discovery inside. It merely assisted the artist by making him more receptive, less hesitant to grasp what came before him.

The surrealist attitude was inspired by the belief that the subliminal message is communicable without benefit of prescribed rules and that the surrealist artist might reach his audience without having to accommodate aesthetic regulation or custom. Surrealists viewed communication as placing the artist and his public on a level where aestheticism can be discarded as totally irrelevant. In consequence, one major problem posed by surrealism for the critics lies in their difficulty in answering the following questions with assurance: Where does the surrealist's talent lie? What is the nature of his gifts? His achievement eludes precise critical evaluation. Or, to put it another way, the features of his work seeming to lend themselves to critical assessment were the very ones to which the surrealist himself remained indifferent, his confidence undiminished in his role and in his capacity to fill it.

Because the methods favored in surrealism were intended

to remove obstacles, dissipate inhibitions, and free the imagination, they did not contribute to artistic growth in the way that
implementing generally respected aesthetic principles is supposed to do. Nor did surrealist methods extend the artist the
opportunity to increase command of this medium. They did
not hold out the prospect of better progress toward set goals
so long as skill, dexterity, and familiarity with reliable technique
underwent development. The surrealist artist's success might
be as great the first time he tried out a given technique as the
second or twenty-second. Moreover, it could happen that the
measure of success achieved the first time exceeded that obtained several times later. In surrealism, practice did not make
perfect; it taught no tricks of which the practitioner might take
advantage. This was the other side of the coin, which appeared
to indicate that surrealists succeeded without even trying because conscious effort rewarded them little, if at all. The surrealist artist's position was such that each time he embarked on
the creative act, he started over from the beginning, without
guarantees and without momentum of the kind that allows a
critical observer to say, when speaking of nonsurrealists, that
they are mastering their craft. Had the phrase been applicable
to surrealist creative endeavor, polishing one's technique would
have been viewed, in surrealism, as falling prey to methodology,
becoming its slave not its master.

Surrealists may appear to have been exaggerating when they
demanded that the poet choose between substance and form,
when they ascribed poetic virtue exclusively to the former. Commentators examining surrealism's poetic principles with suspicion have had no trouble drafting a list of names of poets worthy
of respect whose work reflects a felicitous balance between the
two elements surrealists placed in opposition to one another.
Doing so is no more than the obvious form of protest elicited
by the surrealists' argument. True, we can sympathize with the
position taken by the first generation surrealists. Symbolism,
the established literary mode against which they reacted most
consciously because it was the one that several of their number
had tried and found wanting, seemed to have encouraged its
poets to lay emphasize on form. All the same, an early unsatisfactory experience with Symbolism was not the only reason
why the surrealists would always continue to mistrust the effects
of formal preoccupations. Given their conviction that poetry
makes a valuable contribution to the cognitive process by releasing imaginatively stimulating images, any concern for the mold

in which that contribution happened to be cast appeared to the surrealists likely to impede free expression. In their opinion, however small a price might have to be paid to modify the subliminal message so as to facilitate communication or to render it more elegant, it was too high. Rejection of formal considerations was a nonnegotiable condition of poetic action. As a result, surrealist writers would never have consented to treat the conflict between substance and form as a debatable issue. None of them ever would have countenanced the thought that a poet might go on contributing to surrealism beyond the moment he began devoting himself less to what he had to say than to the manner in which it might be said.

Formal considerations did not merely look distracting. They were seen as diverting artists from valid objectives and ousting concerns that should have been paramount. Behind all that the surrealists wrote about traditional rules, regulations, aesthetic demands, and so on lay the belief that attention to any of these would be an unprofitable substitute for true artistic activity. The more the reader attends to these things, the less time and inclination there is for what really mattered to the surrealists. Certainly, in their eyes preoccupation with form was a tacit confession of a lack of inspiration, the drying up of imaginative resources. Thus in surrealism neglect of form was not a pose. Nor did it reflect deliberate choice. It was a necessary accompaniment to poetic activity, clearly indicative of the nature of the surrealists' priorities. Full understanding of their position and appreciation of what it reveals about their approach to art make plain that any discussion purporting to deal with their aesthetics betrays an incomprehension of surrealism and of the requirements it imposed on its artists.

The surrealist who placed himself at the disposal of the subliminal message had to prove himself worthy of it. He had to hold himself ready to serve that message but never take advantage of it in a self-serving manner. He had to continue to be responsible to it without making himself responsible for it before the judgment of the critics. Fidelity, he acknowledged, must go to the subliminal message with no thought for its possible aesthetic qualities. Submission of his message to some kind of quality control had to be excluded from the communicative process. This explains why the surrealist artist worked with a mixture of pride (at having been chosen as the medium through which the message was transmitted) and modesty born of the knowledge that the subliminal message was not his, though his to share. It would have been unjust to accuse all critics of bad faith, but entirely fitting, surrealists agreed among themselves, to blame any of their own group who allowed his efforts to be influenced by the critics' requirements.

The surrealists' rejection of critical judgment established their situation with clarity. When André Breton and Jean Schuster announced in their 1959 "Art poétique" that the poet is answerable to no judge, they wished to stress his responsibility to the message he had to deliver, not to the public receiving that message. So they denied by implication that the communicability of the subliminal message is subject to restraints of a formal nature that in the past had been customarily taken into account when poetry came under examination. Thus surrealist theory challenged the practice, common among literary critics, of treating poetry as formalized presentation, of looking upon form as legitimately disciplining content that was consequently regarded as enhanced by a form which, lending it a certain shape or structure, somehow refined it. Whereas many readers continued to anticipate refinement through formalization, the surrealists foresaw only unacceptable interference resulting less in improving the poetic statement than in contaminating it.

Refusal on the surrealists' part to bow to the judgment of outsiders needs to be set against commitment to the principles of surrealism if we are not to fall into the error of concluding that surrealists imagined they were placing themselves above criticism. Surrealism did not assure its members so much freedom of action that they would be answerable to no one at all. Indeed, where the surrealist writer—or painter, for that matter—appears to have enjoyed the most complete liberty, or at least to have claimed it, he was divesting himself of certain commonly respected obligations, the better to acknowledge and to meet others. The latter were demanding, in part for the very reason that surrealism's artists turned from the use of aesthetics either, for example, as a measure of success or as an alibi for neglecting content, as defined in surrealism. No approved, inherited, or agreed formal guidelines directed their endeavors. The absence of aesthetic safeguards—to continue to use the same example—soon taught the neophyte surrealist poet that he could take nothing on trust. The illusion that past achievements provided the impetus for renewed investigation of the surreal was soon exploded, as long as the artist was honest enough to admit that repeating past discoveries would bring him no progress. In other works, nothing would have been more injurious to the surrealist

poet than developing mannerisms, whether or not he attempted
to pass them off as elements of a "style."

Looking back in "Position politique de l'art d'aujourd'hui,"
Breton declared in a 1935 lecture: "In particular, the whole
effort of surrealism, for fifteen years, has consisted in obtaining
from the poet instantaneous revelation of those verbal traces
of the perception-consciousness system. . . . I shall never tire
of repeating that automatism alone dispenses the elements on
which the secondary work of emotional amalgamation and of
passage from the unconscious to the preconscious can be undertaken validly" (p. 269). To avert confusion, he went on to insist
that psychic automatism has never constituted for surrealism
an end in itself, adding that to claim the contrary is an act
of bad faith (p. 271). Elaborating this point, Breton then emphasized that the technical procedures put forward by the surrealists
could serve only to "take soundings." In another 1935 talk,
"Situation surréaliste de l'objet," he reiterated, "Therefore all
the technical effort of surrealism, from its origins down to the
present, has consisted in multiplying ways of penetrating the
deepest levels of the mental" (p. 328).

All the things the surrealist word poet aspired to accomplish
combined to concentrate his hopes on the image. Consequently,
in "Du surréalisme et ses oeuvres vives" we read, "the attitude
of surrealism toward nature is dictated before anything else
by the initial conception it formed of the poetic image" (p. 361).
The peculiar virtue of surrealist imagery was to produce an
effect that lay beyond calculation, the surrealists were persuaded. The essential feature of the image was to be revelatory.
Any preoccupation that invited or justified premeditation had
to be excluded, dismissed as reducing the efficiency of the image
by diverting it from its unpredictable course. In essence, then,
surrealist poetry was to be an investigative act, its achievement
to be judged from its capacity to generate surprise, not self-
congratulation.

The unconditional search for surprise proclaimed by André
Breton set a value on the poetic image that literary criteria
do not weigh. So it was the ex-surrealist in Nicolas Calas who
assured readers of his Art in the Age of Risk that the artist
"should achieve that state of grace in which one overcomes
the vain satisfaction of solving purely aesthetic problems."[10]

The guidelines helping direct the littérateur's progress, making sure he is not in danger of wandering from the track laid
out before him, had to be thrust aside in order for surrealists

to advance where aesthetics ceased to be the artist's polestar. In "Prolégomènes" Breton asserted, "there is no great expedition, in art, which is not undertaken *at the risk of one's life*, . . . the road to follow is not, it is obvious, the one bordered by guardrails and . . . each artist must resume alone pursuit of the Golden Fleece" (p. 345). Elimination of personal vanity from surrealist creative effort removed the undertaking of art as risk from the footing on which the *littérateur* may endanger his reputation. If the surrealists had cared about public reputation, then the best safeguard available to them would have been repetition of previously successful creative gestures. But all of them realized how little was to be gained, for surrealism, if art were reduced to a recipe. In "Du surralisme en ses oeuvres vives" Breton reproved the conduct of persons whose claim to be treated as surrealists rested on nothing more solid than a facility for imitating one or other accredited surrealist painter. Long before then, though, Breton had glimpsed the serious disadvantage of complacency.

It was only logical that, with time, Breton himself should have decided that continuing to practice automatic writing routinely could bring no new revelations. Although he did not say as much, there is reason to believe that, in his case at least, abandonment of verbal automatism was less an admission of diminished confidence in automatic technique (still less of growing mistrust of the automatic principle) than an indication of wariness, a disinclination to consecrate any method, however valuable it had already proved to be. Diversion of the surrealist spirit of inquiry into the safe exercise of a proven method, however tempting to some, however profitable it looked, could only discourage investigative boldness, the adventurousness from which surrealism took life.

From the surrealists' standpoint, pursuit of the well-balanced, mellifluous phrase, the telling maxim, and so on would have been a betrayal of the writer's purpose. Instead of furthering the task of self-discovery shared by all surrealists, it would have appeared nothing better than a demonstration of narcissism, a sign of self-satisfaction quite in contradictionwith the surrealist mood and outlook. Surrealists regarded the inclination to acquire, improve, and display literary skills as confining poetry to the application of a prescribed exercise. Undertaken within preordained limits, they argued, poetry simply repeats the past. So it releases the poet from the necessity to venture beyond the known into uncharted regions. Here the only discoveries to which surrealism attached value await the artist.

All this sounds grandiloquent and therefore perhaps questionable. Certainly, if the surrealists were no better than masters
of the art of obfuscation one would have no difficulty dismissing
them and their work. If all they had managed to accomplish
in forty years and more was development of an inflated rhetoric,
unsupported by creative activity of any consequence, then there
would be good reason to ignore them, even to condemn them
as frauds. The complexities of the problem with which surrealism confronts us do not yield to such simple solutions.

By what right did the surrealists presume to shift the basis
for artistic evaluation? Was not their approach closer to being
a hoax—and, as such, a feeble excuse for lack of talent—than
a plea for revitalizing artistic aspirations worth taking seriously?
Hinting more or less openly at these questions, critics have
history and literary tradition on their side. Were the surrealists
to be considered upstarts who had laid a trap that any self-
respecting cultivated observer owed it to himself to avoid and
then might feel duty bound to point out to others?

The fact that the exchange between surrealists and critics
sometimes became acrimonious should not be permitted to reduce radical differences of opinion to the level of a personality
conflict in which, for instance, André Breton is found guilty
of pontificating. The surrealists' attitude toward their critics was
less one of uncompromising antagonism than of disappointment,
often magnified to the proportions of frustration. Being castigated for failing to do something they had made no effort to
do was as aggravating, evidently, as being accused of doing
inadequately other things they had not attempted either. Basi-
cally, the rift between the surrealist creative artist and those
taking upon themselves to assess his accomplishment from outside surrealism was deepened and broadened by the critics'
unwillingness to hear art justified on surrealism's terms. Fundamental to the disagreement hampering acceptance of surrealist
art in critical circles is the absence of an agreed definition of
the function of art, never more elusive, apparently, than when
the meaning and scope of poetry comes under discussion in
relation to the life of man.

Defending their position was never the occasion for surrealists
to explain it with care. Their resistance to applying accepted
critical standards to the evaluation of their own writings (and
paintings, for that matter) was stated firmly enough. Even so,
the grounds for objection were less than clear, in some respects
at least. When challenging the critics' right to appraise works
inspired by surrealism, the surrealists took more trouble to un-

derscore inadequacies they detected in critical judgment than
to specify values they considered appropriate to fair assessment
of surrealist creativity. Thus an objective reader might have
to admit hesitancy after examining the ideas summarized above,
for instance. He might even confess to aggravation after hearing
how the surrealist mind theorized. The difficulties he faces present certain points of concentration, centered on the concept
of surreality as absolute reality and on the surrealists' conviction that imagination, not reason, is the gateway to cognition.
Where does the absolute lie? How is it to be attained? What
is the nature of knowledge brought within reach by imaginative play? These questions have a common denominator. When
invoking absolute reality and referring to knowledge, the surrealists stopped short of precise definition.

Prompted by disappointment or irritation, our first reaction
is to condemn the surrealist mind for being vague. Only extreme
indulgence, apparently, can induce anyone to entertain the hypothesis that the surrealists actually refrained from precision
rather than showing themselves incapable of exactitude. So concerned are we to avoid being hoodwinked that we may miss
the most significant feature of the surrealists' imprecision. It
is, in fact, a consequence of their belief that the surreal has
no foreseeable limits. And what surrealists were sure would
be learned by way of imagination is similarly boundless.

If the surrealists had been fully cognizant of what they might
achieve, they would have prescribed themselves limited goals.
These would have confined surrealist investigative action, setting it a term which, whether reached or not, would have reduced the energy level of surrealist endeavor. Even if reluctant
to accept this interpretation of how the surrealist mind worked,
we cannot deny one thing. This is how André Breton and his
friends themselves saw surrealism, as an expression of faith
in which man is privileged to be his own savior.

The frame of mind in which the surrealists exercised their
redemptive privilege is scarcely of a nature to disarm criticism.
It did, though, release the surrealists from concern over adverse
judgment by anyone at all who, unresponsive to the obligations
going with the central privilege they enjoyed, remained insensitive to the nature of surrealist creative activity. Committed by
inherited views of the function of art to evaluation by criteria
holding no meaning in the context of surrealism, where they
could contribute nothing of value, tradition-minded critics, it
seems, serve surrealism best by demonstrating that a full understanding of surrealism eludes them.

4

Surrealist Poetry in Writing and Painting

The common source of inspiration reflected in surrealist poems and paintings is lost from sight by anyone who, having noted one central fact, ends up misinterpreting it. The fact is indisputable, of course. André Breton was not a pictorial artist but a writer who found space for comments on painting only in a brief footnote to his celebrated 1924 *Manifeste du surréalisme*. Where some people go astray is in believing this fact had a consequence that they regard with disfavor: the imposition upon surrealist graphic art of a character commonly described as literary.

Certainly, the chronological sequence of events must be acknowledged and respected. Among those remembered today as early surrealists it was the writers who commanded attention first. But this is not to say that painters were recruited to the surrealist cause only after they had agreed to sacrifice pictorial ambitions to literary ones. In surrealism, the painter shared common ground with the writer. Both of them took as a prerequisite for all creative action suspicion of literature and of the meaning generally attached to art by people outside the surrealist circle.

All the same, the title of Breton's 1928 volume, *Le surréalisme et la peinture*[1]—assembling essays the earliest of which had appeared originially in the first Parisian surrealist magazine, *La révolution surréaliste*, from 1925 onward—indicated the tentative nature of its author's enterprise: to combat Pierre Naville's argument that surrealism and painting were, if not quite irreconcilable, then perhaps incompatible. The degree to which André Breton gained confidence in painting (more exactly, in its serviceability) may be judged from a remark he made later, in the course of his 1935 lecture in Prague: "There exists, at the present time, no difference in underlying ambition between a poem by Paul Eluard, by Benjamin Péret and a canvas by Max Ernst, by Miró, by Tanguy" (p. 311). Before the mid-1930s surrealism's chief spokesman in France had become thoroughly convinced that a painting was a perfectly appropriate form of communication for surrealism. He now felt sure that the work of certain artists had proved pictorial art to be no less well adapted to surrealism's needs than verbal language, as employed by writers highly regarded among the surrealists. From then on, Breton and those who engaged in the surrealist venture with him were to feel no misgivings. They would retain faith in the capacity of painting and word poems to further surrealism's "underlying ambition" together, and consequently to be mutually enlightening expressions of the surrealist spirit and the antiaesthetic posture essential to surrealist activity.

In a war waged on "art" and "literature," the surrealists did not deem it necessary to divide their forces into battalions, assigned a special role in attacking tradition or convention. Surrealism was never to establish, respect, or imply a hierarchy in which artists from one field must be ranked above or below their counterparts in another. Whichever medium one of their number happened to explore, surrealists recognized a single priority: the attainment of poetic revelation.

In the context of surrealism, the complementary function of painting and writing was not just a curiosity, then, to be noted in passing before moving on to other, more interesting topics. It was a distinguishing characteristic of surrealist creative endeavor. Thus, understanding the surrealist mind—appreciating what the surrealists attempted to do, and why—depends largely on our success in learning why painting and verbal expression went together, why in fact the demands surrealism imposed on its adherents made it imperative that the one complement the other. Even though it may look paradoxical to some observers, the absence (more precisely, the rejection) of an aesthetic program or code encouraged surrealists in the opinion that painters and writers might advance side by side toward a goal all the more attractive because it eluded advance prescription.

Avoiding the rigidity accompanying clearly defined aims, aesthetic in scope, the surrealists were at liberty to devote themselves to the pursuit of ends that did not require them to categorize creative effort in terms that aestheticians would consider valid. This does not mean, however, that, facing surrealism, one must be resigned to dealing with an undisciplined mob of individualists who appear to have shared a sense of purpose only because nothing, really, bound them close enough together to exercise a restrictive influence, either over what they each set out to do or over the methodology employed to seek an individual goal. It is easy enough to misread the declaration placed at the end of Breton's October 1924 manifesto announcing that the future techniques of surrealism did not interest him. Breton's aim was not to reserve surrealists every possible latitude, so that anyone at all might call himself a surrealist, whatever he might choose to do. More than a half-century of militancy would show how quickly surrealists could close ranks against intruders whom they suspected of all opportunism that could do surrealism a disservice.

Whether we call it proof of constancy and perseverance or of obstinacy and prejudice, the surrealists' ever alert defense of their position against all outsiders provided evidence of the strict demands imposed by membership in their group. Indeed, it is fair to say that the tension under which artists lived voluntarily so long as they wished to participate in surrealism was a direct result of the interplay of two elements: freedom to handle certain problems in their own way and accountability, which was the very first requirement for admittance to the surrealist camp. This tension explains the pride that went with belonging to the surrealist group and, no less noteworthy, the nostalgia felt by many who had departed or had been shut out under circumstances that, one might have thought, should have left a few of them with a sense of relief, instead of regret.

It is no exaggeration to say that participation in surrealism brought awareness of the privilege of being among an elite body of men and women and, in addition, a highly developed sense of obligation. All participants were sensitive to the latter, regardless of the medium through which they tried to prove their fidelity. The obligation they accepted taught members, among other things, to have no respect for the boundaries and limits traditionally set upon literature and art. A basic feature from which surrealist activity derived unity was therefore that everyone who drew inspiration from its principles acknowledged surrealism to be both extraliterary and extra-artistic.

Even so, surrealism was anything but a ready-made excuse for painters and writers who had failed to reach acceptable standards in what they had produced. By no means was it a refuge for the *artiste manqué*. Still, its demands were such that they conflicted with those usually applied to literary and artistic endeavor. Respect for conventional rules would have come between any surrealist and his commitment to purposes different from those of schools of literature and painting. Therefore, to the extent that the ends justified the means, in surrealism, the former imposed on the latter demands that took surrealist writing and painting out of the framework with which students of literature and art are acquainted.

All this sounds like a plea for unusual indulgence, not to say a weak argument designed to place surrealism above criticism or beyond its range. In reality, it is a reminder that surrealism needs to be evaluated on its own terms. This is true even though its best known expressive modes (poetry and painting) seem to place surrealism squarely in categories to which we customarily apply standards of judgment that it is easy to demonstrate that surrealists ignore. While the prudent among us would refrain from going (every time, any way) so far as to contend that surrealists had little or no idea how to write, and could not paint either, we can sympathize with commentators sufficiently annoyed to level such charges. One can see on what grounds they object to surrealism. Surrealist anticonformity seems to have evidenced incapacity too often for anyone practicing it to escape entirely the accusation that he fell short of doing something he actually was not trying to do. It is far easier, after all, to perceive in which respects surrealists failed or neglected to measure up to normal criteria than to appreciate that their disinclination to do so expressed determination to meet other standards, which many a critic would have difficulty taking seriously.

One might wonder what the fuss is about. After all, the Fauves met with incomprehension, hostility, and ridicule from commentators who found their approach too revolutionary to approve. Yet the Fauves were finally to be assigned a place in the history of art, duly earned for them by their aspirations and their efforts to realize them. As for the surrealists, they have fared less well. They too have been assigned a niche, but it is one of the critics' choosing, a place to which surrealism has been relegated after being submitted to an evaluative procedure fundamentally out of sympathy with its ambitions and the practices they fostered. The position surrealism occupies in the official history of twentieth-century art is testimony to the influence of two factors: limited comprehension on the part of those who judge it and distortion resulting from incomplete understanding. The resulting discrepancy between what surrealism aimed to be and what observers make of it may be gauged from the following comment: "By surrealist criteria all surrealist writing is perfect, by anyone else's it may be gibberish."[2]

This statement looks more foolish than persuasive. Even so, it is interesting and informative because it sets off rejection by everyone else against the surrealists' implied inability to exercise responsible critical judgment. The fallacy is obvious: the commentator's belief that, because they did not judge the way he does, surrealists were incapable of balanced judgment.

Now Christopher Robinson's point of view would not detain us if it could be attributed with clear conscience to someone quite incapable of thinking clearly. What demands attention is the imbalance it reveals, indicating that the surrealists' ambitions took them out of range of the critical instruments Robinson feels entitled to use. Naturally, the simplest solution here would be to dismiss all surrealists as too misguided to merit attention. Doing this, though, would scarcely permit us to begin dealing adequately with the only twentieth-century movement comparable in scope and influence with nineteenth-century romanticism. It is best to notice that, where the surrealist painter and poet seem to have discouraged critical assessment of their work and even appear to have wished to set themselves above it, they did so for the very same reasons. These provide a point of departure for comprehending surrealism's demands upon its creative artists.

When we examine the surrealists' reasons for adopting an antiartistic stance, we better appreciate the order or precedence marking the earliest phase of their activity. Those who first rallied around Breton shared his disenchantment with the symbolist aesthetic. The mistrust reflected in the surrealists' posture before aesthetic concerns had its origins in their conclusion that symbolism had lost its pertinence.

It is by no means uncommon, of course, for a literary school to find impetus in distaste or disrespect for the one preceding it. The point requiring emphasis, in this instance, is not that the future surrealist writers rejected the symbolist aesthetic. They certainly did. In addition, however, they developed an abiding abhorrence of aestheticism. This was shared by the painters who enlisted in the surrealist movement. Surrealists displayed more than the familiar desire to be free of tradition in order to assert and cultivate independence. They rejected all aesthetic norms as impeding productive pursuit of poetic ends.

Refusal to take aesthetic values into consideration or to grant them any bearing on the creative gesture was not merely the sign by which surrealists gave notice of their aspiration to liberate themselves from the past. It was, more significantly by far, the first step along a path that surrealists expected to be able to take only after the weighty baggage of aestheticism had been jettisoned. And it gave fair warning that surrealists believed attention to aesthetic matters leads to literature (in surrealism given the pejorative value it has in Paul Verlaine's verse, "Et tout le reste est littérature"—all the rest is literature), which they regarded as conflicting with the dedication to the search for poetry. This quest was not to be the goal of the surrealist writer exclusively. Reaching out for poetry would also be the task of every painter who deserved a place in the surrealist movement. In other works, an understanding of what motivated a surrealist to creative action eludes anybody who has not reflected on the meaning ascribed to "poetry" in surrealist parlance.

In the surrealist's lexicon, poetry embraced everything he hoped to attain. Yet surrealist ambitions were never pinpointed exactly enough for anyone (even the poet himself) to be perfectly sure where they lay. In fact, so ill-defined did they remain throughout surrealism's history that no one—least of all perhaps the surrealist artist—could predict where, along a given investigative path, poetic success would come, if it came at all. A vital feature of surrealist poetics was the unpredictability of poetic manifestation. Surrealists were well content to observe that poetry never could be reduced to the studied application of a formula. For this reason, it continued to fascinate them all, making the surrealist reaching out for poetry through one medium of expression responsive to the efforts of his fellows, who were engaged in exploring the poetic through another.

It was characteristic of surrealism that the search for poetry guaranteed its participants complete parity. No expressive medium was assured precedence, either by tradition or by edict. None was esteemed over the others as being richer in poetic potential. Each surrealist, in other words, had to prove himself, though by no standard yardstick of merit. As a result, the surface impression yielded by review of surrealist activity in a number of fields—cinema, photography, and sculpture, among them— presents almost bewildering variety. From this the outsider has difficulty deducing unity of purpose, except in generalized terms of unconvincing vagueness. Only beneath the surface are there clear indications of the cohesiveness of the surrealist movement in aspiring to poetic consciousness through unprecedented and quite unforeseeable revelation.

One can appreciate the vitality of the surrealist group, as demonstrated in its survival for more than forty years and in its power to attract new recruits throughout its lifespan. Yet one can still be dubious. Confused, in any event, about the source of its appeal, one may wonder quite legitimately about the nature of the fascination exercised by surrealism, for pictorial artists no less than poets. Meanwhile, the frequent defections and imperious exclusions from the surrealist ranks leave the observer with some qualms. Did the poetry of which surrealists liked to speak remain tantalizingly unobtainable, capable of firing the imagination for a while but proving in the end too remote from the practicalities of creative effort to prompt sustained interest? The answer the surrealists would have given to this question is not likely to agree with that of someone bent on uncovering a surrealist aesthetic or on proving that a surrealist school of painting or poetry really existed.

The surrealist movement was essentially a movement toward something, not an attempt to realize ideals that could be identified positively and then trapped within a system of ideas or a battery of techniques. This explains why pronouncements about poetry made in the name of surrealism lack clarity of outline. It is not that surrealists sometimes found themselves unable to furnish exact information or even were reluctant to do so. They sounded evasive because it was characteristic of poetry, as they referred to it, to locate itself beyond precise definition, just as it lay on the other side of predictability.

It may seem at this stage as though the surrealists' dissatisfaction with symbolism inspired less innovation than emulation. The surrealist mind appears to have been more inclined to imitate the vagueness in Stéphane Mallarmé's theorizing about poetry than to take issue with it fruitfully. But this objection holds our attention only momentarily. Actually, it serves to bring to light the discord between symbolism and surrealism more than it proves their continuity.

However difficult Mallarméan writing was—André Breton, for one, did not hesitate to castigate Mallarmé for deliberately rendering the meaning of some of his verses hard to penetrate—its function was plainly to embrace beauty. The identification of verbal poetry with its traditional goal, the beautiful, sustains our trust in Mallarmé the poet even where obscurity impedes

understanding. Ultimately, the norms of poetic ambition suffer
no violation, even though the means implemented obstruct some
readers' progress toward that ambiguous response which Mallarmé chose to call "la jouissance." On the other hand, where
poetic effort is not linked by tradition with the attainment of
beauty recognizable to all, the result of creative endeavor may
sound or look so disturbing as to leave the audience unconvinced of the poetic merit of the completed work. Thus it is
from practical necessity, not because we have agreed to accord
the surrealist artist special advantages, that we must approach
surrealist poetry on its own terms.

Dismissing the surrealists out of hand as men and women
who abused the word "poetry" with intent to obfuscate takes
us nowhere. Moreover, it conceals the true source of their refusal
to supply a definition of poetry by which they wished to have
their material judged: the firm conviction that poetic achievement eludes anticipation. To the surrealists, poetry was something other than a reward earned through careful application
of prescribed technique or controlled effect. It was an unforeseen
and indeed unforeseeable manifestation that evaded measurement according to criteria agreed upon in advance.

The absence of a common aesthetic purpose isolated each
surrealist from his fellows while committing him to a risk common to all. Every new created work being a new adventure,
neither the painter nor the writer could expect to enjoy the
comfortable assurance of utilizing acquired skills within a preordained theoretical framework guaranteed to produce admissible
surrealist results. Thus, although many artists who frown on
surrealism also claim to be wary of a recipe for creative action,
none takes more care to neutralize the effects of routine, imposed
regulation and conformist practice than do those for whom remaining worthy of surrealism was a perpetual challenge.

When Max Ernst spoke of "means of forcing inspiration,"
he was not boasting of having mastered a surefire method for
creating graphic images. Rather he was acknowledging that inspiration must escape any artist who does not realize that it
has to be forced to yield up secrets that the surrealists considered
poetic in nature. Here, indeed, a writer has as much to learn
from a painter as he had to teach the pictorial artist working
by his side in the cause of surrealism. The beneficial effects
of automatism can be observed as much in surrealist painting
as in surrealist verse or prose. Meanwhile, restless pursuit of
pictorial means for forcing inspiration (certainly not exclusively

a feature of Ernst's surrealist activity) served as an insistent reminder to surrealist writers that they must avoid the routine application of well-rehearsed methods, however worthy of respect these had proved to be in the past.

Whether we are inspecting the work of a surrealist painter or reading a surrealist text, we are in danger of confusion so long as we ask just how the artist goes about communicating with his audience. To come closer to grasping surrealist poetry, we have to consider why he works as he does. However, the answer to the latter question will surely be inaccurate unless we start out accepting the following. With the surrealists, *why* did not correspond to exactly formulated aims. For this reason, the answer to *why* always remained speculative. It indicated the vitality of a creative endeavor that maintained its appeal, where surrealists were concerned, because explaining *why* meant admitting that they were consumed by a yearning to communicate the previously unexpressed for the sake of convenience designated by the word "poetry."

Now another danger presents itself. It comes with the hasty deduction that, when the surrealists referred to poetry, they wished merely to allude to something so far unexpressed— anything at all, in fact, as long as no one had said or painted it before. In surrealism, though, ignorance of any fact, idea, or phenomenon was not what gave it worth. Had that been so, then gradual elimination of ignorance would have threatened to erode poetry and eventually eliminate it. The surrealist mind was interested in precipitating discoveries of a certain kind, extending knowledge in an area widely distant from that where scientific progress marks its advances.

The distance separating scientific investigation of the as yet unknown from the exploration in which the surrealists were engaged may be estimated if we draw a distinction between science as rational and surrealism as antirational. One may quibble over the first label without disposing of the differences surrealist writers invested with importance as they sought to combat rational speculation with imaginative projection. Those same differences come to light when one turns to surrealist painters. For the most part devoted to representation or figuration, especially during the early years of the movement, surrealism's pictorial artists resisted curbing imaginative freedom on the pretext that pictorial imagery should be either borrowed from known reality or limited to what rational speculation authorizes. Rationalism was the surrealists' *bête noire*. They saw it as a restraint imposed upon imaginative play, confining the latter within boundaries they were quite sure denied access to the poetic.

The more one reflects on surrealist poetics, the more necessary it becomes to grant that among the surrealists poetry designated a perception that has cast off the limitations of past experience as well as those the reasoning mind would project on future experience. Thus when André Breton affirmed that surrealism "is what will be," he linked the present with the future in the here and now of poetic evidence leading outside commonly respected bounds. There the surrealists were able to explore modes of experience to which anticipative reasoning cannot admit us.

Quite simply, the surrealists' motive for rejecting the rational in favor of the antirational was their belief that the latter is more rewarding than the former, more stimulating, better suited to satisfying private desire. And it was private desire that provided surrealism's painters with the *"purely inner model"* to which Breton referred on the fourth page of *Le surréalisme et la peinture*. The importance of Breton's adverb is not to be ignored. The purity of the creative gesture was assured by the surrealist artist's reference to an inner model only. It excluded all concern for what is outside. And what is outside? Something commonly termed reality and allowed to propose itself as a model from which the artist departs—so the surrealists would have argued, and whether he is drawing, painting, or writing— only at the risk of incurring disapproval or even condemnation.

Surrealist poetry lay outside generally accepted norms. In defiance of aesthetic criteria it offered a form of beauty with which André Breton's book *Nadja* (1928) linked the adjective *convulsive*. Breton's choice of attributive was significant, as it emphasized that the surrealists aspired to something other than replacing one mode of aesthetic pleasure with another, more exotic. Surrealist beauty was anything but a shrine at which the writer or painter was expected to worship, fervently but decorously. The all-important adjective used in *Nadja* was not meant to give beauty an intensity similar to that which the concepts of *l'amour fou* (André Breton) and *l'amour sublime* (Benjamin Péret) granted love, in surrealism's name, by concentrating on its mad or sublime aspects. Revealing as were *fou* and *sublime* in the surrealist vocabulary, they contributed less to the originality of surrealism than did *convulsive*, qualifying *la beauté*.

Convulsive beauty was a disruptive force making its presence and influence felt by combating more than traditional aesthetic canons. It militated against common preconceptions about the physical world and man's relationship to his environment. For this reason, the surrealists' idea of the role artists must play in society differed radically from the one assumed by members of this literary *cénacle* or that school of painting. Convulsion denoted more to Breton than dissidence and more than anticonformity also. Indeed, it was not the expression of an artistic attitude at all. It bore witness to a break with tradition and convention (as much in perception, it is essential to notice, as in expression) in which the surrealist might take pride, even when—especially when—its manifestation owed more to the happy intervention of chance than to skillful design and precise calculation.

Drawing sustenance from a search for means of forcing inspiration, surrealist art of every kind was the product of a mental disposition in which two elements combined to the artist's satisfaction. The surrealist's attitude toward the revelatory gesture in which chance had an unpredictable part to play was self-effacing, not self-congratulatory. At the same time, the surrealist took pride in the fact that the creative act put him in fruitful contact with convulsive beauty. Hence the self-assurance that led Max Ernst to believe means of forcing inspiration were within the artist's reach went with a sense of wonder when success followed. The idea of the artist as a privileged medium, which entered surrealist theory in the 1920s, was never to lose its appeal, its capacity to excite.

To say that the surrealists were disinterested in art would be forcing a point, and distorting it in the process. To say, however, that they were interested in art as a means to ends that it appeared fully capable of bringing within reach is much closer to the truth. Moreover, this is the first step toward understanding why, in the face of incomprehension sometimes spiced with calumny, surrealists approached art in a manner peculiarly their own.

On occasion blossoming into open contempt, suspicion of critics, art dealers, and museum curators was typical of the surrealist group. It grew out of opposition to the notion that art of any kind possesses intrinsic worth. The key to surrealist pleasure before a product of artistic activity (in any medium, by the way) lay in the ability displayed by the creative artist to furnish an image for which no model exists in the world about us. This is why Breton referred in a 1936 essay to Lautréamont as "the great locksmith of modern life." Breton was arguing consistently for "the will to emancipate man *totally*, drawing its strength from language, but sooner or later reversible to life."[3] The context that surrealists reserved for creative action was not the mysterious but the marvelous. They saw "pure and simple abandonment to the *marvelous*" exactly as Breton did, as "the only source of eternal communication between men."

One theoretician of surrealism, Pierre Mabille, published two books about the marvelous, on which another, Benjamin Péret, centered his poetic writings in prose and verse. Yet no exact definition of the surrealist marvelous has come down to us. The reason is, evidently, that surrealists shared Péret's view of the marvelous as "heart and nervous system of all poetry,"[4] hence as no more susceptible than surrealist poetry to close analysis. Although unwilling to circumscribe *le merveilleux* within a narrow definition, surrealists had no hesitation about respecting the painter's right and ability to enter the realm of the marvelous, just as the poet may do when working from the inner model.

We miss an essential feature of the surrealist mind if we interpret emphasis on the purely inner model as indicating a tendency supposedly common to surrealists—to shut out the world, to withdraw from contact with the outside. The surrealists saw the latter the way Mabille did in *Le merveilleux*, as "a universe about which it is permissible to wonder if it is not quite different from the way we conceive it habitually."[5] It is noteworthy, therefore, that Mabille went on to quote a poem by Breton. Called "Vigilance," Breton's text (from his *Le revolver à cheveux blancs* [1932]) begins in Paris, with its river and Tour Saint-Jacques. Then it advances out of the familiar urban landscape through an experience culminating in an illumination that brings to mind that mythical guarantee of escape from the labyrinth, Ariadne's threat: "Je ne touche plus que le coeur des choses je tiens le fil" (I touch no longer but the heart of things I hold the thread).

Breton's verses reinforce the description offered by Mabille, who saw the marvelous as summing up, for man, "the possibility of contact between what is inside him and what is outside him."[6] They support also his reference to the marvelous as a "*tension* that is something different from regular, mechanical work: the tension of passion and poetry."[7] At the same time, they lend weight to Mabille's view of the marvelous as "the conjunction of desire and outer reality." If one seeks to probe their origin in desire, reaching out and making contact with the world of physical reality, what one finds in Breton's verses is precisely what one discovers when examining the painting of Yves Tanguy, for example.

Yet this does not mean that a Tanguy stands as the pictorial rendering of verbal imagery, that the inspiration for Tanguy's art was literary after all. Much more important than mere parallelism or a latter-day version of nineteenth-century *transposition d'art* is the equivalence we notice when placing images from a surrealist text next to the imagery of a surrealist canvas. Influence—whether it be the commonly supposed influence of surrealist writing on painting or, for that matter, operating in reverse—is not present to any significant degree. What really needs emphasis is that the varied forms of surrealist imagery originated in desire unrestrained by rational objection. Surrealism took its characteristic forms from an opposition to reason firm enough to release the artistic imagination for free expression, in words and pictures, of innermost desire.

One would have thought that, locating within the artist both desire and the model from which he or she should work, the surrealists must have had very definite ideas regarding the nature of the images meriting attention. In fact, they were no more sure on this subject than they were about the true nature of poetry. As before, though, we find that imprecision—or, to put things more accurately, refusal to delimit goals with precision— is a sign of the strength of surrealist principles. It helps account for the vitality of surrealism. And why should this be? Because surrealism granted special importance to techniques that solicit desires lying at a level below that of conscious awareness.

Fundamental to the attitude prompting surrealist painters and writers to employ techniques for probing their own unvoiced desires was the state of mind revealed by André Breton. Breton admitted in *Les pas perdus* to having always wished to meet a naked woman in a forest. No sooner had he done so than he was remarking that such a desire has no meaning, once expressed. So he was led to correct himself and to avow that he regretted not having had such an encounter. His statements reflect a cardinal principle of surrealism: that desire voiced, consciously entertained, is already compromised, confined by the procedure that articulates it.

A number of factors govern the point of view shared by Breton and his fellow surrealists. Of these one in particular deserves attention. This is the relationship of the use of expressive modes to the revelation of an image nurtured by desire. Here the problem centers, as one would expect, on the adverse effect of reasonable language as a communicative channel. The example drawn by Breton from his own experience gives us occasion to observe what can happen. The process by which desire must be voiced prosaically in the language of reasonable exchange (as Breton tried to share one of his wishes with readers of his *Les pas perdus*) is in his estimation a procedure that inevitably takes the luster off desire. Immobilized in the language of reason (and therefore subject to evaluation by reason), desire can appear wan, even foolish. This is because the medium in which the unvoiced is given communicable shape within the frame of customary discourse, although it may give ideas an outline permitting the rational mind to grasp them, sometimes fails to capture and hold an image stimulating to the imagination.

How, then, can language—verbal or pictorial language—avoid the negative effects so displeasing to Breton? This is a central question faced by the surrealists. That they succeeded in furnishing a response to it is attested by the fact that they did not end up arguing themselves into sterility and silence. Instead, they looked to paintings and written texts, poetic in scope, to encompass more than the artist can know he desires at the moment of painting or writing.

Tension between the known (the recognizable) and the as yet unknown (the so far unarticulated) affects the surrealist artist's use of expressive means. The latter derive value, by surrealist standards, when the use of his chosen instrument of communication takes a writer or painter beyond the limits normally assigned and respected in art. In some instances, a rift opens up most fortunately between conscious intent and the results obtained. Breton alluded to this phenomenon when remarking in his first surrealist manifesto that Stendhal's fictional characters hold our attention where their creator has lost control over them. In addition, however, surrealists gave full credit to artists of whom they approved for exceeding the bounds within which others are content to operate. This is why Breton so admired Yves Tanguy. André Breton made his enthusiasm public on numerous occasions, calling in one text, we should notice, for the revision of the language in which experiences are recorded: "The sensory verbs: to see, to hear, to touch, to taste, to feel demand not to be conjugated like the others. To this necessity correspond astonishing participles: already seen, already heard, never seen, etc."[8]

One detects no strain when hearing Breton refer to elements of language in the course of the discussion of surrealist experimentation by a painter. Rigid classification of the sort that would keep pictorial experiments quite apart from verbal communication had no meaning for the surrealists. They refused to grant it validity in the context of creative investigation to which surrealism's ambitions gave purpose and direction. Hence Breton's statement on Tanguy offers something more significant than simple metaphorical extension of vocabulary usually reserved for the medium of verbal communication. We find here indications of aspirations that linked surrealist writers and painters in one endeavor. Only when common aims spurred these artists on could they qualify as surrealists.

No surrealist artist enjoyed prerogatives that made the task of reaching the goal of poetic revelation less difficult for him or her than for a companion working in another expressive mode. It is safe to assume, indeed, that, had any method presented itself as capable—against all odds—of ensuring poetic discovery every time it was employed, the surrealists would have placed limitations upon its application, as Marcel Duchamp limited the number of his *ready-mades* and as Marcel Mariën did when he terminated his experiments with pictorial *étrécissement*, which he had invented.[9]

If we happened to be dealing with a different group, we might have very quickly come to a persuasive conclusion about motivation for behavior like that of Duchamp and Marien and even Breton who, after all, finally gave up automatic writing. We might infer with confidence that limitation was only an attempt to inflate or at least to maintain, by calculated means, the market value of a given work of art, in a given style. With surrealism, though, we have to acknowledge something other than commercial self-interest. Suspicion of facility went, in the surrealist mind, with total disinterest in style and contempt for "self-kleptomania." The self-kleptomaniac artist is one who, for profit, exploits past discoveries and gives up taking risks, thus losing sight of the greatest virtue that surrealists ascribed to art: its functional character. Any artist who began treating his own work as an end, rather than as a means to an end, had severed his ties with surrealism. His accomplishments thereafter were of no more concern to surrealists than were the later paintings of Max Ernst and Salvador Dali or the postsurrealist writings of Louis Aragon, Paul Eluard, and René Char.

The austere demands imposed by surrealism upon those whose work took direction from its doctrine were no more confining, so far as the writer was concerned, than the painter found them to be. In no instance did fidelity to surrealism engender a reliable "manner," which the artist had only to acquire and then retain at his disposal in order to continue to be a surrealist in good standing. Under the circumstances, it was only to be expected that the surrealists never credited any of their number with talent or with having mastered a craft of some sort. Doing this would have meant denying all they regarded as fruitfully creative in the surrealist artist. It would have implied that the work of this or that artist might serve as an example to be followed by others, so dispensing those who came after from the obligation to take risks for themselves in the interest of surrealist inquiry and discovery. All the same, certain individuals deserve to be cited as having made pronouncements that stand out as especially revealing and setting an example in the most productive way. One is Tanguy, who noted that if he planned a picture beforehand he denied himself the pleasure he sought through painting: surprise. But the value of such statements was that they incited other surrealists to search and find for themselves, not to take over their predecessors' discoveries or to deduce from them a mode of creative action which could be expected to guarantee results.

More than forty years after Breton's 1924 manifesto formally launched surrealism, an active member in the movement remarked, "What is said is more important than what is not said. What remains to be said is more important than what has been said."[10] Like the author of the surrealist manifestoes, the man who spoke in this way, Jean Schuster (named the executor of his estate by Breton), was a writer and editor of surrealist magazines. The author of "battles for surrealism" gathered in his *Archives 57/68* (1968), Schuster published much later a collection of poems, *Les Moutons* (1979). But it was not simply from the standpoint of the writer that, speaking in the name of surrealism, he extolled the virtues of the as yet unexpressed over those of the already expressed.

Schuster openly endorsed the position taken by one of surrealism's painters, Roberto Antonio Sebastian Matta Echaurrén. An outline written by this painter for a presentation he was to give at a conference in Havana in December 1967–January 1968 (at which the surrealists were well represented and where one of their number, the writer-painter Joyce Mansour, gave Siqueiros a kick in the backside "in André Breton's name") included the notation, "Create in order to see." Schuster's comment on these words stressed the links between surrealist painters and writers. It emphasized creation as enlarging "the angle of sight, the angle of vision."[11] Schuster went on to argue that imagination prolongs physical perception "beyond the latter's limits."[12] Where Matta recommended "not flight into the fantastic but constitution of the inner maquis, the guerillero and the inner provo in place of self-criticism,"[13] Schuster echoed his words: "Between the fantastic (false liberty, encouragement of sub-imaginative, sub-creative laziness) and self-criticism (the automatic voice pronouncing the discourse of the instincts, then reflection of that voice by consciousness for considered discourse) is the new man in process of putting himself together. . . ."[14]

Testifying to the presence of the surrealist new man was never considered among surrealists to be the exclusive right of the painter. Nor, for the matter, was it the prerogative of the writer. In surrealism, painters and writers shared that philosophy of immanence to which André Breton referred when bringing Le surréalisme et le peinture to a close. Surreality, they all acknowledged, is contained in reality, being neither superior nor external to it. They were convinced indeed that the reverse is equally true, that the container is also the content. This is to say that they agreed in rejecting all effort—in painting as in writing—to "withdraw thought from life, as well as to place life under the aegis of thought" because, as Breton put it, "What one hides from oneself is worth neither more nor less than what one finds. And what one hides from oneself is worth neither more nor less than what one allows others to find" (p. 46). Surrealism taught that it was each artist's responsibility to find for himself. Naturally, everyone could not be expected to find exactly the same things. Nevertheless all the surrealists would have responded in the same way to a question on the last page of the original edition of Le surréalisme et le peinture, which, posed verbally, evoked visual imagery: "What difference is there *fundamentally* between a couple of dancers and the cover of a beehive?" (p. 48).

André Breton brought to his devotion to the surrealist cause the deep conviction that surrealism would never make its full impact until painters had joined writers in protesting against tradition and in developing a poetic antitradition. On occasion, the consequences of Breton's attitude were less then impressive. We may smile upon learning from Julien Trevelyan's autobiography, *Indigo Days* (1957), that, visited by the organizers of the 1936 international surrealist exhibition to be held in London, one English painter, at least, was granted surrealist status "overnight." All the same, Trevelyan had declared in 1928, "To dream is to create." And he would be the person who opened the 1937 exhibition of surrealist objects at the London Gallery in the guise of a blind explorer. There is something touching in his insistence that, to make his religious affiliation, the word *surrealism* appear on his dog tags when he was drafted for military service in the Second World War.

On balance, the striking effect of Breton's wish to draw painters into surrealism is not that he was signally successful, involving some of the major pictorial artists of his time. It was that, in addition, he opened to those artists a place in the surrealist poetic movement that, but for their cooperation, would have remained woefully empty, denying the surrealist mind access to an expressive mode that soon proved to be indispensable.

5

Painting in the Surrealist Mind

Never more than when painting comes under discussion are we likely to encounter skepticism about surrealism as a vital expression of the surrealist mind. At no time, apparently, do the majority of observers agree more completely that surrealism itself furnished all the proof needed to discredit the hypothesis that such a mind stimulated productive creative activity.

Presumably, commentators share a perspective making it easy for them to view surrealist painting as essentially a matter of technique. Conceiving surrealist pictorial art in technical terms has facilitated its condemnation, or at least has encouraged critics to treat it with condescension. Instead of tracing the operation of the surrealist mind from inside outward—from inspiration to execution—surrealist pictures are reduced to what the spectator notices first, without penetrating beneath surface evidence to explore motivation. In the long term, as well as in the short, the effect is to foster the supposition that, if not quite a hoax, surrealist art is surely facile. This conclusion is apparently buttressed by signs in the work of a number of surrealist artists of affection for pictorial imagery of a kind not fashionable in the twentieth century, which the invention of photography is generally thought to have made redundant.

Few are likely to protest against the injustice of minimizing the influence of the surrealist mind on painting when the surrealists' attention is concentrated on the use of techniques that they themselves termed automatic and that relieved the practitioner of the necessity to plan his pictures, calculate effects, and so on. Should not surrealist painting be regarded as form more than substance? In such a view, the existence of a creative spark is questioned. Indeed, the need for such a spark is swept aside as having nothing of importance to do with the production of a surrealist work or with our assessment of why it has come into being. If technique is really the key to surrealist pictorial art, then that art is no more than a curiosity, its field of operation, scope, and interest are all delimited in an area prescribed by methodology alone. The results obtained—so far as any can be said to have been achieved—are apparently both guaranteed and limited by the methods called into service.

Reduction of surrealism to a variety of techniques routinely applied conflicts with the fact that surrealist creativity was inspired by the surrealist mind and answered some, if not all, of the demands that mind set itself and needed to meet before a work of art could take on value in the context of surrealism.

For anyone wishing to comprehend how the surrealists evaluated painting, the best starting point is provided at the beginning of Le surréalisme et la peinture. Here André Breton confesses he finds it impossible to consider a picture as anything but a window, adding that his primary concern is to know "what it looks out upon." His metaphor makes very clear that, as a surrealist, Breton looked through pictorial art, not at it the way critics do. From the outset, all surrealists evaluated painting in relation to the outlook it provided, the perspectives it offered, the vistas it presented the imagination. And so the quality of a painter was to be measured by his success in making surrealists see.

From the moment when the painted canvas commands attention as nothing other than a window on surrealism a number of considerations, usually contributing significantly to our pleasure before pictorial art, cease to have pertinence. When one looks out of a window, its shape or design is far less important than its location, the latter assuring access to one visually compelling spectacle or another. Things other than "what it looks out upon" take second place to the enjoyment derived from the view granted by the window-picture. Examining a painting by one of his companions, certainly, the surrealist spectator would have been conscious of pictorial technique only so long as it had helped capture an image, bringing him directly into contact with it. Technique that drew attention to itself, on the other hand, was suspect to the surrealist mind, which condemned intrusive methodology as not merely gratuitous but unproductively distracting. As with surrealist poetic writing, concern for the why of painting had to remain paramount. Otherwise surrealist artists might have been tempted by the how of pictorial art into losing sight of the goals which the surrealist mind brought into focus.

Painting in the Surrealist Mind

   To say that surrealism's pictorial artists dep world is well and good, even if this does entail neglec ous artists whose work did not explore a dream univ is another matter altogether, though, to ask why surrea evoked a world of dreams, to establish why they found it worthwhile and even necessary to do so. This is especially the case if one rejects the facile conclusion that the intent was and continued to be no more than escapism. True, the second sentence of the original surrealist manifesto refers to man as a "dreamer once and for all." Hence, at first glance, Breton's phrase seems to reinforce the opinion that a surrealist painter had given all that could be expected of him once he had recorded nocturnal visions. How, then, are we to rank artists in the surrealist movement who did not capture oneiric images? Were they any less faithful to surrealism? Did they qualify any less as surrealist dreamers? What about, for instance, Breton's praise of Max Ernst, taken up in *Le surréalisme et la peinture* (p. 26), as engaged in a "dream of *mediation*"? We cannot weigh Ernst's contribution as a surrealist pictorial artist unless, probing the meaning of Breton's allusion to dreaming, we make contact with the surrealist mind.
   André Breton was not merely playing with words when he referred to dreaming in ways that lend themselves to contradictory interpretations. To Breton, a surrealist artist who exemplified the "dreamer once and for all" was no different from one engaged in a "dream of mediation." Both were linked by common devotion to desire. For it was desire that gave dream its value in surrealism, whether it was the dream encountered during sleep or the dream aspiration pursued in the light of day.[1] As for the surrealist mind, its role was always central, governing the artist's effort to record on canvas his dream as a projection of desire. Hence the range of response, the scale of revelation, so to speak, was neither objectively set nor universally applicable. It was a measure of subjective imaginative vitality, emanating from the surrealist mind.
   Breton, we notice, avoided the trap of all-embracing generalizations while alluding to certain "episodes" of Ernst's dream as involving mediation. Furthermore, he made an essential point clear. He showed that the role of the surrealist dreamer might be active as well as passive. He indicated that the dream did not always come to surrealist artists during sleep, but was often

something they succeeded in causing to manifest itself. Max
Ernst concurred with Breton's estimate of the artist's function,
at least in his own case, when he spoke of using "means of
forcing inspiration."

The fine point of balance to which surrealist creative activity
directs our attention is that in which passivity (willing submission to the creative impulse taking possession of the artist) meets
directed effort expressive of the will to create. At this point
we must grant special significance to Ernstian means of forcing
inspiration. Far from doing violence to inspiration, those means
were utilized in order to give inspiration a jolt, to set it in
motion and—most important of all—to cooperate with it while
avoiding infringement upon its revelatory prerogative. Implementing such means (frottage, for example), the artist had the
satisfaction not so much of summoning inspiration, of calling
it into service at will, but of making himself available to it,
proving his readiness to place himself at its disposal. To the
extent that using means of forcing inspiration indicated that
the finished creation was the result of a collaborative effort,
it demonstrated the folly of believing that the artist made no
personal investment in the creative gesture. It undermined the
false conclusion that anyone at all who sought to attain the
degree of receptivity emphasized in the 1924 surrealist manifesto could be assured of a place of honor among surrealism's
artists.

When the created work becomes an amalgam of the conscious
and the unconscious, the success of the operation, surrealists
would have admitted, depends on the measure achieved in adding consciously to what has emerged from the unconscious.
The danger to be avoided is that of burying the unconscious
contribution beneath the weight of a conscious superstructure.
The essential feature of the procedure should consist in developing the virtualities furnished by the unconscious in a manner
which, in the final analysis, places the conscious at the service
of the unconscious, respecting the integrity of the subliminal
message while still drawing inferences that the artist works
at bringing to the public's notice.

It would be a mistake to imagine the surrealist mind to have
been indecisive. Its principal objective was to push inquiry on
into the as yet unknown, conducting investigation in a fashion
that would rule out no possibility of progress but would challenge the predispositions (prejudices, in the surrealists' estima-

tion) accompanying rational thinking. Beneath Ernst's interest in "means of forcing inspiration" lay the assumption that certain obstacles have to be removed before inspiration will yield its revelations.

Ultimately, of course, Max Ernst sought visual effects through graphic experimentation in collage and frottage. Still, he realized early on that visual response would continue to be restricted by preconceptions formulated in the reasoning mind unless rational restrictions were lifted or evaded. There were locks needing to be forced so that access to inspiration might become possible. Ernst was not merely hoping to revitalize his art, then, to give it new vigor when inspiration was flagging. He was looking for something more: a means to reach beyond past achievements, to surpass them in unforeseeable ways. Therefore although his endeavor engendered new methods, to the surrealist mind its interest was extratechnical, since it was valued as effecting a breach in the wall rising between man and his desire.

At the source of Ernst's trust in "means of forcing inspiration" was a belief shared by all surrealists that chance had nothing to do with the haphazard. Justice might go on being blind, yet to the surrealist chance was illuminating. Far from impartial, as we like to believe justice to be, surrealist chance was excitingly partial in the benefits it bestowed on those capable of taking advantage of its gifts. For this reason, the surrealist mind did not presume to intrude upon the province of chance. But the invocation of chance, when the surrealist artist invited its intervention, signified confidence in its power to reveal something he could never have known without its cooperation. Pictorial techniques like Ernst's frottage were methods utilized by the surrealists to extend knowledge beyond known limits. Chance commanded respect as a stimulant able to activate creative imagination in unforeseen ways, entrusting emergent imagery to control by levels of the mind below consciousness or perhaps above it. In surrealism chance was prized as always potentially beneficent, helping "force inspiration."

A centrally important factor was that chance came under no obligation to provide the surrealist pictorial artist with valuable assistance. It was the artist's place, rather, to make himself available to take advantage of its gifts. This is why numerous "means of forcing inspiration" were respected in surrealism as methods for rendering the painter responsive to chance. The surrealist

mind called for creative activity that would permit the painter
to learn from chance while avoiding the blind alley of attempting
to force chance to meet his or her own demands.

"Means of forcing inspiration" had in common one feature
going beyond the capacity to liberate graphic technique. Basi-
cally, these were all methods that neutralized intellectualism
in the arts. They placed the creative act on a level where, dispensing with reflection and conscious speculation, it grew without interference from deductive thinking out of manual gesture.
The latter was esteemed by the surrealists as unpremeditated,
hence as anti-intellectual, released from unwelcome supervision
inhibitive to imaginative freedom.

The idea that the surrealist mind functioned anti-intellec-
tually is possibly confusing to someone attending to surrealist
painting for the first time, and even for the second. Many people find it difficult to grasp that imaginative play, as reflected
in surrealist pictorial art, was not a consequence of the elimination of mental activity so much as of its reorientation. From
the surrealists' standpoint, imaginative play recorded pictorially
was a sign that the mind had ceased to operate in ways the
intellectul could oversee and was now free to advance under
propulsion from imagination. Surrealists felt assured that submitting the discoveries made under these conditions to evaluation in terms familiar to the intellect would not simply be unfair;
it would be illogical, leading to frustration as much in the asses-
sor as in the artists he was judging. One of the major differences
generating discord between surrealist creative artist and art critics lies in conflicting presuppositions about the justification for
pictorial imagery and about the evaluative basis appropriate
to its appraisal.

When all the evidence is reduced to its common denominator,
the characteristic feature displayed by the surrealist mind is
anti-intellectualism. So the dominant aspect of surrealist activity
in favor of anti-intellectualism was the imposition upon pictorial art of a focus unifying experiments in a variety of directions
and modes, lending them a common function without imposing
a confinement that might have violated the spirit in which the
experimentation had been undertaken.

Investigative surrealism was spared monotony of effort and
accomplishment because the methods its participants implemented were not meant or used to channel mental effort, as
intellectualism inevitably does. Those methods were to open
the door on new possibilities, unforeseen discoveries, highly

regarded in surrealist circles for the very reason that they could not be predicted. For example, the distinguishing characteristic of the surrealist mind in its automatic mode was to make itself available to revelations of unpredictable consequences. These were valued because the methods utilized set a point of departure without ever prescribing a culminating point to delimit the admissible scope of achievement. That was the remarkable thing about surrealist painting and graphic inquiry. They proved capable of breaking out of the limitations that follow upon the deliberate application of paint to canvas which, in the pages of *Le révolution surréaliste*, had prompted Pierre Naville to doubt the feasibility of surrealist painting. Naville's error was to place painting first and then to speculate pessimistically on development of a surrealist form of it. That error was scotched by individual artists who, concentrating on surrealism (the projection of the surrealist mind), treated painting as a medium for its communication, so affording Breton the opportunity to look through their work as through a window.

When Breton declared that surprise must be sought "for itself" and "unconditionally," he was laying down a surrealist principle as important to painters as to writers in the movement. Summarized in his edict, the raison d'être of surrealist painting differentiated progress in knowledge from a deductive procedure on which the intellect relies in its pursuit of cognition. Surprise, as Breton referred to it, administred a dislocative shock beyond reasonable association and projection. Consequently, it was valued by the surrealists as provoking a leap that carried thought further than rational processes are able to do, in directions where reason would not venture and could not move forward. This is why our understanding of surrealist painting improves with increasing comprehension of the surrealist mind, of the ways in which it operated through art, and with what purpose.

Surrealists cannot be accused of having flirted with the antirational in order to shock their audience or draw attention to themselves. The authenticity of the surrealist's extrarational creative gesture depended largely on his freedom from inclination to pose. His undertaking was serious and his effort sincere, judged by the surrealist mind to be necessities, not luxuries, and certainly not attempts to engage in the classic pursuit of French artists for a century and more: *épater le bourgeois*.

The surrealist mind took strength from being misunderstood and opposed. It surely would have lost some of its energy and purpose had surrealism found wide acceptance and general ap-

proval. Beyond question, all surrealists were outsiders thriving
on rejection. Breton, for one, measured the purity of surrealist
aspirations by the suspicion they aroused. To the end of his
life he remained convinced that no compromise with society
was possible, except at the price of relaxing surrealism's standards. To the surrealist mind, then, accommodation would have
necessitated an adjustment of surrealism's demands that was
bound to work to surrealism's detriment. Here, where we might
imagine the surrealist attitude would have been tainted with
arrogance, in reality we face devotion to a cause that, for its
defender, took definition best while it remained outlawed. To
the surrealist, continued antagonism was proof that his vocation
remained genuine.

The surrealists' outlook placed them in an antibourgeois tradition to which they seem to have clung no less firmly for being,
in the main, men of bourgeois origin, several of whom were
not averse to living off women of bourgeois means. But the
surrealists saw themselves as members of the spiritual aristoc-
racy among which the French romantics had placed themselves
(hence the description of surrealism, in Breton's *Second manifeste*, as the prehensile tail of romanticism). Their feeling of
superiority was less the expression of belief in the refinement
of their own sensibility than of their conviction that their demands corresponded to a need to which the bourgeoisie was
sui generis insensitive and consequently hostile. As an essential
ingredient, the purity of the creative act had therefore total
unreserved involvement of the sensibility in the creative process, complete absence of calculated effect. Contrivance and os-
tentation would have been a betrayal of the surrealist mind,
harmful interference adversely affecting its unrestricted operation. The substructure of thought would have been undermined,
and no possibility would have remained for the surrealist mind
to build securely upon it.

Surrealist painting demonstrated unambiguously that surrealism was a state of mind, not simply a position on art supplying
a handful of technical devices that an artist might borrow in
anticipation of passing himself off successfully as a painter in
surrealist's clothing. Equally important, the surrealist's ambition
had nothing to do with disguising himself in painter's clothing.
Surrealist pictorial art could go on being a vital expression of
the surrealist mind only as long as the ends challenged the
means, as long as the latter remained under tension, extended
in the pursuit of goals that the artist was well aware he could

never be certain of reaching. Complacency and surrealism were not merely incompatible; they were mutually exclusive. Meanwhile, deliberately calculated efforts to violate pictorial custom would have been affectation in any surrealist artist. They might even have impeded crystallization of the surrealist pictorial image. What mattered to the surrealist in painting was to surpass traditional requirements. Surrealism's demands on the painter eclipsed all others. To a surrealist, any adjustment of art to nonsurrealist regulations was maladjustment, resulting in malfunction. These metaphors may sound exaggerated, but they are nevertheless appropriate to the situation and fittingly emphasize the distance surrealists found it necessary to maintain from the "art" of painting.

The radical difference separating the surrealist from the art historian or critic centers on the answer each would give to one question: What is the function of art? At least, so the surrealists would have contended, when noting how historians concen trate on elements in painting that they themselves saw as contributing nothing of significance to a picture or even as liable to divert attention from what they felt certain really mattered.

In this regard fully expressive of the surrealist mind, the originality of surrealist painting lay in the functional role assigned pictorial art by surrealism. As long as he persisted in his devotion to the latter, the artist remained a surrealist first and a painter second. So true was this that, almost invariably, when a painter left the surrealist camp or was expelled from it, it was because his "art" had displaced surrealism as his main focus. Surrealist painting exemplified the surrealists' conviction that art is just a means. Anything less would have entailed inviting their audience to admire the window in preference to looking through it. And the result? The example of Salvador Dali indicates what can occur when an artist finally becomes so enamored of his methods that they totally undermine his surrealist purpose.

A surrealist painted canvas did not come into being in order to display painterly skills but to solicit the spectator's participation in illumination through a revelatory image. No longer was it possible for the painter to seek and expect to earn commendation for proving he had acquired and fully mastered a certain number of techniques. Instead, parallel to Breton's metaphor likening the pictorial image to an appealing panorama visible through a window ran Matta Echaurrén's definition of some of his own canvases as representing "inscapes." The surrealist painter escaped inside himself by painting landscapes perceived with the inner eye.

At the core of the surrealist attitude lay the conviction that art as practiced and approved in modern times is, with few exciting exceptions, an art alienated from man's most essential needs. Perpetuating art forms consecrated by their predecessors was pointless, surrealists concluded. More than this, they argued, it was a distortion of the artist's role at a time in history when there was less excuse than ever before for ignoring the function of art, as defined by the surrealist mind.

Promoting art to the status reserved for it in surrealist thought could follow only when reorientation of artistic ambition had been hastened by firm rejection of time-honored rules, of customs and values that surrealism cast aside as prejudicial. It was this outlook, not unmotivated iconoclasm, that provoked surrealist conduct with respect to artistic activity. Directionless rebellion would have brought surrealism back to a position its first advocates had condemned when severing ties with Dada. Under those conditions, the effort made in the name of surrealism would have lost meaning, henceforth deserving no more than a brief mention in histories of modern Western art.

The art that surrealists saw practiced around them dissatisfied them because they saw it as an alienating agent, needing to be transformed into an agent of reconcilation operating by way of imaginative liberation. Because art had its place in surrealism, not surrealism in art, surrealist painting took on meaning as an expression of the surrealist mind. Consequently, art as instrument, not goal, was central to the surrealist concept of painting. A surrealist denigrated established art forms for other reasons than to excuse himself for making ineffectual use of them. He regarded those forms as erecting barriers obstructive to advance in directions where he felt that visionary progress must lie. So it was not by falling short of agreed standards that the surrealist painter must distinguish himself. He had to set himself other standards, according to which he would judge his own work and expect to see it judged. Reviewing surrealist anticonformity with respect to artistic tradition, one can see that the surrealist mind subjected pictorial form to stress less with the purpose of bettering that form than in order to oblige it to meet surrealism's requirements more adequately.

As with writing, in painting inspired by the needs and interests of the surrealist mind the *how* of artistic creation was predicated on the *why*. In the final analysis, then, how a pictorial image emerged was not important of itself. More important were the artist's reasons for resorting to the methods he employed, his hopes and expectations. Particularly significant here was that those hopes and expectations often lacked sharp definition, a situation motivating the artist all the more strongly because he was incapable of projecting results precisely defining the goals to which he aspire. This occurred as a result neither of reluctance nor of insufficient mental or imaginative capacity but because the very nature or surrealist pictorial experimentation was to move beyond predictability into a zone where technique became the instrument of revelation. Technique in itself was not a guarantee of "quality." Nor, for that matter, was it a sure means of attaining it. Technique was valued in surrealism only for the assistance it provided artists in breaking down mental barriers and in gaining access to areas of mental and imaginative activity previously beyond reach. In no way could surrealist methodology in the pictorial arts be ascribed intrinsic worth, as a manifestation of aestheticism, for instance. This is why it could be modified or even abandoned altogether if it ceased to be productive within the framework of ambition nurtured in the surrealist mind.

If we select as an example the affection for academicism apparently common to widely-known surrealist painters, we soon have to acknowledge that, in surrealism contrary to appearances, it was a tool used in defiance of academic goals. It was a method turned back upon itself, its easily identifiable features employed to undermine the purposes with which academicism was associated. Our example helps show why simple enumeration of technical devices fails to bring increased understanding of surrealism and instead actually works against better comprehension. Analysis of pictorial surrealism according to traditionalist canons merely widens the distance between the evaluator's criteria and those inspiring the artist to paint. For the *why* of surrealist painting is to be traced to the surrealist mind rather than to misguided fidelity to unfashionable pictorial methods.

Broadening the issue makes us more aware of the absence of common ground on which artist and critic might agree to situate judgment, there being a considerable distance between surrealist practice and critical expectation. An illustrative case is provided by William S. Rubin's study, *Dada and Surrealist Art*,[2] written on the occasion of a large exhibition at the Museum of Modern Art, New York.

Prefacing his weighty volume, Rubin begins by remarking that most contemporary writing (surrealism was still every active at the time he wrote, yet he relegated it to the past) about "this art" (he makes no distinction between Dada and surrealism) was "the work of poets whose virtually exclusive concern was with its imagery." He continues, "I have tried to balance these iconographic interests with the needs of stylistic analysis. In so doing, I have had to bring into play such judgments as that of quality. These determinations were not simply outside the concerns of the surrealist poet-critics, they were utterly alien to their beliefs."[3] The abrupt transition from judgment to determination is amusing, setting a stamp on Rubin's presentation that provoked an experienced surrealist commentator on painting, José Pierre, to attack his book violently.[4] For the crucial question, as Rubin naively admits, is that of quality. More exactly, it is that of defining the quality of surrealist painting.

Rubin tries to relate surrealism to mainstream art, affirming that "the ultimate survival of the objects in question [in reality, he is talking about paintings,not surrealist objects] depends on the fact that they are art"[5] (p. 7). The circularity of his argumentation cannot escape notice. Meanwhile, his assumption that "the works can be described in terms that make sense for art history in general" typifies the art historian's interpretation of surrealism which Rubin, like his fellows, achieves by isolating surrealist painting from the mental climate to which it belonged, uprooting it from the soil in which its seeds had been sown and reached fruition. With any school of painting, Rubin's approach might pass for permissible, even mandatory. Witb surrealism, it is neither the one nor the other. As a result, the perspective adopted in Dada and Surrealist Art slows our progress toward understanding surrealism, if not confusing the central issues enough to bring our advance to a halt.

It would be inaccurate to dismiss Rubin's analyses and others like them as a betrayal of surrealist painting, since none of those who speak as critics or art historians ever had the opportunity to examine surrealism from inside the movement. All the same, given the peculiar nature of painting of surrealist inspiration, it is scarcely an injustice to measure the distortion presented in those analyses, achieved thanks to a viewpoint confidently defended even by those—Rubin, for one—who recognize that it conflicts with that of the painters under scrutiny. Art historians may not all follow Rubin's example in mocking the surrealists' evaluation of surrealist painting. However, they do agree with him in taking a position remote from that of the surrealists. In this important respect they display a lack of sympathy for the surrealist mind and, more important, a lack of appreciation of it.

There is no denying that the approach common to art critics teaches something about surrealist painting. It is ironical, though, that no surrealist artist ever saw any good reason for his public to learn what it has to teach. The surrealist rejected the judgment of historians on the grounds that their remarks were irrelevant to his aspirations, took no cognizance of these, and set appraisal on a footing far distant from the foundations of surrealist art. Under these conditions, it mattered not at all to the surrealist painter whether he received critical praise or was castigated. Whatever commentators might say about his work sounded impertinent to him. This deserves emphasis because it disposes of the common illusion that surrealists were prompted by arrogance alone to scoff at those who found their work wanting.

Whether implicitly or explicitly, the surrealists' comments on poetry and painting exhibit a unifying theme, which can be summarized as follows. The surrealists were right, while the critics were not and never could be. One might reject such an argument as no more defensible than when critical judgment has been ridiculed by artists whose evaluation of their own work contradicts it. Doing so, however, denies us the opportunity to pursue our investigation of the surrealist mind.

The achievement of the pictorial artist was easy to gauge, from the surrealists' viewpoint, according to a standard that precluded self-deception. In order to learn how successful he had been, as soon as he had finished a picture the painter had only to ask himself one question. What did he know now, thanks to what he saw before him, that he had not known before? Applying this criterion did not measure productive methodology on a statistical basis. On the contrary.

Fundamental to the surrealists' outlook and approach was the notion that anything diverting attention from the picture as image, or detracting from the impact it made on the imagination, thanks to the image it presented, was more than superfluous; it was unforgivable. High on the list of negative facts they considered harmful to the image, diminishing its intensity, were the very elements that hold an art critic's attention. Hence the distinction they drew between critical approval and their own reflected differences in evaluative standards. Convinced that meeting the criteria applied in criticism and histories of art would have contributed nothing to enhancing the image, surrealists found critics and historians to be willfully blind or at the very best uninformed. Thus it was André Breton's intent to state his position as a surrealist unequivocally, when he warned anyone reading a collection of his essays, *Yves Tanguy*, to expect of their author "nothing resembling art criticism" (p. 9). Far from hiding behind false modesty, he was seeking to clarify his position in contradistinction to that of a critic. In opposition to critical norms, he meant to indicate why he regarded Tanguy as a superior painter.

Where the critic might not hesitate to pronounce surrealist pictorial methodology weak or impoverished, surrealists had no complaint to make. Indeed, they were aware more of advantages than of disadvantages in techniques that stimulated reservations in critics. It seemed to them that an artist could concentrate better on imagery when spared the seduction to which art historians expect willing reaction on his part. Poverty of means is a relative concept, obviously—as is seduction, for that matter. We cannot refer to either profitably unless doing so deepens our appreciation of one feature of surrealist creativity in the artistic field. Generally speaking, the surrealists' use of pictorial techniques constituted an act of aggression carried out by men and women less concerned with practicing the painter's art than with capturing images.

It was the intensity of the image obtained that vindicated technique, rather than the frequency with which an experimental method precipitated imagery. Mass production, after all, was never among the surrealists' priorities. Attempting to gauge the quality of surrealist painting on a percentage basis would have been inappropriate, Rubin's inclination to do so notwithstanding. As for relating success to the care with which certain techniques were brought into service, this would have been dangerous. It would have encouraged caution and fostered the delusion that methodology per se was valuable to surrealist art, that there was some virtue in elevating to the status of inviolable rules technical procedures that had been used experimentally before strictly for the revelations they might offer and never as guarantees of acceptable results. For the surrealists, it was imperative to avoid the error of allowing means to displace ends and become their own justification. Otherwise, the surrealist mind would have slipped into dormancy, no longer exerting an influence in the absence of which surrealism would have succumbed to complacent repetitiveness.

One of José Pierre's books, *Le surréalisme* (1979), opens with a subtitle that states the surrealist position simply and directly: "Le surréalisme et sa peinture" (surrealism and its painting). Surrealism claimed painting as its own, without acknowledging any obligation to art. Hence the surrealists reserved the right to demand that the results obtained by a surrealist painter be weighed in relation to surrealist intention. They looked upon his work first and last as evidence of the fermenting action of the surrealist mind. The perspective deemed fitting, in surrealism, was set from the beginning, when in his first manifesto Breton approvingly quoted Pierre Reverdy's dictum, "The image is pure creation of the mind," adopting as his own a definition that would never cease to be pertinent to the surrealists' assessment of creative activity, pictorial as well as verbal.

Criticism that ought to be addressing painting in surrealism usually proceeds in the wrong direction and treats surrealism in painting. It rarely advances fruitfully beyond cataloguing the constituent elements of the pictorial image. Surrealism, though, manifests itself when the painted image presents a mystery that formal analysis cannot penetrate. Here the *why* of the picture resists reduction to rationally comprehensible terms. When the surrealist set brush to canvas, his goal had no more clear outline than the wish to learn. Ignorance rather than knowledge gave him his point of departure. His creative endeavor was spurred by the wish to know more, not by the intention to prove to others what he knew already. To the surrealist, then, painting was an investigative act instead of a demonstration. It was elucidation by imaginative play. The surrealists placed their faith in painting as discovery, which, in their estimation, must replace painting as testimony. And so the criterion for judging artistic accomplishment was illumination instead of confirmation or distillation of an accepted truth.

We respond first, no doubt, to similarities of technique linking certain modes of surrealist writing and painting, the most striking example for most of us being automatism. In the long term, however, what impresses us as important is not so much methodology as the mental attitude to which the popularity among surrealists of this or that technique directs attention. So, to clear the way to better appreciation, we have to rid ourselves of the common mistake of regarding surrealism as a movement, literary in scope, that prompted a number of painters to imitate, as far as this seemed possible, the work of writers they admired.

To do less means failure on our part to grasp a central fact, that the purpose of surrealist writing was to transcend the limitations of literature. And it also means falling short of realizing that as an expression of the surrealist mind, just like surrealist writing surrealist painting was assigned a cognitive role.

Surrealism recorded reality in the process of expanding, embracing an ever-widening circle of possibilities limited by nothing more than man's capacity to respond, explore, and accept. Reality in surrealism ceased to be fixed in its contours. Its boundaries were set, in fact, only by the imaginative receptivity of the individual facing it. Thus, surrealism taught, when the surrealist is aware of reality as oppressively confining and emotionally restrictive, he is really measuring his own limitation, his own mental and emotional confinement. In effect, what the surrealist mind demonstrated is that we are to blame ourselves, not the world around us, if reality is disappointing or frustrating. The essential optimism vitalizing surrealist thought was the conviction that it is man's privilege and right to make the most he can of reality, under prompting from his desires.

Surrealist painting found justification in the eyes of those who practiced it and those who formed its most immediate informed audience, according to a scale of values not meant to violate accepted rules yet coincidentally encouraging their violation. This fact is important in one respect particularly. The surrealist attitude, it bids us note, was not one of negation. Negative features were simply offshoots of a positive program. In order to accomplish what they wanted to do, the surrealists believed they should begin by avoiding whatever was unproductive. Thus, breaking with the past was an affirmation of their faith in the future.

We gain no more than limited understanding of the surrealist mind if we fail to appreciate that its artistically creative expressions denoted salvation earned beyond the framework of religious thinking yet sometimes evoked in terms reminiscent of that thinking within the surrealist group. André Breton's assurance that the surrealists must and would possess the afterlife in the here and now, for instance, reflected a confidence without which surrealist art would have lacked meaning and purpose. The future is now, surrealists claimed, urging the public to concede that its manifestation depends only on the elimination of obstacles impeding our perception of it.

Surrealist painting came into being to provide a foretaste and promise of "what *will be*." For this reason, surrealist canvases solicit a response that offers no resistance to their annunciatory aspects, which are concentrated in pictorial imagery, coming before us as an expression of an enriched and expanded perception of reality: surreality. In the surrealists' opinion, any attempt to measure the worth of such imagery by one or other of those standards in which Rubin (and he is far from alone) asks us to place confidence must distort the work under examination. For it fails to concentrate attention where surrealism required that the latter be directed: on the spirit in which the picture was executed under the direction of the surrealist mind.

The ambition shared by surrealist painters using diversified approaches never varied: to encompass something of the so far unknown, to fix an image of it. In their common pursuit, those artists were all sustained by the belief that the unknown will not be forever unknowable, even if it lies beyond the range of reasoned comprehension. Pictorial technique of whatever kind retained its value, for the surrealist, to the extent only that it helped the imagination escape from confinement by the familiar into the exciting prospect presented by the presently unfamiliar. Use of pictorial technique for any other purpose, surrealists were persuaded, must result in its debasement. Hence such use was not simply discouraged. Surrealism banned it as extraneous to artistic purpose, as a dangerous concession to irrelevant preoccupations vitiating art, of which aestheticism was perhaps the most reprehensible. With the purity of which surrealists were wont to speak, when referring to verbal automatism, went purity of intent in painting, single-minded concern with eliciting and communicating revealing pictorial imagery, with avoiding anything that might divert attention from such imagery, blunting its impact on the imagination.

To the surrealist, seeing with the inner eye did not necessarily mean declining to admit visible evidence perceptible and therefore acceptable to everyone else. It meant being able to glimpse things that eluded vision focused on sights rendered familiar by everyday experience, usually classified as unexceptionable because neither reason nor memory doubts the evidence presented by one of the senses. When the surrealists praised the inner eye, it was for bringing revelation without precedent or parallel in the world of lived experience. As a result, it may seem that their ideal was a radical departure from familiar reality when in fact it was transcendence of the reality we all know. They aimed to surmount the limitations of perception imposed on us all by experience, habit, education, and inculcated moral, ethical, or aesthetic values. In this sense, surrealism marked the repudiation of unquestioned norms, achieved through emancipated vision. Thus it called for a better grasp on the real, to prove more satisfying because it was in closer harmony with desire and uninhibited by social, ethical, cultural, and aesthetic restrictions.

The surrealist looked upon the aesthetician and anyone heeding his word as enemies. For the surrealist mind could not reconcile aesthetics with progress and discovery. Surrealists reproved aestheticism's regulatory demands as being diametrically opposed to art as an instrument of surrealism. The central preoccupations of the surrealist mind laid the foundation of an art serving to illuminate, not refine. Therefore, instead of feeling sensitive to aspects of the painter's *métier* consecrated by the aesthetic tradition, surrealists embraced the idea that the deliberate neglect of aesthetics—its self-conscious avoidance, even— could help place the artist on a pathway along which new discoveries might be his to make. It was not that surrealists nurtured the delusion that sidestepping the obstacle of aestheticism must ensure progress. They were thoroughly convinced, though, that the failure to circumvent that obstacle would place success out of the reach. Not everyone would agree that the surrealist position was unassailable. Even so, we do the surrealists a grave injustice when concluding that their conduct betokened ineptitude, lack of sophistication, or quite simply a spirit of barbarism meriting nothing better than condemnation.

The surrealist mind regarded as confining all painting done according to inherited conventions. Breach of convention, on the other hand, appeared likely to be liberative. However, it was not liberation from control, pursued in the spirit of anarchy, that the surrealist mind sought. Surrealists saw in liberation from restraint an assurance of freedom to act in defiance of the values underlying accepted restraints, and under impetus from desire, urging the painter on to discoveries inaccessible by inherited means. Anyone who regards surrealism as an extention of Dada has failed to identify one of the fundamental differences between surrealism and Dada, originating in the surrealists' dissatisfaction with the Dadaists' demonstrated inability to arrive at a program extending beyond the negative to the positive. Freedom *from*, the surrealists believed, must generate freedom *for*. Indeed, the latter justifies the former, according to surrealist theory. History was to show that disappointment with Dada was the initial stage in evolving a surrealist program

for life as well as for art. In surrealism, it was insufficient to
say no. One had to be able to say yes as well and to find ways
of formulating positive answers not only desirable but feasible.
Thus negativity was no more than a prerequisite bringing the
surrealist artist up against the need and obligation to fill a vacuum with which the Dadaists all too often had seemed perfectly
content. In fine, the divergence between surrealism and Dada
may be traced back to the effort made by the surrealist mind
to fill that vacuum, back to the motivation behind that effort.

The surrealist was a mental adventurer, eager to discover
something new and convinced that the best way to do so was
to turn away from the old. Stated in these terms, his attitude
seems to have been indistinguishable from that at the origin
of numerous ephemeral avant-garde movements. The originality
and durability of surrealism were products of the surrealist
mind's resistance to prevalent assumptions about the artists'
relation to his work and his public. Surrealism marked a revolt
against accepted interpretations of the function of art and the
role falling to the artist. Hence, when engaged in art, surrealists
did not fail to meet appropriate standards. Instead, they rejected
consecrated criteria as inapplicable to their undertaking and,
indeed, inimical to creativity of the kind on which they placed
reliance.

The surrealist concept of purity of artistic achievement was
related to the idea that inherited forms and approaches contaminated purity. More than this, according to the surrealists such
forms and approaches diverted the artist's attention from purity,
when not placing it quite beyond his reach. Their attitude was
grounded in the belief that art as instrument should not merely
take precedence over art as purpose, but ought to eliminate
the latter entirely. A feature essential to the operation of the
surrealist mind, so far as it dictated the surrealist attitude toward
art, was that art had to serve the surrealist mind as well as
express it, thereby rewarding the artist's interest in creativity
manifested in pictorial imagery.

Before it could serve the surrealist mind profitably, art had
to assume purposes and take forms to which that mind lent
significance. Meanwhile, it had to abandon other purposes and
forms that surrealism condemned as immaterial or even objec-
tionable. Less than strict adherence to the principles that invested painting with meaning for the surrealists could well have
increased an artist's chances of appealing to an audience whose
attention surrealism taught, he had no reason to try to engage.

That this happened to be an audience looking for guidance to critics of art, and respectful of judgments passed by art historians, in no way discouraged the surrealist or weakened his resolve. On the contrary, experience led all participants in the surrealist venture to conclude that hostility on a critic's part, in whatever medium of creative action, was an indication that they were managing to remain faithful to their vocation.

There are times when, reviewing their behavior vis-à-vis critics, one finds it unjust to exonerate the surrealists from the crime of having anticipated more hostility than they encountered, from having been intolerant in charging art historians with intolerance. Indeed, one senses beneath the surrealists' intractability a fear that their art might meet wider acceptance and fuller appreciation than would have left them feeling totally at ease. But even here suspicion and mistrust are evidence of the liveliness of the surrealist mind, which we cannot ignore without the risk of miscontruing the role that fell to painting in surrealism.

6
Creativity and Criticism

One pedestrian way of describing the role of criticism with respect to that of artistic creation represents the critic as standing on the outside peering in while the artist is on the inside looking out. Apparently, this seems a permissible way of putting things because it allows us to begin with a truism by and large applicable to the posture adopted by all responsible critical commentators where all forms of art are concerned. However, we move beyond the safe realm of banality when we become cognizant of one crucial fact. Where surrealism is in question, the person looking out and the one peering in usually do not see the same thing.

We are all aware of the arrogance with which artists traditionally greet attempts to elucidate their work from outside, especially where, in their estimation, these only distort what they have tried to do or actually accomplished. When surrealism comes under consideration, we find comparable arrogance on the side of the critic. He is sure in his own mind that surrealist artists must be trying to achieve something that he, as expert commentator, deems worth attempting. So he chides or even attacks them when—as it usually happens—they fall short of aims he believes are to be ascribed to them, quite regardless of the fact that surrealism fostered ambitions different, or even altogether contrary, from those he has in view.

The situation is aggravated, naturally, by a feature of art criticism that has gained prominence in our time. This has grown out of these critics' self-confident conviction that they do not merely come before the public as reliable arbiters of taste but also are entitled to dictate what the artist shall try to do with the means he adopts. According to their reasoning, technique in any form of art is deserving of appreciation and merits validation only when and where its results warrant the approval that it is their prerogative to bestow. Claiming every right to pass judgment in matters of technique and relying at all times on their own estimate of what surrealist art ought to have aspired to accomplish, somewhat paradoxically critics are misled even further by the self-evident disconcerting simplicity of many of the verbal and pictorial investigative methods developed and implemented under impetus from surrealist aspirations. The critic's ability to respond profitably is further impaired by the stress that surrealists so often gave to play in the creative act. Because surrealism did not exclude fun, it appears from where the commentator stands that, in surrealist works, the high seriousness of art and literature is patently compromised, sometimes being excluded entirely. Tacitly associating simplicity of means with lack of worthwhile ambition, the critic looks upon these methods as merely trivial.

The foregoing may sound grossly exaggerated. It is even likely to be taken for evidence of prejudice against the critics, who are by no means as villainous or imperceptive as they have been represented. Rather than accusing them of arrogance, in fact, we should be speaking more sympathetically of the misunderstanding and shortcomings that are the consequences of their inclination to share a perspective markedly different from the surrealist point of view. Nevertheless, all too often observers outside the surrealist movement overlook the central importance of one basic fact. The surrealists' sense of wonder at creative achievement was intensified by their pleasure at seeing how little it takes for wonder to be released. And their enjoyment was all the greater because, in true surrealist artist, proprietory feelings were minimal at the very most. Ideally, they were nonexistent.

Yves Tanguy would very often turn his canvas upsidedown after painting it and before signing his name. He is reported to have said on one occasion, "I found that if I planned a picture beforehand, it never surprised me, and surprises are my pleasure in painting."[1] On the level of painterly exploration, the radical difference between Tanguy and, shall we say, Raoul Dufy, lies in this forthright statement. Meanwhile, among the surrealists' aspirations Tanguy's were hardly unique. One cannot place too much emphasis on the fact that artists using methods as diverse as Jean Arp's and Max Ernst's all have proposed titles that constitute deeply subjective interpretations of the paintings and sculptures they have executed. As for René Magritte, it is noteworthy that his custom was to let others—Paul Nougé, especially—interpret his pictures by naming them in his place.

A distinguishing feature of surrealism is that artists devoted to its principles very often leaned heavily on techniques that may be termed mechanical. Indeed, this is why surrealists—whose lead the critics obviously are quite disinclined to follow—looked upon Benjamin Péret as their greatest poet. Without reservations of any sort, Péret consistently surrendered to verbal automatism, both in his verse and in his short stories. His writing method was consonant with the techniques employed by certain prominent surrealist pictorial artists who favored such methods as frottage, decalcomania, and grattage. Speaking of pictorial automatism, André Breton described it in a 1941 essay, "Génèse et perspective artistiques du surréalisme" (in *Le Surréalisme et la peinture*), as "the skiff always at the same time lighter and more reliable," on which certain painters (Breton mentioned Frances, Matta, and Onslow-Ford) have set out "on the conquest of a new morphology that will exhaust in the most concrete language the whole process whereby the psychical has repercussions in the physical" (p. 82). Thus painterly techniques here termed mechanical, placing at the artist's disposal new means of expression that Breton likened to a new language, were the counterpart of automatic writing. In this respect, they usefully cast light on the scope and nature of surrealist endeavor.

The mechanical means the surrealist painter turned to advantage were used in protest against the *art* of painting. In other words, where a surrealist resorted to methods requiring no professional skill, he did so because he rejected the controls that professional training necessarily imposes.

Acquired expertise generally helps the artist arrive at a finished product that, to some extent any way, takes no account of the public's expectations. Yet, deep perspective in the pictures of Salvador Dali or Conroy Maddox notwithstanding, technical mastery (or even, more modestly, elementary proficiency) appeared to many a surrealist irrelevant to his function and unsuited to furthering the ends he pursued. Quite simply, he aimed to arrive at that "pure psychic automatism," advocated in the 1924 *Manifeste du surréalisme*, which grants the creator of images release from the deleterious effects of egocentricity, firmly ruled out by the surrealists when they echoed Lautréamont's outburst against *tics*. Surrealists found that automatism has the supreme advantage of giving the artist a sense of privilege, as it makes access to the image-making process possible. Modesty is a virtue in the critic that anyone can recognize and see as beneficial even when surrealism is not the object of his attention. Still, it is not easy to grasp why surrealists insisted that the artist must efface himself before his work.

At one extreme, the surrealists believed, failure to meet this requirement produces only premonitory tics, revealing mannerisms. But at the other extreme, critics are within their rights in detecting evidence of what they term style. Here, surrealists argued, method has ousted vision. Now original insights yield to platitudes, just as in the postsurrealist work of Dali, where external signs of surrealist technique survive, ironically, long after surrealist inspiration has ceased to be operative.

André Breton brings us back to essentials when, in his "Génèse et perspective artistiques du surréalisme," he explains that the essential discovery of surrealism is that "without preconceived intention, the pen that runs to write or the pencil that runs to draw, *spins* an infinitely precious substance not all of which perhaps is material for exchange but which, at least, appears charged with everything that the poet or painter has by way of emotion inside him" (p. 68). These remarks prepare us to be attentive to Joan Miró's confession that he did not feel accountable for the paintings he executed during the early 1930s. And they remind us that Benjamin Péret was unable to recognize his own poetry when it was read aloud to him. In short, they point to the surrealists' rewarding sense of discovery through their own work.

Approaching surrealism, critics who—whether knowingly or not—treat art as externalizing the artist's ego invariably underestimate one highly important factor. We are made aware of its nature when reviewing the case of Max Ernst.

Speaking of "means of forcing inspiration," Ernst was not confessing to being worried about finding ways to whip his jaded imagination into one more productive effort. Instead, he was concerned about a serious obstacle that arose before every authentic surrealist artist, whatever his medium happened to be. Inspiration—to pursue Ernst's metaphor—needs to be forced, the way a lock sometimes does. "The driving belt between the individual and the collective—and this is perhaps at the same time a vital gear-wheel in surrealist activity, its most original characteristic—has been stretched, neither too tight nor too slack, once and for all," commented one surrealist. "This being so, the means of ensuring the development of surrealism depend, in large part, upon the determination of each of us to force his own locks."[2] The trouble is, though, that a major obstruction still lies in the artist's conscious predisposition. It makes its unwelcome presence felt through his insidious inclination to reiterate previous artistic statements, to repeat past accomplishments. This is why we hear Breton, in the preface to an Ernst exhibition held in May 1920, raise an important question when wondering if we are not preparing to escape, some day, from the "principle of identity." The first step, evidently, is suppression of vanity.

In this connection, Ernst's remarks on his discovery of the technique of frottage stand out as quite significant. They stress that the person making a frottage is no more than a spectator, present at and assisting in (the French verb *assister à*, used in Ernst's 1936 article called "Au-delà de la peinture," is fruitfully ambiguous) the manifestation of an image. In the final analysis, regardless of the disappointment it gave some people to learn that Luis Buñuel arrived accidentally at the visual parallel we are shown in *Viridiana* between the disciples gathered in da Vinci's *Last Supper* and the beggars assembled at the dining table the important thing is that Buñuel took care to acknowledge publicly that chance had intervened beneficently in his movie.[3]

The satisfaction a surrealist derived from producing a poem, film, object, painting, or piece of sculpture with the welcome assistance of chance—solicited very often through the application of unsophisticated operating methods—lets us see him looking outward in eager anticipation from the creative act to whatever it might accomplish. The contrast is only too clear when we bear in mind how suspicious or confused are critics who consequently find themselves denied full understanding of what surrealism affords its primary audience the opportunity to witness.

Increasingly fascinated by the *how* of art, critics are brought to a halt by questions to which they would like to have firm answers. For instance, how exactly did chance intrude, and to what extent, to make Buñuel arrange his beggars at table in such a way that the horrifying blind man evokes da Vinci's Christ? Natural predisposition is obviously a factor in the total effect of Buñuel's scene ("I didn't try to blaspheme, but, of course, Pope John XXIII knows more about that than I. Chance led me to show impious images; if I had pious ideas, perhaps I'd have expressed them too.") Yet the mystery remains. Meanwhile, critics drift more and more into misunderstanding the wherefore of surrealist art. Their approach is less than adequate

to the task of dealing with surrealism and leads predictably
to distinctly unsatisfactory results. The reason for this is not
hard to trace. It has to do with the critic's underlying confidence
in his theory that assumes creative processes follow a pattern
from which typical surrealist creative acts frequently diverged
radically. We see what can happen if we consider the critical
analytical method known in France as *explication de texte*.

André Tinel has emphasized quite correctly that *explication
de texte* concentrates on working method. This leads him to
the firm conclusion that "everything it tries to discover, to render
perceptible, is foreign to surrealism."[4] No less an authoritative
spokesman for surrealism than André Breton indicated why this
is the case. Ridiculing the "ultra-debilitating regime" of *explication de texte*, he remarked appositely, "It is amusing or disconcerting, according to one's humor, to observe—when all who
know something about it agree in proclaiming that the virtue
of a poem depends as incompletely on what it 'means' literally
or seems to mean as that of a painting on what it 'represents'
that textbooks . . . are overloaded increasingly with commentary
aimed, at all cost, at re-establishing the primacy of understanding over feeling."[5] And what are the consequences? Undertaking
to explicate Breton's poem "Au beau demi-jour de 1934," first
published in *L'air de l'eau* (1934), Roger Cardinal reveals the
pitfalls that open up before the critic's feet by falling head first
into them.
    To begin with, Cardinal has no qualms about misrepresenting
the material he is examining. Accepting implicitly that he has
in front of him an example of automatic writing, he hastens
nevertheless, to credit its author with having "recognized the
need for a certain degree of *arrangement en poème*, as Eluard
called it—the need to give some shape to the *materia prima*
of poetry offered by automatism."[6] Wondering where Cardinal
finds sanction for his unsupported contention that Breton tail-
ored his poems out of the material of automatic writing, one
cannot but notice that, indirectly, this commentator invites us
to ignore Breton's declaration that he did not set aside the automatic principle before writing his *Ode à Charles Fourier*, published only in 1947.[7] Reading Cardinal's *explication de texte*
of "Au beau demi-jour de 1934," we soon see why he was
prompted to do such a thing.
    Before long (p. 270), Cardinal has ceased to confine himself
to discussing the presence of words like *rouget* in Breton's poem.

He is speculating upon the poet's choice of such words. By now, he is entirely taken up with intentions he attributes to Breton, despite the fact that he has spoken of "the process of careless metamorphosis that goes on in Surrealist poetry" (p. 265), despite having formulated, too, this damning criticism: "One of the weaknesses of the Surrealist poetic method is that it does not allow for careful elaboration of a theme that will arouse the reader's more slothful responses and convey a recognized emotion" (p. 261). Cardinal finally gives the game away when, stopping at the word *oursin*, and claiming that in the verse collection *L'air de l'eau* allusions to such creatures as the sea urchin, turtle, and axolotl are "gratuitous" (no longer the result of choice, then?), he confides in a footnote, "I prefer to take the present reference as a sexual one, . . ." (p. 271). If any features mark Cardinal's *explication* from end to end, they are sustained effort to bend André Breton's text to a coherent, consecutive, rational interpretation and the supposition that readers will not doubt that this is faithful to deliberate intent on the poet's part.

By what right, though, does Roger Cardinal presume to know just what Breton's automatic text—a text produced by means that eliminate conscious controls—was "intended" to convey? To answer this question, we have only to turn to a statement of faith made by a longtime adept of the method of *explication de texte*.

In a study of "five modern French poets," Bernard Weinberg offers an introductory section outlining general assumptions about "the art of poetry" by which he argues that the methods he employs in analyzing individual texts are "justified":

> My first assumption is that an art of poetry does exist. I am not sure whether, for the individual poet who uses it, it is a set of principles, or a collection of habits, or a complex of feelings about the "rightness" or "wrongness" of elements that might go into the making of the poem. But we know that as the poet composes, he constantly makes choices: where to begin his poem, how to continue it, where to end it; the object of the work or the figure to be developed; the emotions to be aroused and directed. These choices result from his art. They are not accidents, they do not just happen. In each case, the choice depends upon a conception or an instinct relative to the form that the whole poem will ultimately take, and the "art" consists in determining, at every point, which of the alternative solutions is to be adopted. . . .
>
> Second, I assume that, as a product of the art, any poem is the

possible objective of an analysis that will discover, not by what creative process it was made, but what it is and in what particular form it exists. The assumption here is that it should be possible to describe that final form which, as the ultimate goal of the poet, determined his individual choices.[8]

It means even more. For Weinberg lays down guidelines for tracing the *how* of a poem back to a preexistent *why*. Having done so, he has the good sense to refrain from attempting to apply his method to analyzing even one surrealist poem.

A case—not easily disputed—may be made for the surrealists' suspicion of anyone placing faith in the *explication de texte* method. Evidence available to everyone supports their viewpoint that *explication* takes as its premise assumptions about the nature and structure of verbal poetry quite inapplicable to a surrealist poem. This is why attempting to analyze surrealist poetry according to the rules of *explication de texte* brings only strictly limited success. The best it can do is assemble findings to which the surrealists would have attached no real significance. In an essay written in September 1924, a month before the publication of his first surrealist manifesto and published three years later as *Introduction au discours sur le peu de réalité*, Breton poured scorn on the unnamed editor of an anthology who had taken upon himself to explain certain of Saint-Pol-Roux's images. The surrealists' contempt for the presumptuousness at the source of *explication de texte* derived from their disinterest in any statement, passed off as poetic, for which a prosaic paraphrase readily suggests itself. To presume to judge poetry is already, they thought, to degrade it, to reduce its stature. For they resisted the idea that the poetic is susceptible to prosaic restatement. They were firmly opposed to the notion that prose can infringe upon the domain of poetry, thereby invading the territory that is poetry's by right.

We only distort Breton's "Au beau demi-jour de 1934" if we fail to acknowledge that it conforms to surrealism's basic articles of faith. These stipulated that the poet may place his trust in a mode of verbalization practiced outside the region over which reason exercises tutelage and imposes censorship. Automatism makes it possible for poets to speak after breaking the bridges by which reason hopes and expects to advance along the road to comprehension. To progress with "Au beau demi-jour" and other texts of the same inspiration, one must therefore realize that these poems bypass routes congested with reasonable traffic.

Hence an instructive aspect of Breton's poem is that the narrative voice it lets us hear displays no critical sense while recounting the experience it places on record. Even after the event, the poet continues to be unable to explain to reason's satisfaction what exactly has occurred. A single present tense interrupts a narrative otherwise offered in the past, and this admits the poet's incapacity, now, to explain what happened then: "I do not know how he held on," the poet remarks of the squirrel that pressed its belly to his heart.[9]

Just as important as the surrealists' disaffection for the explicative mode of literary commentary is the following. At no time did even one surrealist try to promote a counterproposal for locating and identifying qualities by which surrealism makes it presence felt in poetry. To the already established fact that the surrealists rejected traditional critical methodology must be added another: they offered no alternative method. They made it clear, albeit only by inference, that poetry, as they responded to it, had nothing to do with the successful implementation of a formula. Poetic creativity in surrealism was an inimitable gesture, beyond definition as it was beyond advance projection. Thus one theme runs through the aphorisms by Breton and Jean Schuster, published under the title "Art poétique." It is that the poet's work, by its very nature, places itself above criticism, outside the range of critical judgment, beyond the reach of explicative evaluation. Instead, all the aphorisms composed by Breton and Schuster bear the same underlying message, stressing that the poetic statement remains impenetrable; "One does not penetrate their secret. Wishing desperately to do so, one renders their beauty more unfathomable."[10] Highlighting this essential characteristic of poetry, the authors of a surrealist *ars poetica* underscored by implication the futility of bringing critical instruments to the task of measuring surrealist poetic achievement. Eliminating the need for critics, they placed response at a level of receptivity where conventional critical values have no contribution to make.

Are we left, now, with confirmation of a widespread belief that surrealism was meant to evade comprehension and thus unworthy of our effort to appreciate it? One can begin to combat this erroneous conclusion by probing the hypothesis that a valid interpretation of a surrealist poetic text promises to be the privilege of the reader who has recognized in Bernard Weinberg's approach the very opposite of that which yields a valid assessment of surrealist writing. In other words, one may start by admitting the surrealist to have been an antiartist, so far as he refused to see his function as orchestrating effects after the manner Weinberg and Cardinal both presuppose. The surrealist poet did not deliberately and knowledgeably select the elements from which he could carefully assemble a poetic text, so guaranteeing anyone devoted to reversing the procedure, through *explication*, the assurance of being able to take a given poem to pieces once more in order to test its mechanism without impairing its efficiency.

Scrutinizing a surrealist text with the purpose of facing its *wherefore*, we should be unwise to suppose that the answer we seek lies in conscious purpose, necessarily antedating the poem's composition and rigorously or even intermittently controlling its development. While *explication de texte* proposes to trace the poem back to its origins and presumes these to have clear outline, characteristic surrealist poetry demands that we grant less attention to determining the poet's point of departure than to finding where he is going, and especially where his poem leaves us (and him, also), when it is over. For the concept of the poetic statement—a term broad enough in surrealist parlance to embrace paintings, sculpture, objects, plays, and movies—as adventure was fundamental to the surrealist's undertaking. Poetic thought thus may be defined, in its surrealist expression, as thought managing to "throw itself into a possibility of which the end will never be determined in advance."

Such a definition of poetry—summarized, as it happens, by a former disciple of Breton's—poses basic problems, as far as criticism of surrealism goes. These problems are not the concern solely of the commentator who, surrendering to the evidence, finds himself obliged to question the usefulness of the *explication* method as a reliable instrument for weighing the qualities or defects of this or that surrealist poem. Whatever the surrealist's preferred medium, longterm aims could not be predetermined because he did not cherish or entertain any with precision. In the circumstances, creative activity could not be measured in relation to an identifiable purpose more precise than a "possibility." Moreover, all hope of gauging results by universally acceptable objective standards was absent.

In short, it is not in the least surprising that participants in the surrealist movement had nothing but contempt for traditional modes of critical evaluation, epitomized in *explication de texte*. All of them firmly rejected the analytical procedure by which critics generally hope to understand and to explain.

They looked upon such analysis as the result of gravely erroneous presuppositions about artistic purpose and creative
method. Yet this is not to say that those men and women undertook to impose a critical canon of their own. Presenting a "first
annotated edition" of Lautréamont's *Poésies,* two surrealists,
Georges Goldfayn and Gérard Legrand, had as their declared
goal to "keep the 'future' of surrealism alive with certain texts."[11]
However, they emphasized in their preface that their project
"will grow out of exegetical methods only to the degree that
everything needs to be done over again on the subject of Ducasse's work," adding, "But it is precisely the exceptional situation
of that work with respect to surrealism that impels us to think
that exegesis is almost nothing in such a field, where everything
will constantly have to be done over again in order to create
the laws of our thought and action" (pp. 11–12).

The conclusion put forward here established a noticeably
strong link between creativity and commentary in surrealism:
"Thus, the wish for total coherence and the always narrower
connection between 'criticism of poetry' and poetic creation
itself have seemed to us to characterize the present-day fate
of surrealism" (p. 14). Even though clarity of expression eluded
Goldfayn and Legrand, one thing is plain. As we have heard
Schuster intimate, these commentators, examining what the
writer had produced, were no less concerned than the artist
himself with opening their own locks. The work before them
engaged their attention so far as it confronted them with locks
they still had to open for themselves. As Goldfayn and Legrand
described what now happened, "surrealist thought is not a reflection on the combat of others: it is itself combat" (p. 15).
So, as they comment on works of special interest to them in
terms that shed light on the creative process peculiar to surrealism, those serving the surrealist cause afford us the opportunity
to observe how creativity and criticism illuminate one another
in surrealism. At once, though, their remarks produce a situation
that seems discouragingly fraught with paradox.

Surrealists were convinced that creativity promises to be most
productive when the artist surrenders self-critical control over
his actions. If, then, creation and analysis are indeed incompatible, should not criticism of any kind be regarded as impertinent
at best and at worst a real impediment to enjoyment of whatever
creativity has yielded? More than this, how can one expect
reliable guidance from commentators who make a point of emphasizing their abiding hostility to rational expression the way

surrealists did? Does it not seem likely as a consequence that, when sharing their impressions with us, they will succumb to incoherence or even glory in it? In view of surrealism's preference for the irrational, Julien Gracq suggests in his *André Breton: quelques aspects de l'écrivain*, its proponents could scarcely be expected to offer anyting resembling an argument. May we not sympathize, then, with Frederick Brown who, having taken upon himself to discuss surrealist criticism, loses his nerve and, ignoring it entirely, simply talks instead of earlier poets, Lautréamont and Rimbaud?[12] A glance at the evidence leads us to conclude that Brown capitulates too hastily when he implicitly agrees with Gracq's implication that we must resign ourselves to seeing Benjamin Péret express himself no less antirationally than in his poems while writing his cogent essays on the nature of poetry, when prefacing his *Anthologie de l'amour sublime* (1956) and his *Anthologie de mythes, légendes et contes populaires d'Amérique* (1960), or when conducting his polemic *Le déshonneur des poètes* (1945).

One thing must be established at once; otherwise both the nature of criticism as surrealists practiced it and its relationship to creativity in surrealism will elude identification. There was no conflict, no incompatibility, between creation and criticism, for surrealists. One of their number has shown how criticism can fill a role accessory to that reserved for creative action. In "A l'ordre de la nuit," Schuster explains, "Our activity of reflection, distinct, it has to be, from our activity of creation, defines the object of subversion according to its constants and variables."[13] This is not to say that surrealists wished to "promulgate laws for art and poetry in the illusory hope of rendering them more efficacious; very much to the contrary, our selective criteria, where they are concerned, are, it so happens, based on their capacity to anticipate and on the natural intuitive movement carrying them, sometimes, without any assistance from outside, toward the most clandestine but not the least deadly forms of oppression to confront them." Thus, Schuster asserts, "the activity of reflection, in surrealism, will follow the activity of creation and will be set up in relation to it as necessary and subordinate."[14]

There is something else, too, that we have to bear in mind when asking what the art of criticism became in the surrealists' hands. As early as 27 January 1925, the Bureau de Recherches surréalistes in Paris issued a declaration proclaiming, among other things, the French surrealist group's disinterest in literature and drawing a sharp distinction between literature and their primary concern, poetry. No comprehension of surrealist values is even possible without some understanding of the reasons behind this distinction and, specifically, of its effect upon surrealist critical practice.

The celebrated announcement made in Breton's 1924 surrealist manifesto—that language has been given man so that he can make surrealist use of it—anticipated by nearly four decades Jean-Louis Bédouin's praise of Benjamin Péret's early collection of poems, Le passager du transatlantique (1921) as "pure" because uncontaminated by literature.[15] Over the years, the main problem facing surrealists was not how to establish a new form of literature but how to save poetry from sinking to the level of literature, from falling prey to literary critics.

Here we touch on one of the underlying themes of Breton's first volume of essays, Les pas perdus. It is a theme that predominates in the letters Antonin Artaud wrote to Jacques Rivière between 1923 and 1924.[16]

From the beginning identified in the surrealist mind with mere amusement (la distraction), and with the vulgar pursuit of public recognition, literature seemed to be represented by the work of writers like André Gide, the very embodiment of the littérateur in surrealist eyes. The first-generation surrealists were much more impressed by enigmatic peripheral figures like Arthur Cravan, Raymond Roussel, and Jacques Vaché. One of them spoke openly of his preoccupation with what he called "some manifestations of spiritual existence."[17] From the 1920s onward, the surrealists associated literary success—usually measured, they noticed, by the yardstick of technical competency— with both contrivance and the complacent display of its facile benefits. They steadfastly defended the belief, voiced by Péret, that the true poet is an "inventor for whom discovery is only the means of attaining a new discovery."[18]

Meanwhile, Pierre Mabille pointed out in his Le merveilleux that society is suspicious of the élan poétique. For this reason, he argued in an extended essay on the poetic marvelous, society has created rules of versification, at the same time defining modes of expression and norms of taste and beauty, "in order to dam it up and discipline (!) it."[19] Questionable though it must appear to all who find the surrealist conception of poetry unacceptable, Mabille's point remains an important one. It highlights once again something noted already: surrealism distinguished between literature—the exercise of talent within approved formal limitations—and poetry as a mode of discovery. It goes further, too. Mabille spoke for all surrealists when suggesting that rules and conventions (by which literary critics, just like art critics, tend to measure accomplishment) constitute a menace to the purity of poetic expression.

Considering in the perspective of literary commentary the inferences to be drawn from Mabille's statement, we now can make a valuable deduction. The surrealists defended an essential nonliterary criterion, one for which literary critics could not be expected to have any regard at all. Once we view poetry as "activity and need of the spirit," then, remarked Jehan Mayoux (who borrowed from Péret this phrase so reminiscent of one by Artaud) we must give up the idea of art for art's sake as well as the notion that poetry is an instrument to be put to this or that use. To do otherwise, Mayoux contended in his article on Péret,[20] is tantamount to confusing poetry with versification.

If there is one word that sums up the activity and need to which Mayoux referred, it is revolt. At least, Bédouin points out, it seemed to the surrealists that "where this revolt proves to be missing, poetry loses its way,"[21] leaving us with what Breton contemptuously termed "literary games" in his prière d'insérer for Paul Eluard's Capitale de la douleur of 1926. In other words, the distance separating true poetry, as surrealists referred to it, from the exercise of literary skills is too great for possible compromise. Breton and Eluard demonstrated as much when publishing their Notes sur la poésie in the twelfth and last issue of La révolution surréaliste (December 1929). There certain aphorisms appearing over Paul Valéry's signature in Commerce the previous summer were adapted without acknowledgment, their sense being reversed or significantly distorted. For instance, Valéry's definition of a poem as "a feast of the Intellect" became "a debacle of the intellect." While Valéry had called poetry literature reduced to the essential of its active principle, Breton and Eluard affirmed that it is the contrary of literature. Later on, Péret was to indicate his complete agreement when, in La parole est à Péret (1943), taken up in the preface to his Anthologie des mythes, he refused to define the marvelous, despite his conviction that it is "the heart and nervous system of all poetry." His unwillingness to discuss method was a token of Péret's belief, as expressed in La parole est à Péret, that poetry can be neither manufactured nor produced according to a recipe.

Mayoux interprets Péret's attitude as denying the influence

of artistic preoccupations upon the creative act and deems this sufficient to raise Péret above Eluard (for whom automatism was, indeed, only the first stage in the process of writing a poem) as a poet. Meanwhile, commenting on Péret's major verse collection, Le grand jeu (1928), Bédouin insists in Benjamin Péret that its author's method, "or rather this absence of method of composition, in the classic sense of the term" is not "an original literary procedure." Instead, "it is justified by a conception, radically new for the period, of the relationships an individual maintains with his own thought." This means that "it implies new rights and duties in matters of expression."[22]

Out of mistrust born of their dissatisfaction with French symbolist poetry, no doubt, surrealists repudiated poetry as form. They gave their confidence to poetry as vital content, which demanded an outlet regardless of the restraints of form, never thanks to its salutary influence. Persuaded that formal concerns are inimical to poetic expression, they had as their avowed aim the liberation of poetry from literature. They sought to leave it free to accomplish something they believed cannot be attained within the constrictive framework of prescribed structure. Only when we have discarded the controls that delimit the literary horizon, they contended, can poetry ready itself for the task of discovery and exploration to which they felt sure it must be dedicated.

When a surrealist spoke of liberation, when he equated revolutionary activity with dreaming and defended the pleasure principle, he was promoting a special form of subversion. Subversion was the "great reservoir of new strength" judged by André Breton capable of protesting against absurdity, inertia, and iniquity in every form. Thus in surrealism the focal point of attention can be detected where negative elements unite with positive ones, where revolt in the face of restraint becomes at the same time the expression of aspirations reaching out to something that promises to be accessible only when and where revolt and the assertion of freedom have cleared the way. This is why, in Le deshonneur des poètes, Péret treated poetry as "the source of all knowledge and that knowledge itself in its most immaculate aspect."[23]

If, as Péret implied, poetic activity must be an act of faith, evaluation of that activity—of what he has accomplished—rests upon agreement between the creative artist and the interpreter of his work that art is feasible only so long as it is capable of making knowledge take a step forward, as Breton put it in *Les pas perdus*. Time after time, therefore, we come upon the term *la connaissance* in surrealist critical writing. It carries both the sense of knowledge and of the cognitive act, the surrealist commentator showing himself attentive to any poet engaged in helping man arrive, in Péret's phrase from *Le deshonneur des poètes*, at "an ever-perfectible knowledge of himself and of the universe."[24]

Like the well-publicized experiments in the simulation of insanity published in Breton and Eluard's *L'immaculée conception* (1930), the fruits of automatism—whether verbal or pictorial—had no special virtue in themselves. They were subjected to critical examination directed at estimating their contribution to the "general revisions of modes of cognition" about which Breton spoke in *Les pas perdus*. Here as always, emphasis fell on knowledge and gaining knowledge rather than on literary or artistic achievement. The spiritual adventure to which Breton promised attention in his abortive "Collection révélation" for the publisher Gaston Gallimard closely resembles that of which the young Artaud spoke. It would guarantee no revelations, naturally. But it still presented the compelling attraction of conveying man's need to know more than at present he can know.[25] In surrealism, men and women permanently opposed to what Julien Gracq has dubbed in his *André Breton* "the fetishistic cult of logical intelligence" advanced from the premise that man's effort must take a new direction: "to the French knight Descartes we prefer the Percevals who, with heart full of anguish, plunged into the dark wood, in search of the impossible."[26]

While assuring the artist the right to complete independence of outside supervision, the surrealists encouraged also a critical posture of a special kind. Ado Kyrou demonstrates some of its consequences, both in his *Amour-érotisme et cinéma* (1957) and in his *Le surréalisme au cinéma* (1953), where we read, "Watching a movie I necessarily carry out an act upon that object, I transform it then and, starting out with the element given, I make it *my thing* in order to withdraw scraps of knowledge from it and to see into myself better."[27] Kyrou returned to the same theme when affirming, "Poetic, frenetic criticism, which would take account of all that is invisible, of all the mystery of a movie is the only one for which the necessity makes itself felt imperiously," arguing too that the critic "ought to start out from his aggressively personal impression, from the shock produced by the encounter of the object-film with the subject-self, to objectify the hidden beauties."[28]

Such an idea of film criticism was by no way exceptional among surrealists. We appreciate this as soon as we examine the Romanian group's tribute to the involuntary surrealism of Mario Soldati's *Molombra* (1942) or an experiment conducted by the Paris group into the "irrational enlargement of a film," Joseph von Sternberg's *Shanghai Gesture*.[29] Indeed, the perspective formally recommended by Kyrou dates back to the synthetic-critical mode of film commentary pioneered by Louis Aragon in the early 1920s, a fitting counterpart to the cinematographic poems being written at about the same time by Philippe Soupault. An English surrealist has commented pertinently that the synthetic-critical method was "an attempt to extract the latent dream content from the dream thoughts that make up popular cinema."[30] This is to say that the film "is no longer a 'closed' work, a mere object of contemplation using the limited resources of reason," because the synthetic-critical text "opens up its reading, the dialectic is set in motion, and we are on the road to surreality, the 'point of the mind' where contradictions cease to trouble us."[31]

What really matters, then, is that, as defined by Kyrou and practiced by others as well as he, surrealist film commentary is fully representative of the surrealist concept of criticism. The very same attitude also underlies Eluard's *Donner à voir* (where, incidentally, the appended poems dedicated to painters are evocative in the same way as Aragon's synthetic movie commentaries), Breton's *La clé des champs*, *Perspective cavalière*, and the successive editions of his *Le surrèalisme et la peinture*, just as it does Jean Schuster's *Archives 57/58*, frankly subtitled "battles for surrealism." It has never been outlined more explicitly than in the *avant-dire* written by André Breton for a collection of his essays, *Yves Tanguy*:

> Let no one go looking below for anything resembling art criticism. . . . Excluded *a priori* from these pages is any didactic intent. They are presented as a succession of echoes and flashes which this work has succeeded in setting off in one person at moments fairly distant from one another. . . . Their deeper unity comes from the fact that they mark out an uninterrupted quest for emotions through this work and, beyond those emotions themselves, tend to locate a series of *indices* likely to cast light albeit from flickering

flames on the route taken by man today. . . . As such, . . . [this quest]
in no way transgresses the principle: criticism will be love or will
not exist at all. (P. 9)

To the objection that Breton has just told us what criticism
is not—so far as he implies that a critic must surrender all
objectivity—the surrealists would have replied that for them
creation and commentary were collaborative acts. Artist and
commentator must have in sight the same goal: elucidation of
a phenomenon which the former has had the privilege of helping
into existence and the latter then has the opportunity to help
interpret. In the first text offered in *Yves Tanguy* (reprinted
from the 1928 edition of *Le surréalisme et la peinture*) Breton
remarks, "I am eager to join Yves Tanguy in that place he has
discovered" (p. 11). What really matters is this: "To recognize
(or not to recognize) is everything. Between what I recognize
and what I do not recognize there is myself." This, in effect,
is the significance of criticism, as a form of love: "There is
in what I like that which I like to recognize and that which
I like not to recognize. It is, I think, to the conception of this
most fervent relationship that surrealism has risen, and held
(p. 11)."

In a 1939 essay, "Des tendances les plus récentes de la peinture surréaliste," first published in the 1945 edition of *Le surréalisme et la peinture,* Breton made it clear that the surrealist
critic's task was no less demanding for having its roots in love.
In fact, he showed that Tanguy's painting presents an especially
enlightening example of surrealist creativity because it actually
resists explanation: "If . . . Tanguy's star is still rising higher,
it is because he escapes by his nature from all kinds of compromise. Tanguy's painting has hardly surrendered, so far, more
than its charm: it will deliver its secret later" (p. 21). It was
Breton's belief that "the manifest elements in Tanguy's painting
which remain uninterpretable and among which, later, memory
has difficulty managing to choose, will be elucidated with the
help of imminent action of the mind" (p. 21) He defined those
elements, therefore, as "the words of a language which we do
not hear yet, but which soon we are going to read, to speak,
which we are going to verify is the one best adapted to new
exchanges" (p. 21). And this is why Tanguy's work suggested
a succinct definition of surrealism: "WHAT IS SURREALISM?—
It is Yves Tanguy's appearance, wearing on his head the grand
emerald green bird of paradise" (p. 22).

Coming to critical commentary by way of private response to Yves Tanguy's painting, Breton was no less true than in the *proses parallèles* he wrote for Miró's *Constellations* to the non-explicative principle that led Goldfayn and Legrand to treat Lautréamont's *Poésies* the way they did in their *édition commentée*: "At the risk of comically wishing to 'shed light' from above on a work without equal, we have preferred that of adding—in all modesty—enigma to enigma" (p. 19). The risk is obvious. A surrealist commentator was in danger of passing for an obscurantist delighting in irresponsible obfuscation, a practical joker, even, going to elaborate lengths to teach us that it would be foolish to take him seriously. But answering enigma with enigma is not begging the question, surrealists felt sure, when one is dealing with an artist who—to borrow a phrase from a 1942 essay that reappears in Breton's *Yves Tanguy* under the title "Ce que Tanguy voile et révèle" (What Tanguy veils and reveals) —"throws himself out of the window of his own eye" (p. 36) and who, like Tanguy, "abstains from any declaration regarding the aim he proposes to attain, gives away nothing about his intentions, is very much too disdainful to give the lie to those attributed to him" (p. 38). The critic who has studied the work of Tanguy must count himself fortunate to have glimpsed "Yves behind the bars of his blue eyes" (p. 45).

Here is the key to the surrealist mind's reaction before all forms of art. The technical merit of a given work (literary or pictorial, it made no difference) appealed far less than the relationship the work sets up between subject and object, as Kyrou used these terms when speaking of cinema. A surrealist's imaginative sensibility was attuned above all to the creative act capable of establishing a relationship that shatters reliance on the habitual, challenging the latter's ability to limit our power of creative-critical conjecture. Poetry is alchemy's twin sister, according to Bédouin who, in support of this claim, appositely quoted in his *Benjamin Péret* Breton's tribute to Péret: "He alone has fully realized on the *word* the operation corresponding to alchemical 'sublimation' which consists in provoking the 'ascension of the subtle' by its 'separation from the thick!'[32]

The alchemical analogy is quite familiar to anyone who has read some of the essays in which surrealists discussed poetry. It is no surprise, therefore, to find that, in the medium where Breton saw Péret as having intervened "as a liberator," the *thick* is manifest as "that crust of exclusive signification with which usage has covered all words." As a result, there exists, now, a "narrow compartment that opposes any entry into relationship between the significative elements frozen in words today." Its effects can be resisted, Breton suggested (using the word *jeu* in two senses) only by associative play.

When recalling how the surrealists were impressed by creative work like Péret's, we have to take into consideration two important factors. First, Breton spoke for all his associates while dismissing lucidity in *La clé des champs* as "the great enemy of revelation" (p. 10). Second, every one of the surrealists agreed with the "Art poétique" by Breton and Schuster that "the poet has to exculpate himself before no judge." A statement Breton made while prefacing Jean Ferry's *Une Etude sur Raymond Roussel* (1953) brings into clear focus the question still facing us: "I have always maintained that a certain number of poetic works and others have value essentially from the power they possess to appeal to a faculty *other* than intelligence"[33] By generally accepted standards, it must seem that Breton was determined to put critics out of business, condemning their efforts as not merely superfluous but quite irrelevant. In reality, he was inviting them to change the tools of their trade. And what mattered was that, speaking from the surrealists' standpoint, he was assured of having every reason to do so.

In surrealism, intelligent judgment was not the critic's prerogative any more than it was his obligation. This did not mean, however, that, responsible to nobody for what he created, the artist remained above all criticism, entirely free to enjoy the shallow satisfaction of self-indulgence because he was answerable to no one qualified to impose objective criteria by which he had to abide. We are dealing with a closely-knit group who observed one another's activity attentively and assessed the results unsentimentally. Over the years, the best-known of them, André Breton, was able to assemble a four-hundred-page volume of essays on surrealism and painting, at which we shall look next, without for all that ceasing to consider painting as "a lamentable expedient." To the surrealist, all modes of artistic expression were but tentative. He saw them as valuable so long as they approximated to standards and answered demands formulated outside art with less regard for the scope and limitations of a given medium than for the exigencies imposed by surrealist imperatives. In his *Second manifeste*, Breton wrote apropos of surrealism, "One would not wish it to be at the mercy of the humor of these men or those; if it declares itself able, by its own methods, to wrench thought from an increasingly hard serfdom, setting it again on the path to total comprehension, to return it to its original purity, that is enough for [surrealism] to be judged on what it has done and on what it still has to do to fulfill its promise" (pp. 154–55).

This statement is coherent enough. Yet its meaning is elusive, not to say obscure. Everything hinges on the phrase "total comprehension," given no more exact definition by Breton than is *la connaissance* (both "knowledge" and "cognition") by any of the surrealists who used it freely. But it did not trouble a surrealist in the least that someone brought up on Descartes can make little sense of the writings of a critic who delights in following Perceval and takes pleasure in the consternation that the latter's mission releases in the minds of reasonable people. In his *prière d'insérer* for Péret's *De derrière les fagots*, Paul Eluard offered a categorical statement with which all surrealists agreed:

> One of the principal properties of poetry is to inspire in frauds a grimace that unmasks them and lets them be judged. Like no other, the poetry of Benjamin Péret encourages this reaction, as inevitable as it is useful. For it is endowed with that major accent, eternal and modern, which detonates and makes a hole in the world of prudently ordered necessities and of babbling old refrains. For it tends with its extralucid images, its images as clear as rock-water, evident like *the strident cry of red eggs*, toward a perfect comprehension of the unwanted and toward its use against the ravages of malignant exploitation by stupidity and a certain form of good sense. For it militates insolently in favor of a new *régime*, that of logic linked with life not like a shadow but like a star,
> It is my pride to know only men who love as much as I this specifically subversive poetry which has the color of the future.[34]

Not the least noteworthy aspect of Eluard's remarks is that they draw and maintain a firm distinction between insiders (responding as surrealists) and outsiders, those in whom the inability to share the others' response is proof that perfect comprehension—however that phrase is to be understood—eludes them and, we may infer, always will.

No surrealist looked upon the occasion to comment about poetry as an opportunity to practice conventional criticism, an activity to be approached with detachment and carried out with benefit of objectivity. Far from granting that their own attitude revealed weaknesses, the surrealists would have contended, and with pride, that it gave commentary the only value it could have. In reality, we might add, surrealism never boasted a critic in its ranks, if one interprets that title as it is commonly understood. Yet the surrealists never shirked their responsibilities as commentators on matters poetic. From where they stood, responsibility took on a complexion very different from the one generally supposed to lend dignity and purpose to the critic's role. With the love demanded of critics by André Breton went, no less significantly, detestation, abhorrence, even hate of whatever placed an obstacle in surrealism's path or tended to turn the artist away from that path, directing his attention elsewhere.

Surrealists had no interest in reaching a civilized compromise with anyone whose standards they rejected. They were radically opposed to tolerance of the values underlying those standards. Hence, for them the merits of poetry were not subject to discussion; adjustment of critical criteria was not only pernicious, it was a meaningless undertaking. Even if achieved, compromise would have represented nothing better than contamination of poetry through contact with concerns the surrealists proclaimed antipoetic. Any accommodation, they felt sure, could only be harmful to poetry, and so is unworthy of anyone who, having gained a sense of the poetic, takes guidance from it when measuring his own responses.

The longer we review the observations published by surrealists, praising some artists and disparaging others, the more obvious it becomes that one question cannot be indefinitely ignored. Accepting the proposition—with which only a surrealist, perhaps, would have taken issue—that, as with any other work of art, a variety of critical perspectives is more likely to illuminate than obscure a surrealist work, we have to ask for what reason the surrealist approach in particular should hold our attention. Under normal conditions, such a question would appear redundant, the insider's view being acknowledged as providing irreplaceable insights that could come from no one else. However, given the surrealists' consistently uncompromising attitude and their adamant refusal to concede any merit at all to evaluative standards other than their own, we cannot examine their remarks without wondering whether prolonged study will teach us anything worthwhile.

Is there something to be gained by persisting, by accumulating proof that surrealists denied the value of any viewpoint differing from theirs? This is a question which the surrealists' unwilling-ness to compromise, to grant the admissibility of an interpreta-tion departing from their own, and to engage in even the briefest dialogue does nothing but bring into sharper focus the more evidence we assemble. Is all we gain, then, additional proof of inflexibility, for which no apology was ever offered or indeed considered necessary? After all, it was always an unabashed subjective assessment that the surrealist presented, whether talk-ing of verse or of painting. Making no effort at all to curtail the influence of subjective reactions on what he had to say, he declined to engage in gentlemanly discussion with anyone dissenting from his opinions. Are we to conclude therefore that those opinions deserve to be set aside once they have been classified as indications of unyielding obstinacy?

There was a good reason—or so the surrealists thought—for them to adopt and maintain a posture far removed from that of critical detachment. And there seemed an equally good reason not to defend a posture adopted after neither reflection nor hesi-tation. The surrealists held the views they propounded to be in harmony with indisputable truths about the nature and func-tion of art, which they saw no excuse for questioning. Thus, for them, subjective evaluation in keeping with surrealist princi-ples and values called for no defense or apology. A surrealist had no cause to argue with his opponents. All he had to do, he believed, was affirm the truth as he perceived it.

The point, therefore, is not whether the surrealists were so right that critics could not hope to be anything but wrong. What matters is the profound rift that opened up between the surreal-ists' ideas—the way these affected judgment of artistic effort and the concept of artistic integrity—and those that usually guide critics in their estimate of the worth of artistic endeavor. Even more important is the significance of that rift, the reasons why it opened up and why the surrealists showed no inclination, ever, to close it or throw a bridge across it to people standing on the other side. In the surrealists' estimation, the distance separating them from the critics could never be bridged. The thought of producing and maintaining what might be termed a just equilibrium had no more appeal for them than that of trying to balance, without falling to the bottom, over the chasm separating the two sides.

It was, of course, their denial of any hope of reconciliation with critics whose opinions diverged from their own that made

the surrealists appear narrow-minded. Had they been charged
with intolerance, they would have put up no defense, convinced
that no better one was needed than their conviction that a point
of view other than their own must lead us all astray, when
it does not actually betray poetry, defined in the only terms
to which surrealism lent credence. They felt no obligation to
excuse themselves for defending the truth as they saw it. Guilt
could fall only on the other side, to be compounded, inevitably,
by the critics' incapacity to see where they had gone wrong
and why. We falsify the evidence beyond a doubt if we succumb
to the temptation to read surrealist commentary as proof of
complacency.

To declare that, conducting themselves as they did, all those
who spoke as surrealists betrayed ingenuousness, or even uncontrolled naïveté, may afford surrealism's detractors satisfaction.
Yet this is a very small victory indeed. After all, it is easy
enough to interpret the surrealists' unwillingness to yield as
revealing their inability to do so. This is why identifying characteristics like intractability seems to authorize condemnation of
surrealism's spokesmen as obtuse and rigidly obstinate. What
do we learn, though, from surrealist conduct about the mentality
common to surrealists, about the reasons for surrealism's long
survival as a seminal influence, and at the same time about
receptivity in their primary audience? When our motive is to
gain better appreciation of the operation of the surrealist mind
rather than to pass negative judgment the angle of perception
changes noticeably.

Usually reprehensible defects, ranging all the way down to
the least subtle expression of intractability—verbal rudeness—
may be no more easily pardoned in the surrealists now than
before. But they take on fuller meaning as we recognize in them
something better than lack of sophistication. More instructively,
they may be seen as indications of the operation of the surrealist
mind, never doubting itself and acknowledging no reason to
consider itself either misinformed or misdirected. No greater
error could be made by someone contemplating the surrealist
mind, as it grapples with questions touching on the meaning
and role of art, than that of imagining it to be the mind of
an insensitive, uncouth terrorist. What the surrealists had to
say, when facing writings and paintings that attracted them
(or, again, that they found repellent), reflected their loyalty
to a point of view that in the long run permits us to discover more about the surrealist mind than about the works it

judged, sometimes lauding and sometimes ridiculing them.

It would be a costly mistake to interpret departure from familiar critical norms and flat denial of their pertinence to the evaluative process as aggressively assertive acts by which surrealist
commentators on poetry and painting sought merely to draw
attention to themselves. These men and women were anything
but intellectual exhibitionists. They were people convinced that
fidelity to surrealism left no room for compromise with values
that they resisted and condemned as injurious to art. When
taking issue with the critics or challenging the latter's judgments, surrealists were not giving way to an uncontrollably
disputatious temperament. Intellectual debate afforded them no
stimulation. On the other hand, neither an agreeable mental
exercise nor a pastime, discrediting opinions they condemned
was an obligation. It was an expression of a concept of art
they simply refused to discuss and considered beyond debate.

Commenting on the surrealists' interest in "the savage heart,"
one of their number, Vincent Bounoure, affirmed, "what was
at stake in Oceania and the Americas was an altogether different
dimension of the mind which had madly ventured into the
jungles of dreams where scarlet birds rule."[35] Art that ventures
into a "different dimension of the mind," the surrealists asserted,
does not yield its secrets under analysis according to traditional
standards of aspiration and achievement. Any attempt to apply
those standards entails, they argued, removing art from the dimension it had now made its own, in an effort—whether conscious or instinctive—to situate it in a dimension to which it
does not belong.

So caught up are we likely to be at times with the aggressive-
ness characteristic of the surrealist's manner when expressing
his views that we are in danger of imagining that, typically,
the surrealist commentator's approach to works of art of all
kinds alternated between two extremes. At moments he seems
to have been capable only of effusion, as he promoted this or
that artist to a status so high that any reservations became,
apparently, unthinkable. At other moments, he seems to have
been content to dismiss a writer or painter so contemptuously
that we incline to suppose him more interested in giving offense
than in passing judgment. Whichever direction his comments
took, they may leave us speculating on the motive behind them.
For, to the extent that a pattern emerges from their published
remarks, the surrealists appear to have been disposed to praise
with least restraint artists for whom the critics have little or

no respect, while attacking with manifest gusto other artists whose reputation in critical circles was well established, even quite high. Are we to infer that, so far as there was any method to the surrealist approach, it was nothing more complex, hence nothing more significant, than a willful inversion of critical values intended to undermine confidence in those values, to discredit them and yet replace them with nothing truly viable?

In their published remarks about artists whose work either attracted or frustrated them, what is of lasting value is that the surrealists' preoccupations with "a different dimension of the mind" placed a special emphasis on their assessment. Now rejection of respected evaluative criteria became a precondition of judgment, neither its goal nor its justification. Hence, to the surrealist commentator, objection to his point of view signified no more than unproductive nostalgia, a return to critical positions he felt sure must be abandoned forever and renewal of premises that he himself had deemed it essential to discard once and for all.

In the perspective adopted in surrealism's name, replacement of old values by new was not designed to rehabititate criticism, to sharpen the tools of the critic's trade prior to putting them to more efficient use. A new standard of assessment was thought to be a requirement, not merely an available option, an alternative that might be chosen freely. The criteria now set were formulated in light of a dual necessity: to respond appropriately to the achievements of exciting artists and to react responsibly to demands made upon art by ambitions prescribed in surrealism. It was illogical as well as unfair, the surrealists were persuaded, to measure art as risk (and not as self-indulgence or the complacent display of acquired skills) except with the determination to appraise the risks taken by the artist against the most demanding conditions of acceptability defined in the surrealist mind.

It would be a waste of time to dispute that surrealist commentary was unashamedly biased, just as it would be fruitless to defend *explication de texte* against the surrealists unyielding opposition to the way it functions and to the purposes that give it meaning. Instead of protesting that the surrealists displayed nothing but unintelligent obstinacy and an annoying lack of subtlety, we should acknowledge that their refusal to compromise was a measure of the rigor of surrealist thought and of the surrealists' scorn for anyone seeking acceptance through accommodation. With full commitment to surrealist principles went a strong dose of fanaticism, whose contribution the surrealists tried not to minimize and whose effects they left uncontrolled. Thus fair evaluation of surrealist critical commentary has nothing to do with returning severity for severity on the grounds that the surrealists had no one to blame more than themselves for such treatment. To proceed as though judging surrealist commentary were the equivalent of a punitive raid into territory invaded and annexed by an enemy would be particularly unfortunate and quite unproductive. It would deprive us of a valuable opportunity to bring a few things (Breton's assessment of certain painters, for example, or the surrealists' approach to the avant-garde) into focus. If we confine ourselves to protesting the surrealist's intransigence, we may easily miss what is most enlightening here about the surrealist mind: once stimulated to creative activity, it found acceptable—and pertinent—no evaluative response other than its own.

As little is gained by ridiculing the operation of the surrealist mind in its critical mode as by denying that, the way an outsider would see it, the surrealist mind was not really functioning critically at all. Intermittently and without a fully concerted plan, the surrealists were openly conducting a campaign that drew unity of purpose from a deep conviction, born of fidelity to surrealist thought and from devotion to the demands it formulated and aimed to satisfy.

7

The Critical Example: André Breton on Painting

Which came first, painting or surrealism? Posed in chronological terms, this question is too foolish to be worth raising. However, asked with slightly different emphasis, so that we may establish precedence and fix surrealism's priorities, that seme question helps situate André Breton's approach to pictorial art.

From his youth Breton reacted with considerable excitement to the work of a few painters, notably, Gustave Moreau and Odilon Redon. By the early 1920s he was already confessing in print to a deep admiration for certain artists. Among these Giorgio de Chirico, Marcel Duchamp, and Max Ernst stood out as figures to whom he would allude repeatedly after the existence of the surrealist movement had been formally announced in October of 1924. There appears little reason to doubt that Breton's interest in graphic artists would have persisted, continuing to prompt him to comment on art, even if he had not helped found surrealism. It seems just as true that, carrying into adult life a fascination with painting, Breton would have come to treat art differently had he not been a lifelong militant surrealist.

André Breton never once commented at length on any artist whose work he did not like. Negative criticism was not so much foreign to his nature as, in his estimation, redundant. He elected to discuss only artists he respected. The things he had to say highlighted the virtues he ascribed to those men and women. This does not mean that he was blind to defects, involuntarily or voluntarily. Rather, his articles and catalogue prefaces illustrated all along a maxim that he was not to put into words until 1946. At that time, writing the foreword to his own collection of essays, *Yves Tanguy*, he alluded to a guiding principle: "Criticism will be love or will not exist at all" (p. 9).

It might be argued that Breton, forced in the end to confess

that he had never really practiced serious criticism, finally had
to face up to his deficiencies. True, the prefatory remarks to
Yves Tanguy frankly warned its readers not to expect "anything
resembling art criticism." But André Breton was still a long
way from admitting that when he came to the work of Tanguy
(or of any other artist, for that matter), he knowingly surrendered
the right or obligation to apply value judgments. His concept
of criticism as an expression of love did not preclude evaluation
while submissively consenting to grant painters full license
to do whatever they liked in whatever manner they saw fit.
Nor was it out of self-defense that Breton denied being an art
critic. The foreword to *Yves Tanguy* was hardly an implicit plea
for indulgence, intended to shift the ground for assessment of
Tanguy's painting and, by extension, for appraisal of Breton's
remarks on the work of any other painter. Breton was neither
taking refuge behind a mask of false modesty nor seeking to
head off attacks by accredited art critics. Really what mattered
to him was trying to indicate how the texts he had written
about Tanguy over the years should be read in 1946, and indeed
ought to have been read when they were first published.

Everything falls better into place if we ask what induced
André Breton to love this or that aspect of some painter's
achievement. Then we appreciate more fully that commentary
in the form of love may not always bring out elements to which
the art critic is customarily attentive, or even reveal the most
characteristic features of a given painter's work. But it offers
something useful nevertheless, if the commentator happens to
be a surrealist. It tells more about surrealist values, about the
surrealist mind, than about the qualities any spectator at all
might be expected to detect in an artist holding his or her attention.

The essential question of priorities was the one Breton wished
to raise when announcing that he was not engaged in art criticism. André Breton eschewed "all didactic intent," stressing
that the unity of his remarks lay in "an uninterrupted quest
for emotions" undertaken with reference to Tanguy's pictures.
He went even further when he talked of assembling "a series
of *indices* likely to cast light albeit from a flickering flame on
the route taken by man today" (p. 9). In other words, his response
to Yves Tanguy led him through two stages that—separately
and, even more obviously, together—revealed one fundamentally important fact. Breton looked upon the painting of Tanguy
as providing an occasion for experiencing emotions liberated

in one viewer (himself, as he emphasized) by the spectacle before him.

His book about Tanguy is the only volume in which Breton
ever gathered essays previously published about a single artist.
Still, *Yves Tanguy* marks no departure from the position Breton
set about defending from the moment he wrote, in 1925, the
very first article in a succession of texts that were to result
in the original edition of *Le surréalisme et la peinture*: "So
it is that I find it impossible to consider a painting other that
as a window about which my first concern is to know what
it *looks out upon.* . . ." (p. 2). Whatever other concerns he had,
Breton did not enumerate them. Evidently, they were—and
would continue to be, so long as he went on commenting about
painting—distinctly secondary considerations.

André Breton's interest in graphic art was narrow in scope.
If challenged, he would have admitted this freely, no doubt
citing it as a clear sign that criticism was not the object of
his writings about the painters who had fired his enthusiasm.
Many of the elements affecting an art critic's judgment of a
painter's accomplishments were actually irrelevant to the viewpoint that surrealism induced Breton to defend energetically.
At the same time, those features of a technical nature which
did catch his eye received attention solely because they enabled
him to look out upon something visible only through the window of a canvas. Far from seeking to hide what underlay his
own approach to painting, Breton prided himself on the self-
centeredness of his preoccupation with art. To put it simply,
in his estimation art existed for the viewer to use, not admire
respectfully. Breton looked to artists to elicit emotions more
than ideas. In so doing, he tacitly argued that the emotions
released in a spectator need not be the ones consciously solicited
by the painter. If betrayal of the artist's intent follows, so be
it. The spectator still will reward the painter's effort, not with
understanding every time but with love, certainly.

One may incline to infer that arrogance affected Breton's posture before the work of art. But doing this quite distorts his
relationship with painting. In statements about his own reaction
to Tanguy's pictures, emphasis on emotion is not merely additional proof that surrealism was that prehensile tail of romanticism that Breton acknowledged it to be in his 1929 *Second
manifeste du surréalisme*. Twenty years and more after his original surrealist manifesto, he reaffirmed that surrealists believed
we progress farthest and most quickly along antirational paths.

Hence learning, extending knowledge, coming to know more and better—all these were considered steps most easily taken when rationalism has ceased directing our effort to advance out of ignorance into understanding.

At the point where surrealist doctrine makes its influence felt on André Breton's observations about art and artists we may expect to have to face a dilemma. How can anybody—even a deep-dyed surrealist, assuring us that he does not want to prove anything—comment pertinently on art so long as he remains convinced that understanding presupposes the denial of rationalism? There was apparently in the surrealist mind a conflict that situated the goal of comprehension beyond the range of rationalist interpretation. Actually, this conflict places in our hands a key to surrealism. Specifically, it facilitates appreciation of the mental state in which Breton looked at painted canvases.

Noteworthy in this connection is the fact that love does not designate a response at which the individual arrives by a deductive process, hence by rationally explicable means or stages. As passion, love ignores rationalism, brushing the latter aside in contempt of its benefits and of its exigencies also. Love encompasses rewards and advantages that rationalism cannot embrace. These derive from a commitment that excludes the rationalist's careful weighing of evidence, both for and against. Here lies the importance of Breton's foreword to *Yves Tanguy*. It separates commentary from dispassionate assessment according to objectively defensible standards. Here, on the contrary, surrealist evaluation is identified with impassioned involvement. And this involvement has little or nothing to do with an assessment of the painter's working method but draws strength instead from his demonstrated ability to let us (make us) witness something to which the surrealist mind attributed value.

Breton's insistence that didactic intent was absent from his published remarks on Tanguy revealed that he was not seeking converts to surrealism. Nowhere do we encounter in his essays about Tanguy or other artists any attempt to conduct an argument intended to sway the skeptical or convince the vacillating. Moreover, Breton did not presume to speak for anyone but himself when reflecting on art and artists. Reading his assessments, we have no trouble believing he considered the subjective focus not only natural but fully justified. Still, his position at the head of the surrealist movement in France lent his voice authority, and not because he chose to pontificate or proved unable to resist doing so. To the exclusion of all else, surrealist ideas governed his outlook giving force to his statements. He never pretended to speak ex cathedra. Yet, in speaking for himself, he spoke for surrealism.

The authority that André Breton's opinions carried with his fellow surrealists in France may be estimated from one curious detail. His indifference to music and even suspicion of it discouraged any effort among the French surrealists to embrace music in their program of revolt against tradition and convention or in its liberation of the imagination. Thus, although— aside from Breton himself—the Parisian surrealists were to have among their number one truly significant commentator on art in José Pierre, none of them discussed music from surrealist perspective, let alone composed. As for the breadth of André Breton's influence on the surrealist movement worldwide, it may be judged from statistical evidence. Jaroslav Jezek in Czechoslovakia, Paul Hooreman, and especially André Souris (both in Belgium) were surrealism's only musicians. In contrast, the list of surrealist painters and of surrealists having had something to say about pictorial art is a long one.

When asking how painting could find a place in surrealism, Breton himself took the initiative by responding optimistically. The importance of his determination to dispute Pierre Naville's reservations about a surrealist form of painting was soon clear. Not long after the first manifesto came out, its author began asserting in print that surrealism and painting were truly compatible. Breton took a significant step indeed when, replacing its editors Naville and Benjamin Péret, he assumed direction of the Parisian magazine *La révolution surréaliste* and, at once ran a series of essays on surrealism and painting. Surrealism, which had had its origins in a new method of writing, was not to be confined strictly to experimentation with verbal modes of expression.

Turning his attention to painting, Breton aimed to do more than widen surrealism's perspective. Of course, it would be naive to discount tactical considerations altogether. Nevertheless, we misjudge the value of painting, as Breton saw it, if we imagine he hoped to recruit painters to the surrealist group merely in order to swell its ranks. Fundamental to the idea of surrealism that he cherished was the conviction that all modes of creative expression must be treated as potential means for expanding knowledge. Logically, therefore, Breton was eager to assemble evidence demonstrating how graphic artists could

contribute to the surrealist program no less actively and positively than writers could. Indeed, one may go further than this
to note that unless painting were shown to have a place besides
writing in surrealism's cognitive program, the viability of the
surrealist undertaking would have been open to question and
in fact seriously undermined. Representing Breton's pioneering
discussion of art as a virtuoso but accessory performance is
a deformation that can lead only to inaccurate conclusions.

From the time surrealism asserted itself as a point of view
on life, André Breton was inclined to think and look about
him strictly from the surrealist standpoint. The attraction he
felt to painting could not be, he felt sure, in conflict with his
devotion to the task of realizing ambitions invested wth meaning
by surrealist principles. It seems fair to suppose that to the
implied proposal that painter be excluded from the surrealist
camp he reacted by wishing to refute Naville's argument even
before a basis for refutation was properly formed in his head.
All the same, Breton's confidence in pictorial art was not to
stand out as a curiosity unique or atypical of the surrealists.
It was to have long-term consequences of such scope that years
before his death, the general public had become more aware
of surrealism's presence in painting than of the achievement
of surrealism's writers, among whom Breton himself was the
most prominent.

Reviewing the articles, essays, and catalogue prefaces brought
together between the covers of the definitive edition (1965) of
Le surréalisme et la peinture, one observes some evolution in
the material presented. The changes are not so much signs of
shifting attitudes as indications that Breton's confidence in pictorial art increased with the passage of time. Meanwhile painting
took on sharper focus for Breton—not necessarily as he saw
it practiced around him, but as he came to think that it might
be and ought to be practiced.

At the beginning, André Breton advanced quite tentatively.
He appears to have been inclined to affirm his trust in a few
artists, none of whom needed support from the surrealist group
before they could make headway with the public at large. In
fact, remarks about Pablo Picasso, Georges Braque, and André
Derain looked oddly out of place, even impertinent, in the first
edition (1928) of his Le Surréalisme et la peinture. Breton left
himself open to accusations of opportunism when commenting
on these already established artists and placing on a comparable
footing a number of his friends, painters who were not so much

neglected as patently obscure. He seemed bent on claiming for Max Ernst, André Masson, Joan Miró, and Yves Tanguy greater stature by far than the majority of his readers were likely to be willing to grant them.

In addition, by the time *Le Surréalisme et la peinture* had gone through two expanding editions, a singular discrepancy had emerged in the earliest essays. Above all, this discrepancy appeared to suggest that André Breton had been more disturbed by Naville's strictures about painting in the context of surrealism than he would have been ready to admit openly. Naville had questioned the adaptability of the technique of verbal automatism to the medium of pictorial art. According to Naville, the purity so admired in automatic writing by those who had enlisted in the surrealist movement promised to have no direct equivalent in the graphic field. Reluctant to face this contention directly, Breton set about looking for points of contact between surrealism and painting (hence the cautious phrasing of his book's title; *Le surréalisme et la peinture*). And he presumably felt more at ease doing this as long as—changing his position from the one he had held while drafting his first manifesto—he did not represent surrealism in the guise of automatism. Anyone picking up *Le surréalisme et la peinture* immediately after reading the *Manifeste du surréalisme* is bound to notice one thing. The cornerstone of surrealism as defined in the October 1924 manifesto, automatism was barely mentioned in the volume about surrealism and painting that appeared in February 1928.

The curious imbalance visible when *Le surréalisme et la peinture* places Miró close to Picasso and Masson next to Braque is a consequence of two factors in particular. The first of these is Breton's discovery that André Masson and Joan Miró already had come closer than anyone else of his acquaintance to adapting automatism to pictorial expression. The second is his hesitation to make automatism the yardstick for achievement in painting with the assurance he displayed when equating surrealist writing and verbal automatism.

The results speak for themselves. In 1928 *Le surréalisme et la peinture* singled out Miró in one regard (the use of automatism) as perhaps "the most 'surrealist' of us all" (p. 37). As for Masson, it was not until 1941, in "Génèse et perspective artistiques du surréalisme," that Breton explained, "From the beginning of the surrealist movement, fully committed to the same struggle as Max Ernst but searching much earlier for principles authorizing him to build on them in a stable fashion, André

Masson right from the start of his route encounters *automatism*" (p. 66).

If one were to remove from the first edition of *Le surréalisme et la peinture* the pages devoted to Miró, or even excised no more than the first paragraph about his work, nothing would remain to link surrealism with painting via automatism. Breton's discussion of Masson alludes to "common considerations" as being "at the basis of everything we avoid and of everything we undertake" (p. 36). While shedding light on a strong bond between its author and Masson, this remark is more cryptic than illuminating. Its vagueness is obviously an effect of Breton's disinclination to specify what he had in common with Masson: faith in the ability of automatism to bring enlightenment. Thus when Breton borrows Edgar Allan Poe's phrase "the chemistry of intelligence" in order to refer readers to Masson's "science" (said in *Le surréalisme et la peinture* to produce "inevitable and dazzling 'precipitates'") he comes closer to creating a smokescreen than forthrightly identifying the importance of Masson's painting. There can be no doubt that, given the orientation of surrealist investigation at the time of the *Manifeste du surréalisme*, André Masson was within his rights in complaining later that Breton had been unjust when he granted him less attention than he gave Max Ernst in the first edition of *Le surréalisme et la peinture*. Masson could persuade himself all the more easily that he had a legitimate grievance when recalling that the section of *Le surréalisme et la peinture* that reproduced an essay from numbers 9–10 (1 November 1927) of *La revolution surréaliste* treated his own painting in three paragraphs—less than a page—while almost five pages were devoted to Ernst's work.

Masson surely was convinced he had reason to feel slighted by André Breton's treatment of his painting. Jealousy of Ernst stood between him and the realization that Breton's motivation was tactical, not personal. There were clear strategic advantages to bringing out a book on surrealism and painting as soon as possible after the 1924 manifesto. This is why the volume appeared within four months of the text in *La révolution surréaliste* to which Masson took exception. All the same, even if we discount the ambiguity of Breton's position, once he found himself inclined to speak of other matters than pictorial automatism, a rapid examination of the 1928 edition of *Le surréalisme et la peinture* is enough to reveal something noteworthy. Breton did not have the leisure to plan a campaign, to marshall evidence about painting, and to present it as purposefully as he would have been able to do a few years later.

During the ten-year period after 1925, Breton's thinking about pictorial art took a distinctive direction. It was swayed more than he cared to admit by the contention (not Pierre Naville's alone) that the painter is less likely than the word poet to be able to revolutionize his working method by recourse to automatism. Hence Breton opened the first of his essays on surrealism and painting with a statement of principle on which he felt sure he could built without protest from any of his fellow surrealists: "The eye exists in an untamed state." Having started out with the theory expounded in his *Manifeste du surréalisme* aimed at releasing creative writing from dependence on rationalism by the intervention of automatism, Breton now sought to establish a parallel with pictorial art by insisting that the eye is not an instrument of reason. He chose to ignore the fact that the human eye is more than a simple camera so that he could introduce his readers to the following idea. Certain painters— the ones he enjoyed, it goes without saying (his example was Pablo Picasso)—work from "a *purely inner model*." Neither reference to the outside, then, nor objection from the reasoning mind can modify that model during the procedure of pictorial communication. Without asserting in so many words that the writer and the painter travel the very same road, Breton was able to intimate in this fashion that their routes run parallel, at least until they reach a domain where imagination reigns uncontested. Yet parallelism is only suggested, never affirmed. *Le surréalisme et la peinture* spares us the obligation to face it directly, just as the book relieved André Breton of the necessity to defend it.

On the informational level, the version of *Le Surréalisme et la peinture* published in 1928 is singularly lacking in detail. The painters discussed are few in number. The amount of time devoted to each is so restricted that one might easily conclude that Breton had so little to say because of constraints on space. But there were no limitations while he was writing, other than those he himself chose to place on the texts first offered in *La révolution surréaliste* and subsequently reprinted—without revision or expansion—in a volume that William S. Rubin, in *Dada and Surrealist Art*, uncharitably (and inaccurately) has relegated to the status of a "booklet."[1] The true purpose of *Le surréalisme et la peinture* was not to assemble data, incontrovertible facts about this or that artist. A series of apparently unrelated essays, the book exemplified its author's approach to painting. Therefore it was intended to prove nothing. In the final analysis, André Derain and Francis Picabia appear to have been cited only because their work presented negative proof of the viability of the surrealist perspective on painting. All the same, taken together, the various sections of Le surréalisme et la peinture tell readers little. Yet they imply much more, making their impact in ways to which conventional art criticism has not accustomed its audience.

Le surréalisme et la peinture is somewhat difficult to read, though not because it confronts us with technical jargon we are untrained to interpret. The problem lies in the contrast between our expectations (fostered by conventional critical practice) and the material placed before us here. It is not the substance of the book that will leave many readers confused. It is the author's departure from the norms of commentary accepted and generally approved, both among critics and by those who turn to criticism for assistance. Comprehension eludes anyone who has not perceived that the various sections of Le surréalisme et la peinture present a succession of images inspired by André Breton's response to pictures he had seen. Reviewing the 1928 edition (to be increased ninefold in the definitive version, published thirty-seven years later), we are struck by the brevity of Le surréalisme et la peinture and its density.

When talking of Picasso, André Breton introduces a simple metaphor, that of the "mysterious route" illuminated in the Spanish painter's work by "a powerful searchlight" (p. 5). With this metaphor goes another, first used on the very same page: "What is there at the end of this agonizing journey, will we even know it one day?" In its turn, this rhetorical question ushers in an allusion to "a future continent," of which the mind is said to speak to us, and also a reference to accompanying "an always more beautiful Alice in Wonderland" (p. 6). In short, what Breton deemed admirable in Picasso's work (between 1910 and 1925) was something other than an affiliation with this or that school (cubism, for instance): the painter's ability to take to its highest degree "the spirit not of contradiction, but of evasion!" As for Georges Braque, fearing that in a year or two he no longer would wish to pronounce that artist's name, Breton hastened in 1925 to salute in him a man who had followed, for a while, the very same "path" as Picasso (p. 10).

Turning elsewhere, Breton lamented the recent orientation of Giorgio de Chirico's work while still praising him for having "carried out in his youth the most extraordinary voyage there can be for us" (p. 16). In this way, the image of traveling along a mysterious route becomes linked in Le surréalisme et la peinture with that of passage, of movement from one form of response (the visual) to another, beyond precise definition or accurate description. Breton's method of dealing with the artists he loved does not transform de Chirico into a surrealist. Even so, it helps us appreciate why surrealists were to regard de Chirico's early work as exemplary, why Breton could sum up its effect (its effect, we notice, not its intent) by quoting a subtitle from F. W. Murnau's silent film Nosferatu, eine Symphonie des Grauens (1922): "When he got to the other side of the bridge the phantoms came to meet him."

Central to the 1928 edition of Le surréalisme et la peinture is the section on Max Ernst. Passing by way of the image of "a few tempting locks without a key" to that of "the irreconstitutable pieces of the labyrinth" (pp. 24–25), Breton has arrived at a new figure of speech. He refers now to Ernst's artistic activity as "like a game of patience with creation," in which no particular magnetism draws together pieces that "try to discover new affinities with one another." Breton's conclusion?–"The rationalism and mysticism which quarrel over the softness of Derain's felt hat are under Max Ernst's feet" (p. 27). Hence the contention that "surreality not reality will reclaim its rights" (p. 30). As before, while we read the image of passage comes to mind in connection with the work of a painter whose dream, according to Breton, is "a dream of mediation" (p. 26). We encounter now a reference to "an admirable passageway" and to Max Ernst's "passage to another and to still another period" in his creative activity (p. 30).

Strictly speaking, there should have been no place for Man Ray in Le surréalisme et la peinture, even though two of Ray's canvases were to be reproduced in the definitive edition. When Breton first turned his attention to the American's work it was to concentrate on photography. In Le surréalisme et la peinture there is no break in the sequence of images, however, as Breton goes on to argue that, with Man Ray, photography engages in "the exploration of that region which painting believed it could reserve for itself" (p. 33). In Breton's view, it was as explorer that Ray had earned himself a place of honor in surrealism.

After a section on Miró, Breton places one in which the benefits of movement out of the familiar are highlighted in connection with Yves Tanguy's painting. The latter is described as a night journey, undertaken "by the sole gleam of the siphonophore" (p. 43), into a world that Tanguy is credited with having discovered all alone. In themselves, then, Breton's successive images display no originality. They certainly do not draw attention to themselves ostentatiously. Their role is merely to bring out the character of the writer's response to painting. To put it more exactly, they betray the demands Breton made upon the painter, reflecting the satisfaction released in him by this or that pictorial artist.

As we review the stages through which the Le surréalisme et la peinture enticed its readers we are impressed by the logical development of a theme, where the circumstances of the original publication—at irregular intervals, in a surrealist magazine— would have led one to expect haphazard presentation, devoid of system and order. By the time, apropos of Hans Arp, Breton speaks, close to the end of his text, about "that great crime which is today the crime of treason against reality," two things should be clear to anyone who has read him attentively. First, Breton did not see anything criminal in turning against reality. Second, the reality in question was that of appearances, fixed in their supposedly static forms by familiarity, habit, routine, our passive acceptance of their presence and prescribed function. In other words, from the standpoint adopted by André Breton, le crime de lèse-réalité was a necessary step in acknowledging that surrealism enjoyed certain rights to which he considered it fully entitled. Among those the most important, surely, was the right to consider the surreal as the real. Breton's belief in that right accounts for the words appearing on the last page of Le surréalisme et la peinture: "In reality, if you know what I mean by that, a nose is perfectly in place next to an armchair, it even adopts the shape of the armchair" (p. 48).

Setting forth his impressions of the painting of Yves Tanguy almost at the end of Le surréalisme et la peinture allowed Breton to make his point of view quite clear in 1928: "Everything I love, everything I think and feel, inclines me to a particular philosophy of immanence according to which surreality is contained in reality itself, and is neither superior to it nor external to it. And vice versa, for the content is also the container" (p. 46). He went on to add, in anticipation of the subject matter of his Les vases communicants (1932), "It is almost a question of a communicating vessel between container and content" (p.

46). He was now ready to affirm the parity between painting and writing in a respect that for the surrealists was centrally important: "This is to say that I reject with all my strength attempts which, in the field of painting as of writing, could have the limited consequence of withdrawing thought from life, as well as of placing life under the aegis of thought" (p. 46). Thus, although more space goes to Max Ernst in Breton's text, nothing to be found in *Le surréalisme et la peinture* tells as much as his remarks on Tanguy about how painting could fit into the surrealist scheme of things, about the way in which one surrealist *looked*, when facing a painted canvas. For this reason, *Le surréalisme et la peinture* leads the reader beyond traditional critical values, letting him witness a form of communion between spectator and artist, taking place on a level to which Breton referred when writing of his "particular philosophy of immanence" (p. 46).

Imagery having to do with travel into the unfamiliar and also with discovery reaches its climax in Breton's observations about Tanguy reprinted first in *Le surréalisme et la peinture* and later in *Yves Tanguy*: Tanguy's painting is placed "at equal distance from those ancient cities of Mexico which the impenetrable forest conceals no doubt forever from human eyes . . . and from an 'Ys' to which he has rediscovered the key," halfway, then between the geographically exotic and the mythologically remote. Only now does Breton open up the question of the artist's relationship to his audience with this comment: "To see, to hear, is nothing. To recognize (or not to recognize) is everything. Between what I recognize and what I do not recognize there is myself" (p. 44). In this manner, *Le surréalisme et la peinture* links the idea of the artist as investigator of the unknown with the notion of self-discovery in the spectator. Departing from the criterion termed reality, Tanguy neither judged things nor expected them to be judged solely by the scale of the familiar. Hence Breton found in his paintings "the first *nonlegendary* glimpses of a considerable stretch of the mental world at the stage of genesis" (p. 46).

Reflecting on Breton's achievement in the original *Le surréalisme et la peinture* gives us occasion to notice how consistent his position would remain, for nearly forty years, where painting was in question. Understanding all that his 1928 volume has to offer sends its readers back to the foreword to *Yves Tanguy*, which makes us witnesses to the emotions released in its author at the sight of Tanguy's canvases. The excitement Breton strove to share in Le surréalisme et la peinture reflected an experience that had turned his attention inward, to self-discovery, not outward in a display of erudition.

We cannot begin to penetrate to the core of André Breton's essays about painting while supposing them to have been written as nothing more than propaganda. Breton was not bent on proving a point. He was devoted to self-exploration, which his encounter with the work of certain artists afforded him the opportunity to pursue just a little further, in hope and anticipation of fruitful discovery. Realizing this allows us to situate Le surréalisme et la peinture with respect both to its author's perception of pictorial art and to writings with a focal point other than painting.

Showing how he thought surrealism and painting came together, Breton was motivated by something other than a compulsion to justify his own enthusiasm for pictorial art to his fellow surrealists and others. In Le surréalisme et la peinture his intention was of greater significance than if he had written simply to bring painting within the frame of surrealism, as an expressive mode no less amenable to manipulation by pictorial artists seeking acceptance within the surrealist circle than the language mode was to manipulation by individuals deserving to be known as surrealist writers.

To qualify as surrealist, any creative work had to demonstrate its relevance to surrealism's program. From the start, the fact that in surrealist context, qualification and relevance were not so much objectively demonstrable as subjectively perceptible invested Breton's idea of painting with a character for which conventional art criticism provided neither precedent nor justification. The point of reference was and would always continue to be inside the spectator, not outside in canons of beauty on which everyone might agree.

With other surrealist commentators of painting André Breton stood on the common ground of aspiration. All defended a concept of art neither arbitrary in its demands nor again so private as to leave the public in bemused ignorance of why one canvas met with the group's approval while another was to be dismissed as nonsurrealist or even antisurrealist. Essential to surrealist discussion of painting was an avoidance of a predetermined program. There never was to be, for surrealists, a recipe of any kind, established on the theoretical plane and consistently applied by aspirant surrealist painters or, for that matter, by those already acknowledged to be so.

To the examination of any painted canvas suspected of being surrealist the ill-informed public—or, more exactly, those allowed to point the way in discussions of surrealism—bring certain preconceived ideas about the forms surrealism assumed in art. These people communicate with one another on a level where the ersatz adjective "surrealistic" sounds precise enough to be meaningful. In contrast, those who had the right to use it about their own work never employed "surrealist" in order to trigger a conditioned reflex that would dispense readers or listeners from the obligation to think for themselves. Indeed, Breton was the first to make clear that applying the qualifier "surrealist" to a picture was anything but an invitation to one's audience to classify some artist once and for all, to assign his production to a pigeonhole of memory. It was on the contrary a challenge to the spectator to determine, by looking for himself, how the artist in question had evaded or surmounted the limits of so-called reality.

André Breton started to open the doors of surrealism to painters who might wish to pass through them when he proposed a standard for painting that would remove the art of imitation altogether from the scale of values by which success must be judged. Others, outside surrealism, had already revolted against imitative art, of course. The special importance of Le surréalisme et la peinture has to do with the direction in which it pointed. Breton's texts evidenced a determination—soon to be typical of surrealist commentary on art—to elevate antirealist content above all else. Technique was to be cast in a dual subordinate role; not only to communicate content but in some instances also to aid the artist in his or her discovery of content.

Absorbing painting into surrealism meant to Breton adjusting the function of art to surrealist requirements, persistently treating art as a means, not an aesthetic end. This is why, introducing his Yves Tanguy years after publishing Le surréalisme et la peinture, he managed to remain fully consistent when evaluating pictorial art by extra-artistic standards. Throughout Breton's adult life, in his surrealist mind recognition was dissociated from acknowledgment of the reality of things familiar. It was located, instead, at the level of subjective response. There it owed more to the capacity of the work of art to capture an image of desire than to its fidelity to objective reality. In fact,

Breton would never cease to castigate "the art of resemblance," to look upon it as not simply false but as a betrayal of art.

Paying tribute to a number of artists who had captured and held his attention afforded Breton an occasion to face the question of painting's role in surrealism. Thus *Le surréalisme et la peinture* grew neither out of the wish to draft a blueprint for surrealist art nor out of a theory calculated to guarantee painters right of entry to the surrealist camp. Far from offering proof of an assured critical posture, clearly designed, carefully argued, and persuasively presented, *Le surréalisme et la peinture* brings before us a series of intuitions from which its author gained his perception of pictorial art as a serviceable means of surrealist investigation. Under the circumstances, hindsight granted Miró greater importance for surrealism than would have been his had he proved only that painting can rest on the automatic principle. The example set by Miró was to lose none of its appeal when the surrealists (Breton among them) arrived at the conclusion that automatism had its limitations. With a flair for going to essentials unequalled in any other surrealist commentator on art, André Breton unerringly singled out the gift that would make Joan Miró a significant artist for surrealism. In an image that *Le surréalisme et la peinture* had well prepared its readers to appreciate he described Miró as "that traveler always in the greater hurry for not knowing where he is going" (p. 40).

Le surréalisme et la peinture developed out of the assumption that keeping on the move will take the painter forward, not backward. Behind this assumption lay the belief that progress is measurable only by reference to content. In turn, this belief implied yet another: that, distracting attention from content, concern for technical matters must impede progress. With the latter seemed to go this deduction: knowing what one is doing or trying to do, through reliance on techniques already used profitably in the past, slows down or even halts advance. To the surrealist traveler in a hurry progress came most quickly, we infer, when he advanced in ignorance of the as yet unknown.

Could it be that, still unsure in 1928 of surrealism's capacity for inspiring and engendering techniques appropriate to pictorial art, Breton elected to give priority to subject matter over methodology in surrealist painting? Anyone inclined to think so would be well advised to turn back to the first manifesto, where Breton declared that "the future *techniques* of surrealism" did not interest him (p. 60). For those equating surrealism with a handful of techniques, such a statement is tantamount to an admission that Breton cared only about surrealism as practiced in 1924. Really, it is a sign that, giving all his attention to the surrealist spirit, he conceived fidelity to surrealism as having nothing to do with hemming oneself in within the limitations set by an array of techniques, however varied. Surrealism, he preferred to believe, had a better chance of proving viable and retaining vitality if its advocates concentrated on subject matter as the pathway to surrealist experience. In short, the "absolute nonconformism" the *Manifeste du surréalisme* claims that surrealism expressed must guarantee that the artist avoid the trap of conformism to proven surrealist methods as much as to any others.

One of the major lessons to be learned from *Le surréalisme et la peinture* comes to light as we notice how diverse are the forms of pictorial imagery in the work of the painters discussed. Not only is variety of technique represented in the artists who inspired Breton's collection of essays, but the content we encounter—even if we go no further than glancing at the illustrations in his volume—defies reduction to one or two kinds of subjects. Moreover, as we review the texts assembled here, we observe that the writer does not linger over the description of the images peculiar to this or that artist's painting, let alone undertake to identify parallels, draw comparisons, or set up enlightening juxtapositions. Indeed, the figures of speech running through *Le surréalisme et la peinture* alert its readers to general aspirations—a need to progress, an impulse to explore, and so on—rather than specify where exploration is to take place, how, and to what extent progress is made. Someone in whom skepticism easily breeds suspicion will conclude that André Breton remained vague because he continued to be uncertain—even though he would soon prepare a *Second manifeste du surréalisme*—of surrealism's influence on painting or, in fact, of painting's adaptability to surrealism. But if his text fails to offer clear directives to artists coming under surrealism's attraction, this is because Breton took care not to avoid closing surrealist painting off from future developments still unforeseen and even unforeseeable in February of 1928.

On balance, examination of the material brought together in *Le surréalisme et la peinture* three and a half years after the appearance of the original surrealist manifesto makes one thing plain. We should be in error to suppose Breton's mood between

1925 and 1928 to have been one of hesitancy brought on by uncertainty of purpose. All the evidence, explicit and implicit, points to hope and confidence, and especially to the writer's determination to remain true to surrealism as a vitalizing spirit. Such a spirit, as the discussions assembled in *Le surrélisme et la peinture* stand to prove, could never be confined within a short-term projection based on the example provided by past experience.

Breton never repudiated *Le surréalisme et la peinture*. Nor did he allow it to drop out of print in the hope that it would be forgotten. When, during his exile in New York, the opportunity presented itself to bring out a new edition, prior to doing so he undertook no revisions (not even stylistic ones, like those he made later for a new edition of another 1928 book, *Nadja*). Instead, he appended to the 1945 edition an essay he had written in 1941 under the title "Génèse et perspective artistiques du surréalisme." This brought *Le surréalisme et la peinture* up to date, so to speak, without correcting it. Breton saw no reason to apologize for or rectify earlier statements about painting. What could have been more fitting, to stress the continuity between the essays published in 1945, than the opening sentence of "Génèse et perspective artistiques"? Using the example of Columbus discovering the Antilles while on a voyage he hoped would take him to India, Breton returned yet again to the image of the voyage of discovery. And he showed the latter to be a journey offering revelation beyond the scope of conscious projection, conducted with the beneficent assistance of chance and leading to entry into a new world outside the limitations of the old.

8

Perspectives on the Avant-Garde

Is there not something just a little disturbing about a snapshot taken in 1912? It shows André Breton posed in the embrasure of a wall of the castle that Ferdinand Cheval had spent a third of a century building from stone and cement. One cannot altogether escape the impression that the presence of the author of the surrealist manifestoes is intrusive, even if it is perhaps meant to authenticate the Facteur Cheval's edifice. That impression may not be well founded, of course. Nonetheless, it does bring into focus one fact of note. The surrealists sometimes established a relationship between the image they were intent on projecting and the creative activity of isolated individuals, a number of whom, we can be sure, would have declined close association with the surrealist group or remained totally indifferent to the supposed benefits of affiliation.

At times, recognition from within the surrealist circle looks more like annexation than a fraternal gesture. We have occasion to observe that a number of contemporaries appear to have felt that acceptance into the surrealist group might be more confining than liberating: the Mauritian poet Malcolm de Chazal, for instance, and Hans Arp, poet, painter, and sculptor.

Some people—they are mainly persons who have wandered away from the surrealist camp or who have been banned from reentry—have complained that the surrealist air was unbreathable. Others, meanwhile, could not imagine drawing breath except in the rarefied atmosphere peculiar to surrealism. The latter give the avant-garde a meaning that challenges our customary view of it.

I confess that my own introduction to the idea of the avant-garde was neither literary nor artistic; it was strictly military.

Defending queen and country, I found myself involved in a daytime exercise that has stayed in my mind. I recall watching as one unfortunate was detailed to guard the rear during a rest period. While we all lay about, he had to kneel with his back to us, rifle at the ready though unloaded, just in case something menacing emerged from the sewage fields behind us. Once our squad changed direction to return to base, my vigilant fellow recruit ceased to be our rearguard. For just a moment or two, he held a forward position. But we soon reached and passed *that*, without anything noteworthy having happened in what our serjeant major termed a farm; of a bluntly specified kind, need I add?

Later, I discovered in myself a marked reluctance to serve as a scout, even before my company commander was killed by the Mau Mau. All the same I came to appreciate the *cachet* of the avant-garde, the aura first of the vanguard writer and then of the painter enjoying comparable status.

In 1949 a *pion* in the French school to which I had been assigned (having been in the Resistance, he had something heroic about him) assured me that one day soon Jean-Paul Sartre's *Le Mur* would be on the academic curriculum. Such an idea was to do more for me in the end than my attempt to ape the fellow's bodybuilding success. Yet it seemed farfetched at a time when the favorite reading of an elderly landlady of mine (who, whenever she referred to "la Guerre," was alluding to the Franco-Prussian War), *Paul et Virginie*, was still on the *programme* leading to the *Agrégation*. Yet nowadays Bernardin de Saint-Pierre, whom I had been compelled to read in high school, is behind the rearguard—the decoration he received from Napoleon notwithstanding. And Sartre? Well, today he scarcely ranks as a vanguard writer. It may be unkind to say that we have advanced beyond the position that was his lookout post. But we certainly know where that position is; we have it circled on our campaign maps.

One may quibble about Sartre's candidacy for avant-garde rank without, I believe, disposing of the point I wish to make. With time, the Fauves have come to look quite tame. Futurism has fallen into the past, Vorticism has ceased to leave anyone giddy. Action painting is no longer where the action is, and *les extravagants* may now leave us yawning but surely not wide-eyed.

The advance guard and even those who move ahead as scouts, it seems, do not all qualify by any means as Baudelairian *phares*. Still, they have served as *éclaireurs* of sorts, moving along paths by which we join them eventually. It was Edouard Dujardin's destiny to pave the way for James Joyce, so earning little more in the end than a footnote in literary history.

What about Joyce, incidentally? Here is part of what we read in the 1941 edition of *The Concise Cambridge History of English Literature*, published the year of his death. My copy is stamped, "For use by H. M. Forces. NOT FOR RESALE." I have no reason to suppose, though, that the version that went through four printings in the next three years and was available to the public at large differs in any significant detail: "If mere quantity of discussion and shrillness of assertion offered any true test of quality, James Joyce (1882–1941) and David Herbert Lawrence (1885–1930) would have to be regarded as the greatest novelists of their time. But we must not mistake the fervid claims of coteries for the calm voice of general judgment" (p. 970). "Much could be written in praise of *Ulysses*; but in dispraise the one fatal word must be uttered: it is unreadable. It would never have a public, even if copies were given away like tracts. The wild enthusiasm of its immature readers can therefore be dismissed as a pretence. . . . *Finnigans Wake* (1939) is equally experimental and even more successful" (p. 972).

As for the assessment of Lawrence in the same reputable work of reference, it yields this gem: "He felt he was one of the unclassed (Oxbridge speaks!). No Scotsman similarly placed would have been conscious of the least inferiority" (p. 973). I regret to have to report total lack of success in establishing the origins of the author of these lines, one George Sampson. I must conclude that he belongs to the obscure but fiercely proud Clan Sampson.

It is not the thorny question of value judgment that preoccupies me here—whether, for example, Sartre or Borges is more deserving of the vanguard title than Queneau or Cortazar. My attention goes rather to the capacity demonstrated repeatedly by literature and painting to overtake the avant-garde and, if not always to move on far enough to transform it into the arrière-garde, then to absorb its innovations and assimilate its boldness, taking the latter as the basis for further progress, out of which—on occasion—vanguard expression once again derives. However, one cannot reflect on this phenomenon without noting that, generalized though it seems to be, it does not apply in every instance. A number of exceptions come embarrassingly to mind, discouraging universal application of the theory that the avant-garde is simply tomorrow clamoring for attention today.

One truism of literary history is that its practitioners have a knack for betting on the wrong horses, for neglecting at least a few of the truly important writers while touting many of the also-rans. So true is this that any author secretly aspiring to immortality must surely tremble when granted wide recognition in the here and now. As a boy, I read a book about contemporary English poets called *Eight for Immortality*—only one of whom I have heard of since. I wonder if that is what Samuel Beckett's Vladimir would call "un pourcentage honnête" ("a reasonable percentage," in Beckett's own translation).

As for painting, it is a field where flaws in critical judgment stand out so plainly that, in recent years especially, commentators have deemed it advisable, by the look of things, to give up evaluation in favor of cautious conciliation. This course seems likely to offer more promise of success in identifying what is worthwhile because nobody anymore dares take the risk of denouncing an apparent charlatan or an incompetent for fear that the latter turns out ten years from now to be God's gift to the post-Picasso era.

It is true that we have quite often seen commentators on literature and art display the decency to try to make amends for past errors and also to repair omissions—acknowledging finally the value of neglected figures who merit notice. A pendulum swing in opinion has afforded us an opportunity to reconsider the importance of Pierre Loti and Lautréamont. Yet some nonconforming artists of vanguard tendencies have proved to be unassimilable. They do not beckon to succeeding generations urgently enough, it would appear. Hence, when not ignored entirely, they are treated as anomalies from which no progeny is to be expected. Such a writer was a man who never doubted his own genius, his indisputable right to eternal glory, Raymond Roussel—still a marginal figure despite Alain Robbe-Grillet's tribute, Michel Foucault's, and the special issue of a magazine called *Bizarre*. Such a writer too, is Maurice Fourré—even more marginal, in spite of André Breton's open admiration for his work, or possibly to some extent because of it.

Generally speaking, there seems to be a pattern, somewhat erratic in rhythm, linking the progress made by art and literature and the advances attributable to the avant-garde. We witness the operation of an integrative principle to which, even if the word "progress" looks suspect the vitality of the arts can be ascribed. Much of what shocks, even outrages, today, will be accepted tomorrow or the day after. Thus, taking the long view persuades us less of the disruptive role of the vanguard than of its necessity for keeping creative action on the move. Certainly, those who resist the call of the avant-garde too long must pay the penalty of being dismissed as reactionary. And this is only as it should be, the rest of us agree, as we feel obligated to explain to those coming after us what looked so alarming, exactly, in the work of this or that painter as to warrant calling him a Fauve, or what it was during the early 1950s that persuaded certain filmmakers in Britain to speak gravely, albeit vaguely, about a Free Cinema.

In the long run, it is not innovative effort that most of us come to admire in this or that avant-gardist. We prize, finally, the anticipative nature of his or her investigation. In time, we salute prescience where at first we were sensitive to nothing more than open conflict with tradition and customary usage. In fact, we apply the term *avant-garde* most readily to artists whom we have begun to overtake, who—although perhaps only silhouetted on the skyline—are yet within our purview. In other words, attribution of the title *avant-garde* is already for most people an earnest of approval. Its use is reserved for creative personalities we already foresee being brought into the mainstream of art or literature. To put it somewhat differently, in terms that may sound dangerously negative, by the time society's guard dogs (the critics) have caught the scent of a vanguard artist and have commenced growling or barking, the person of whose presence they warn has slowed down, permitting the rest of us to begin catching up.

Not all who have enjoyed the reputation of belonging to the avant-garde are as objective or as honest, for that matter, as Eugene Ionesco, who conceded that his work had lost its momentum (let us say, to be accurate, that it had lost a certain kind of momentum, taking it in a certain direction) when he caught himself writing for an audience already exposed to his *anti-pièces*. Where the antiplay becomes the play, the dramatist's relation to his public can remain the same no longer than can the public's relation to his theater. Eventually, the *nouvelle vague* breaks on a seashore where cinema audiences are assembled and waiting, responses primed, heads poised for nods of complicity. In the shock of the new, we discover over and over

gain, the novelty is shocking, all right—but transient nevertheless. In the mid-1960s I sent a postcard to a correspondent
of mine, Jean-Jacques Lebel, one of the promoters of happenings. Posing the query, "What's happening to happenings?" I
received no reply. Lebel never wrote me again. I was left with
the "collected works" he had sent me once: the bottom half
of a paperback American sex novel, in a box designed to contain
suppositories.

It might be argued that the term *avant-garde* can be used
in good conscience only when the creative activity so identified
is a sign that one artist has forged ahead in a direction where
others surely will follow. The vanguard is thus a promise of
things to come. This is to say that where an artist, instead of
opening up a new exploratory path, seems to be headed into
a dead end—going somewhere we are unlikely to follow or
even to want to follow—the avant-garde label looks inappropriate. By the standards implied here, Maurice Fourré is not a
vanguard writer at all. He is a perverse one, a novelist who
must pay the price for trying to return to fiction after a forty-
three-year layoff.

However objectively formulated unfavorable criticism of exceptional people like Fourré may appear, it restricts the concept
of the avant-garde, confining it to limits in which thoroughly
responsible commentators and their public can feel comfortable
placing trust. It suggests that the vanguard artist and everyone
ahead of whom he strikes out are part of the same evolution-
ary movement, advancing in the same direction. In this way,
it renders the idea of the avant-garde tolerable, even welcome.
The assumption is that the vanguard artist is equipped with
sharper instincts than anyone coming behind, presumably blessed with intimations that surprise in the short term yet prove
to be sound and acceptable over time. There is no place in
the scheme of things for individuals who never cease to surprise, whom the rest of us never overhaul, and whom we see
no advantage in chasing after. The attention we are prepared
to grant the vanguard is so selective that we impose on the
avant-garde a meaning that salutes only certain virtues in the
unconventional artist while other characteristics are branded
aberrations or even vices.

It would be foolish to mutter of a conspiracy on a grand
scale. What strikes us instead is the following. The avant-garde
is a generally acceptable notion as long as those who have moved

ahead can be seen one day as having made explicit something at present only implicit, either in our grasp on human experience or in our way of rendering it. Underlying our sense of the avant-garde is a usually unarticulated belief in the permanence of the matter of art and in the necessity of periodically reviewing the manner in which that same matter is to be communicated. Thus the vanguard artist startles us when reaching for a communicative mode that, upon our first contact with it, appears to function so strangely as to leave us at a loss, unable to participate because we are not yet attuned to the investigative procedures the artist has made his own.

Mention of surrealism in all this may sound anticlimactic. I should like to bring surrealism into the picture, nevertheless. My purpose is to test the hypothesis that there exists (side by side with something I term, for convenience, the respectable avant-garde) one that has not attained the status of respectability or at most is judged respectable only on terms laid down by the critics. And when the artist does not meet the critics' standards? Well, he runs the risk of being dismissed, as René Magritte was dismissed by Carlo Ludovico Ragghianti, who as late as 1954 called his work "brothel painting."

At the risk of being accused of employing a vocabulary that is prejudicial, not to say inflammatory, I would call the avant-garde I have been describing up to now the official avant-garde. This is a form of vanguardism that is assigned and indeed actually can be seen to play a role in the evolution of art. It is quite appropriately named, then, legitimately bearing a label for which there is ample justification. I have no excuse either for quarreling with the official avant-garde's designation or for questioning its relationship to art. Some might contend that therefore I ought to be casting about for a name that could be applied without danger of confusion to what I am going to call the unofficial avant-garde.

To whom could the term *unofficial avant-garde* apply? It identifies, for me, individuals in whose work anticonformity is not to be denied, persons who unquestionably forge ahead. These are people, though, whose advance appears of doubtful value, whom the majority of writers and painters (to say nothing of those who speak for them) see no advantage in following. If these artists must be acknowledged as having managed to strike out on their own, the consensus is that they have blundered into one cul-de-sac or another, where it would be pointless to follow. Thus they fail to meet the conditions under which the official avant-garde figures in the scheme of things. Their investigations are denied validity on the grounds that they offer to lead where no one else could imagine wishing to go. In other words, there is no place for them.

At this point, I offer a date, not quite an arbitrary one, I think: 1907. That year Maurice Fourré brought out a short story— his last publication before 1950. Henri Rousseau's *La charmeuse de serpent* was on display at the Salon d'Automne in Paris, Pablo Picasso completed a canvas called *Les demoiselles d'Avignon*, and Clovis Trouille, then eighteen years old, painted his *Palais des merveilles*. Who painted what? One has only to ask this question to be aware of the difference between the official avant-garde—in which not only Picasso but the Douanier Rousseau occupies a position—and the unofficial avant-garde, which has no history yet.

Clovis Trouille's name occurs in just one paragraph of John Weightman's *The Concept of the Avant-Garde* (1973). There he is identified inaccurately as having "the admirably Surrealist name of Claude Trouille" and is described as "an elderly French Surrealist painter."[1] We can be sure that Trouille would not have been mentioned at all in Weightman's three-hundred-page volume had he not given the name *Oh Calcutta!* to one of his 1946 canvases, which Weightman was apparently unable to recognize in reproduction on the backdrop of a stage show, *Oh Calcutta*, and on the front cover of that show's program.

In 1930 Trouille would paint *Remembrance*, describing it as "the anti-everything picture." Shown at the Salon des Artistes et Ecrivains révolutionnaires that same year, it was his first exhibited work (he was forty-one years old already), attracting the attention of the French surrealists, who reproduced it in black and white on the final page of the third issue (1931) of their magazine, *Le surréalisme au service de la révolution*. Although awarded a Médaille d'Honneur du Travail by the mayor of the eighteenth arrondissement for thirty-five years' service as a touch-up artist for a Parisian firm manufacturing wax figures, Trouille (from choice more than neglect) did not hold a one-man show until 1963. To avoid "any blasphemous scandal," admission to the exhibit was reserved for guests bearing the invitation catalogue as a kind of passport. By that time, Clovis Trouille was seventy-four years old. No indeed, Fourré and Trouille have not fared quite as Piccaso and Henri Rousseau have done.

Let me go back now to a reference made earlier to André Breton's admiration for Maurice Fourré. When Breton's preface to Fourré's *La Nuit du Rose-Hôtel* came out with the novel in 1950, an article appeared in a French periodical recording the opinions of celebrities who had been asked to name the ten leading painters of the first half of the twentieth century. Breton had named artists about whom nobody else had ever heard. Moreover, readers learned, that was only to be expected of the man. *La Nuit du Rôse-Hotel* inaugurated a series to be edited by Breton under the heading *Révélation*, for which the cover design incorporated a Baudelairian lighthouse. Evidently, André Breton was running true to form in launching a series (intended to complement Albert Camus's *Espoir*, for the same house of Gallimard) with a fictional text by a neglected writer in his seventies.

It was typical of Breton that in his second surrealist manifesto he should have identified surrealism as "the tail of romanticism," but only, he stressed, on condition that the prehensile quality of that tail be acknowledged. There are moments when it seems that, facing surrealism, we witness the tail wagging the dog. A similar impression may accompany scrutiny of the tradition in which the surrealists gladly took their place. One is readily persuaded that surrealist taste was predictable to the extent that it looks quixotic, quirky. Surrealists obviously inclined to revere the outsider, the anticonformist, the isolated creator who apparently had no literary or artistic successors other than (occasionally, anyway) they themselves. Or again, the features of an artist's work commanding the surrealists' attention and drawing praise from them are those in which reputable critics have shown little or no interest.

To argue that the surrealists were by definition more perceptive commentators than other people, endowed with more subtle sensibilities, would be no more informative than convincing. It would merely separate the believers from the skeptical. What matters at this point is less the peculiar nature of the surrealists' affections than the viewpoint nourishing those affections.

Turning to the preface Breton wrote in 1949 for *La Nuit du Rose-Hôtel*, we see what motivated him to plan the *Révélation* series. "It is a matter," he explained, "of bringing into the light of day a certain number of works that are really *apart*. Approaching them does not always fail to present certain difficulties but their virtue is to make us look *out to sea* in the life we think we are leading, in this way to preserve from stereotypy and sclerosis the vital forces of understanding."[2] His use of medical vocabulary (the respected and lucrative career that Breton, like Louis Aragon, had abandoned for poetry) helps uncover the basis on which surrealists judged the revelatory character of "a certain number of works." What is more, the interpretation placed on revelation by Breton was consistent with the position he defended (and from which he attacked, too), as a surrealist.

Even though no titles were added to the *Révélation* series after *La Nuit du Rose-Hôtel*, it is worth reviewing the criterion Breton had in mind. He proposed to include texts from the past that had not attained "the desired resonance," as he put it, either because of limited circulation or, more significantly, because they went deliberately "against the current." Now those conditions present no novelty. They might be met by a wide variety of works in which people on the track of the official avant-garde could take some interest but in which the surrealists detected no particular virtue. The principal condition of acceptance for *Révélation* was announced when Breton spoke of "a new manner of envisaging man's situation in the world," of deducing means for freeing man from constraints inherent in the routine mode applied more and more generally, according to Breton's text, "in the formation of the human mind."

This still sounds quite vague. To trace Breton's line of thought a little farther, we have to look outside his comments on *La Nuit du Rose-Hôtel* and consider also the title of one of his catalogue prefaces, "L'art des fous: clé des champs" (insane art: roaming free). It was not art that attracted Breton in drawings and paintings by the insane. Nor was it madness, really. His title culminates in a phrase later used to name a collection of his essays, gathered in 1953: *La clé des champs*. Through art André Breton sought liberation.

In the first paragraph of the volume on surrealism written for an *Histoire générale de la peinture* published in Lausanne, fellow surrealist José Pierre insists appositely: "Speaking pictorially and poetically, the notion of a 'school,' as it is current in literary history and the history of art, is fundamentally incompatible with the will to liberation from mental habits, formal conventions, technical routines, the profound 'anti-sociability' of the individual creator, poet or painter. On this plane, surrealism has deliberately held to the 'buissonnière' attitude."[3] Looking "out to sea"; "la clé des champs"; "l'école buissionière (playing hooky)"—complementary metaphors direct our attention to the same need, essential in the surrealists' estimation:

a need to elude control, to assert freedom in the face of imposed authority, and to find in *la sauvagerie* not merely a social posture but a source of creative energy.

It would be unproductive to suggest that art could appeal to surrealists only after it had ceased to be art. It helps, though, to notice that the surrealists' attention was engaged, their enthusiasm fired, when art became—in their eyes—more than art. So far as art managed to exceed functions prescribed by tradition, it held promise for the surrealists.

The surrealist standpoint is most comprehensible—in many respects, anyway—when we observe how often surrealists took encouragement from Marcel Duchamp's dictum that it is the beholder *(le regardeur)* who makes the picture. Much that is apparently arbitrary and even confusing in what they had to say may be traced to the assurance with which they claimed for the spectator/reader the right to invest the created work with a meaning of his or her own. Hence the title of another introductory essay by André Breton, who prefaced his anthology of black humor with a text called "Paratonnerre" (Lightning rod). Surrealism, we infer, attracted certain electrical currents in the air, conducting them in a direction of its own. The surrealist interpreter chose a path divergent from that taken by other commentators on painting or literature, who therefore are at a disadvantage in their effort to evaluate surrealism. He judged the things he saw and read by extra-artistic values.

Such a remark sounds like begging an unstated question. All the same, it explains why surrealists admired, for instance, the work of Fourré in which literary criticism can detect nothing to admire. It explains too why they were responsible to a number of eccentrics, to borrow (reluctantly) a term that immediately classifies negatively persons like Ferdinand Cheval and Léon Corcuff, the inventor of aluminum shoes and collapsible beds, for whom there is still no assigned place in the world where Tinguely has found a public more awestruck than comprehending.

Even if inclined to make fun of Corcuff, we must admit that his creative activities fall outside the frame that usually defines the avant-garde. At best, artists such as he may be saluted as *inspirés* (the word is from Gilles Ehrmann's 1962 photo collection, *Les inspirés et leurs demeures*,[4] for which Breton wrote the preface—a book in which the taxi driver Corcuff does not appear, though the facteur Cheval does). But that is a long way from being recognized as *illuminati*. By and large, the achievement of such people is adjudged curious rather than seminal.

Surrealism, of course, did not offer a permanent haven or even a temporary refuge to any artist who, being outside the limits set by accepted convention, failed to earn a niche in the official avant-garde. Rejection by everyone else was by no means a guarantee of approval by the surrealists. Indeed, the latter were strict in their demands, in imposing conditions under which innovative departure from conventional modes of thought and expression was condoned. To the degree that surrealism defied convention, betokened suspicion of literature, and was wary of what the art of painting had become, it stood for the revitalization of poetic communication.

Now, surrealisms did not presume to change every artistic dead end into a pathway to the new. But it did teach that the absence of some of the virtues regarded by critics as essential to artistic expression and discovery, even in the avant-garde, needed not be an impediment to progress. Everything hinges, then on the meaning attached to "progress," on the possibility remaining for advancement in a zone beyond that of artistic communication. It is here that the surrealists showed themselves responsive, while commentators alert to the official avant-garde continue to be unimpressed.

The problem is that seen from outside the surrealist circle, the kind of assessment offered by Breton—of Raymond Roussel's theater, shall we say, or of Henri Rousseau's painting—seems out of focus. In reality, it is focused differently from the sort of commentary we have learned to expect of critics whom we trust to steer our judgment along lines laid down by the integrative principle usually controlling response to the avant-garde. One has only to listen for a moment to Breton discussing Kandinsky in *Le surréalisme et la peinture* in order to notice that the basis for judgment used is markedly similar to that upon which the abortive series *Révélation* would have been erected: "The line is by [Kandinsky] returned to its true necessity: it is the Ariadne's thread which allows one to find oneself again in the labyrinth of appearances, setting aside that which can constitute from the outside the individual unity of objects" (p. 286).

Naturally, Breton could hardly have claimed to have discovered Kandinsky all by himself. But he surely can be credited with having had reasons for admiration that—while not detaching Kandinsky from the official avant-garde—link him with the unofficial vanguard exciting to the surrealist imagination. Similarly, it would be foolish to assert that the Douanier Rousseau's reputation as a representative of the official avant-garde is enhanced by Breton's remarks about his work. Even so, emphasizing Rousseau's ability to demonstrate how ridiculous are artistic means that can be taught (qui s'enseignent), André Breton was able to relate the Douanier to a branch of the unofficial vanguard from which surrealists drew inspiration. Here so-called primitive painting rests on "the cornerstone of ingenuousness" to which le surréalisme et la peinture attributes the work of self-taught artists: "a fascinating decantation of the real" (p. 293).

Kandinsky and Rousseau are two of a number of artists who may be described as straddling the official and unofficial avant-garde paths. Their names have been introduced here out of a necessity to stress a feature of the surrealist approach of the greatest importance. Even when surrealists appear to have been in agreement with the critics, approving the very same artists, the grounds on which they voiced satisfaction were not shared. Wherever a surrealist saw cause for praise, we find he had reasons of his own for singling out this writer or that painter. The same reasons underlay his enthusiasm when he spoke with admiration of other vanguard writers and pictorial artists deemed unworthy of serious attention in critical circles.

Neither André Breton nor those—José Pierre, notably—who evaluated creative achievement from the same point of view can be accused of capriciousness when defending positions from which some artists appeared worthy of praise while others were treated with contempt. When the moment came to assess some manifestation of the avant-garde, the surrealist's voice was raised to endorse qualities by which surrealism validated art. Thus surrealists were sure why they approved the work done by Giorgio de Chirico roughly between 1910 and 1919 when, according to José Pierre, he was "the perfect model of the surrealist artist, or even of the surrealist pure and simple."[5] They were just as sure why they should condemn everything the Italian painter did after 1920 or so, with the exception of his novel Hebdoméros, which they began to praise upon its publication in 1929.

Affection and esteem were elicited from the surrealist membership by qualities to which their common ambitions made them sensitive. Trouille could affirm his independence of all movements, schools, and factions with the declaration, "I adhere only to myself." Surrealists would not have denied him that right or withheld their support because he asserted it. Devotion to the cause of surrealism was never to breed fickleness or even pettiness, despite things one hears from former affiliates of whom one, Georges Limbour, wrote to André Breton in 1929, "It would give me pleasure to see your nose bleed."[6]

When the surrealists surveyed the avant-garde, they did not embark on an anxious guessing game referred by posterity. They did not care whether a writer whom they had rescued from obscurity (Lautréamont) or one they themselves had discovered (Gisèle Prassinos) would catch the attention of observers whose criteria surely differ radically from their own. It did not bother them (very much, anyway) that a painter might end up, like Max Ernst, capable of biting the surrealist hand that had once fed him. It was of little or no concern to them that after a time an Eugène Ionesco or Fernando Arrabal might find that he could publish elsewhere than in surrealist magazines or that Antonin Artaud's concept of a theater of cruelty took him away from their ranks and enshrined him in the official avant-garde, thanks largely to the inability of enthusiasts to understand what he meant by *la cruauté*.

Meanwhile, no surrealist saw any cause for alarm in the discovery that Raymond Roussel was an admirer of Pierre Loti as well as of Jules Verne, that Clovis Trouille adored Titian and Giorgione. Nor were the surrealists disconcerted to learn that the work of each of these contemporaries betrays signs of the indebtedness frankly admitted by him. Surrealists did not seek to regiment the unofficial avant-garde or even that part of it they judged interesting. When they responded to solicitations from the work of certain artists in the van, they invariably revealed predispositions that in the final analysis are more enlightening than the commendation dispensed. This was true of André Breton's motives when he included Jean-Pierre Brisset in his anthology of black humor. As Breton saw it, Brisset's deeply serious writings introduce us to "a vertiginious succession of word equations" in which "great hallucinatory value" is to be detected.[7] Thus considering the writings of Brisset from the angle of quite involuntary humor enabled Breton to situate them along a line linking Jarry's Pataphysics with Dali's paranoiac-critical activity. And that line, of course, set in surrealist perspective everything it joined together.

"The fact is," writes Christopher Robinson in the preface to his 1980 volume *French Literature in the Twentieth Century*, "that Time imposes an orthodoxy of value judgments with which the prudent concur and against which the bold revolt."[8] In their stance before the vanguard, the surrealists never ceased being in bold revolt against accepted values. Indeed, remaining true to surrealism required them to go on being impenitently imprudent in their perspective on the avant-garde.

A 1931 snapshot taken at Hauterives is proof that André Breton made a pilgrimage of sorts to the Facteur Cheval's *Palais idéal*. Another photo, dating from 1949, confirms that he did so more than once.[9] Some observers will contend that in 1931 egocentricity or vanity drove Breton to strike a pose. These obviously are people who share the suspicion prompting Roger-Jean Ségalat to comment disparagingly when discussing a photograph dating from the same year.[10] Yet when he took up his pose with his head turned to the right, Breton—who never considered his facial features photogenic—displayed the heavy chin he detested. Moreover, he was photographed from far enough away to allow Cheval's baroque architecture to figure prominently in the picture. As a result, we are not free to concentrate exclusively on the man. We see him in a setting rather than against a background.

At first glance, the snapshot is nothing more than an example among many testifying to a mania for keeping photographic records that, far from being peculiar to André Breton, was shared by other members of the surrealist group. Yet the significance of the 1931 photo exceeds its documentary worth as a memento of a visit to Hauterives, complementing the poem entitled "Facteur Cheval," included the following year in Breton's verse collection *Le revolver à cheveux blancs* (The whitehaired revolver). Visually, it sets up an exchange between the poet and the builder. A communication is established that finally helps us learn more about the former than about the latter. In this regard, it is appropriate to attach special meaning to the picture of Breton at the Ideal Palace.

Of course, the placement of the camera and the angle from which Breton was caught in 1931 may have owed everything to the photographer's intentions and nothing to the wishes of his subject. Nevertheless, by raising no objection to reproduction of the snapshot in a selection of his own texts, accompanied by photographs of historical interest gathered by one of his followers, Breton approved its inclusion. If chance had had anything to do with the composition of the photographic image, then Breton gladly accepted the gift of *le hasard*, just as Buñuel did when filming the supper at the home of Viridiana's deceased uncle. The element of choice brings out the significance of Breton's decision to let himself be photographed (or of his wish to do so) in a physical environment externalizing another man's dream. It is worth emphasizing, therefore, that we see him *in* the Ideal Palace, not in front of it, like its creator and proprietor, who is dressed in a mailman's uniform and cap, in two photographs reproduced in Gilles Ehrmann's *Les inspirés et leurs demeures*.

If André Breton was content to appear framed by part of the building Ferdinand Cheval left behind, it was because he regarded the country mail carrier—who had died the very year the first surrealist manifesto appeared—as "the incontestable master of mediumistic architecture and sculpture."[11] For this reason, the architectural elements surrounding Breton and occupying the upper two-thirds of the 1931 photo do not confine him, even though they dominate the picture. The building's presence is testimony to the admiration Breton felt for Cheval's unique accomplishment. Looking again, we appreciate better that Breton was not attempting to strike a pose by any means. About to be photographed, he turned away from the camera toward the wall on his right, giving his full attention to the ideal palace. Examination of the snapshot preserved in *Poésie et autre*, which seems at first to demand that the viewer concentrate on a human figure, actually invites us to imitate the latter and to contemplate the work of Ferdinand Cheval. In other words, Breton does not impose himself on the palace. Instead, he is our link with it. We see and think about it because he wants us to look at and reflect on it.

Did Breton make the ideal palace his own, after the manner of Ado Kyrou, who made certain movies his own through an assimilative response to them? Not quite, perhaps. Yet the end result is analogous. For Breton tried no harder than Kyrou to arrive at a detached interpretation of the object of his attention, instead devoting himself entirely to the reaction it elicited from him. Perhaps then a comparable effect would have been achieved with less ambiguity if Breton had removed himself from camera range, allowing the photographer to concern himself exclusively with the ideal palace, as others have done, among them the surrealist Jacques B. Brunius in his film, *Violons d'Ingres* (1939). Certainly, avoiding the impression that André Breton was intruding upon the scene would have eliminated ambiguity. At the same time, though, the resulting photograph would have denied us the opportunity to witness Breton paying his respects to Ferdinand Cheval, acting in fact as a medium between viewers of the snapshot and the mailman's ideal palace.

Is it fair to say that Breton's presence, off center in the lower third of the photograph is essential to sharpening our awareness of and receptivity to Cheval's achievement? Clearly it is not. Even so, noticing this does not impose the conclusion that when all is said and done his presence is intrusive and must be condemned accordingly. At no time did any member of the surrealist group in France argue that approval by his companions and himself was necessary to the authentication of the Facteur Cheval's building any more than of Raymond Roussel's writings. To the surrealists, demanding more attention for an individual belonging to the unofficial avant-garde was never an attempt to engineer his or her promotion to a respected place in the official avant-garde. Without reluctance, they all would have acknowledged that such a person's contribution owes as much to his or her anticonformist instincts as to anything else. Urging universal or even broad acceptance would have been a superfluous gesture for which no unofficial vanguardist would have felt or expressed gratitude in any case.

Although not necessarily characteristic, the example of Raymond Roussel is enlightening. Recalling having attended the opening of two stage adaptations of Rousselian novels (*L'étoile au front* in 1924 and *La poussière de soleils* in 1926), Breton confessed without shame, "[I] certainly do not claim that the passionate approbation I gave the performance rested on an immediate understanding of the text sufficient in every detail."[12] Among the surrealists, full comprehension was never a prerequisite for admiration, any more than success in elucidating every detail was a condition of appreciation. What is more, they had no hard feelings upon hearing that Roussel found them to be "a little obscure."[13] In consequence, we should be unwise to conclude that Breton imagined he could induce all viewers of one or two photographs of himself, on the evidence these provided, to admit that the achievement of Ferdinand Cheval was important enough for them to take careful note of it. Persuasion was and had to remain an unattainable goal for someone as well aware as Breton that understanding eluded him and who, in addition, could not deny that the brief exegetical studies of Rousselian writing published by Brunius and even the longer pieces by another surrealist, Jean Ferry, were patently incomplete. Breton would never have presumed to attempt to explain the Ideal Palace. On the contrary, he would have regarded this as a profitless and, even more important, meaningless undertaking.

The 1949 snapshot taken of Hauterives lets us look down from above a Breton walking along a pathway in the Palace grounds, followed by an unidentified young woman (his daughter, Aube?). Like the 1931 photograph, this one is ambiguous. Similarly, too, it is open to interpretation as having little intrinsic appeal. Visiting Cheval's strange edifice, Breton could be described as having yielded to the curiosity that might prompt anyone passing through the Drome region of France to stop (though without any encouragement from the French tourists' vade mecum, the *Guide Michelin*, in which Hauterives is not mentioned), to look and snap a photo for the family album. Yet how many tourists would have shared his admiration— recorded in his preface to Ehrmann's photo collection—for people, Cheval among them, who have managed to "provoke the spectacular, saving explosion of desire"?[14] This question obliges us to separate the tourist mentality from the surrealist mind generating in "Belvédère" a typical Bretonian image that traces spectacle and salvation to their source in explosion.

How to account for that explosion without pausing over the word *desire*? And what hope is there of comprehending Breton's meaning if we fail to weigh the significance of desire in surrealist parlance? No sooner does this second question take form than we sense what really matters here. It is something at which the 1931 photograph appears to hint: that the value of the environment against which we catch sight of the author of the surrealist manifestoes relates to the meaning surrealism encouraged him to grant that same environment while he traveled—to borrow his own phrase—"from dream to reality." Cheval had made a discovery to which neither Breton nor any other surrealist could have remained indifferent: "The word impossible no longer exists." Whereas Cheval spoke of his dream, Breton preferred to talk of desire, not to contradict the Facteur or correct him but in order to indicate that, as a surrealist, he himself took dream and desire to be interchangeable, interpretable in terms that surrealism made available and pertinent.

Physical entry into the concrete expression of another man's dream (a dream realized, we learn from notes scrupulously kept by Cheval, with the use of four thousand sacks of whitewash and cement—a thousand cubic meters of masonry, "that is to say, 6000 francs") was not an invasion launched with a view to annexation. It meant, rather, penetrating a world which, to Breton's great satisfaction, instead of leading back to familiar reality, carried him forward under impetus from desire to a reality transcending the familiar, for which he and Philippe Soupault had chosen the name surreality.

Now this does not compel us to suppose that, with André Breton in the lead, the French surrealists regarded Ferdinand Cheval as one of their own, and Raymond Roussel as another. Yet Roussel's unyielding refusal to join the Paris group never led them to complain and certainly did nothing to erode their respect for his achievement. If obscurity on their side helped convince Roussel to keep his distance from surrealism, obscurity in his published texts did nothing to undermine their confidence in him. On the contrary, no doubt, Rousselian writing's impenetrability to rational explication contributed substantially to the fascination it exerted over the surrealists. We surely may include the latter among the "small number of minds on the outside" mentioned in Breton's essay, "Fronton virage," as being attracted to works subversive, unusual, "or simply 'difficult'" (p. 9). In Breton's estimation, at all events, the writings of Roussel belong next to a certain number of poetic works valued for the power they have to appeal to "a faculty other than intelligence" (p. 14). And this is so even though, in the case of Rousselian writing, Breton had to admit to moving around it as if it were "a fascinating machine for which we did not know the use" (p. 16).

In the circumstances, Breton could not expect Ferry to have explicated the six hundred lines of Nouvelles impressions d'Afrique discussed in Une étude sur Raymond Roussel. Instead, he made a point of stressing that the enigma of the Rousselian message studied by Ferry remains complete "and even thanks to him becomes incomparably more pressing."[15] Breton's reaction to Roussel complements his reaction to Ferdinand Cheval, as he writes apropos of the former, "One dreams, in the presence of certain deliberately veiled works, of entering, after analyzing then, into possession of a secret owing nothing to previous knowledge, largely divulged or not."[16]

By his faith in a faculty other than intelligence as laying the groundwork for response Breton's allusion to a machine fascinating in the measure that its use cannot be divined is brought into proximity to his reference to works embodying an unexplained secret. Breton did not put a name to that faculty while discussing Roussel. Indeed, he never defined it except obliquely, as when, for instance, he recalled in *Nadja* one of his visits to the flea market at Saint-Ouen in search of "those objects one finds nowhere else, outdated, fragmented, unusuable, almost incomprehensible, perverse, in short, in the sense that I understand and like."[17] As an example, in *Nadja* he cited a sort of irregular half-cylinder, presenting bumps and hollows "without significance for me." Close examination dissipated its mystery, however, as Breton guessed he had purchased some kind of statistical record of the population of an unidentified town. Therefore, even though he reproduced a photograph of it in his book, the object in question evidently no longer appealed to him. Its perversity had been drained away by its utilitarian function, as the purchaser was obliged to "admit" regretfully to its usefulness.

For Breton the regrettable connection between utility and the existence of an unfamiliar object was established on the plane of rationally explicable function. The latter intervened between him and the appeal of the "perverse" as a challenge to the notion that practicality is the only admissible raison d'être for manmade things. In contrast, the Facteur Cheval's ideal palace would have appealed to a faculty different from intelligence in the man who had written the surrealist manifestoes, if only because it was patently uninhabitable—like the glass castle imagined by Breton himself.

Raising the question of the surrealist attitude toward found objects in the course of a discussion of the avant-garde, we may appear to have wandered from our main concern. Yet to the surrealists the interest of objects presenting a "perverse" aspect—but not of all found objects, by any means—bears comparison with the value they ascribed to the work of a few, but not all, vanguard artists. The attraction of the unofficial avant-garde was not merely its unquestionable status as outsider art. Like that of the perverseness of this or that object discovered by chance, its fascination lay in its ability to elicit favorable response in the surrealist mind.

The surrealists never took it upon themselves to authenticate the achievement of one vanguardist or another. Nor for that matter did any one of them seek to claim credit, to a greater or lesser extent, for whatever that artist had managed to accomplish. This is why adherents to surrealist principles were neither disgruntled not offended when an individual creative artist, having earned their respect, shied away from association

with them. He or she was, in their eyes, no more responsible
to surrealism than an object that stimulated their imagination
could take credit for the perverse quality it displayed. In order
for the surrealist mind to react sympathetically to the work
of a few artists, it would have been no more necessary for those
same artists to be dedicated to the pursuit of surrealist aspirations than for an object found in a flea market to be aware
that its attraction to the surrealist mind lay in its being perverse,
in the sense (never precisely defined) that Breton gave the word.

In none of the pronouncements coming down to us from
within the surrealist movement on the subject of avant-garde
art—whether broadly or narrowly defined—can evidence be detected that the purpose was to recruit converts to the cause
of surrealism. From the outset, it was plain to members of the
Paris group that they would never be successful in inducing
a fiercely independent vanguardist like Raymond Roussel to
pledge allegiance to surrealism or even, more significantly, to
persuade him to see some benefit in consorting with men and
women who had already taken that step. What hope, then, could
they have had of drawing into their circle a man as unsophisticated as Ferdinand Cheval?

It is a waste of effort to presume that André Breton or any
other surrealist was consumed with proselytizing ardor and for
this reason directed his energy from time to time to advancing
the purposes of surrealism by publishing remarks about peripheral artists, despite the fact that seeking widespread acceptance
for such an individual was a thankless task, sure to fail. Only
when we detect in surrealist commentary on the avant-garde
proof of compulsion rather than of strategy do we perceive its
true value, appreciating now what is to be learned from the
things the surrealists had to say. Only then can we expect to
be able to set the surrealist viewpoint in perspective.

Passing judgment on the position taken by the surrealists and
on its consequences would seem likely to commit us to siding
with or against them. It would be necessary to decide, apparently, whether the avant-garde in which they were interested
and which they defended so vigorously was more or less worthy
than the official one to be designated the true vanguard. In
such a process, we risk being led to conclude, one way or the
other, on the basis of sympathy or antipathy for surrealism.
As for evaluating, instead, on the basis of taste—contrasting
the surrealists' taste with the critics—none of the surrealists
would have recommended or even condoned our taking this

step. All of them would have been too sensitive to the danger of employing a substantive that, opening the door on aesthetic criteria, would have clouded the issue in their estimation, if not confused it entirely.

To many who pause to examine it the surrealist perspective on the avant-garde is no more than a curiosity, unlikely to affect their own attitude, let alone modify it radically. Or again the surrealist attitude vis-à-vis general tendencies in the evolution of poetry and painting may seem indicative of preoccupation with peripheral phenomena, too far removed from central concerns to influence these to any measurable extent. Others, of course, will dismiss that attitude as fundamentally mistaken and therefore unworthy of their attention. Yet demonstrating (or claiming, for that matter) that the surrealists' outlook was right or wrong, profitable or misleading, is less pertinent by far than acknowledging that they were firmly confident of being in the right. If we acknowledge, further, their privilege to judge in the way they did, we are better placed to grasp how their judgment of the avant-garde sheds light on the surrealist mind.

9

"A Certain Point of the Mind"

André Breton opened his *Second manifeste du surréalisme* with the assertion that surrealism would have to be recognized as having tended to provoke an intellectual and moral *"crisis of consciousness"* (p. 152). From the intellectual point of view, he went on, surrealism's task was to make people aware of "the meretricious character of the old antinomies hypocritically intended to forestall any restlessness on the part of man, if only by giving him a poor idea of the means available to him, by defying him to escape in valid measure from universal constraint."

So much space, subsequently, went to recrimination and complaint that Breton's second manifesto is best remembered even today as a quarrelsome polemical work, abusing old allies gone over to the enemy by 1929, its tone later regretted by the author himself. The *Second manifeste* has contributed substantially to establishing Breton's reputation as an irascible man, tolerating no criticism, even from friends and associates. Yet—and this deserves to be said, despite the vagueness we have already encountered in Breton's phrase "in valid measure"—it stands as a far more valuable document than has been widely acknowledged. Its merit lies as much in what it does not state openly, in its involuntary revelations, as in what it actually tells us.

Who intended certain unspecified antinomies to keep man confined? And by what authority did André Breton dismiss as hypothetical the intent in question? We are never told, although evidently objectivity was not a criterion that mattered to Breton. His second manifesto reflects a frame of mind distinctive of surrealism's principal theoretician. For this reason, the words we have just read help prepare us for a celebrated declaration made later in the very same paragraph: "Everything leads to the belief that there exists a certain point of the mind from which life and death, real and imaginary, past and future, communicable and incommunicable, high and low cease to be perceived in contradiction. Now it would be futile to seek in surrealist activity any motive other than the hope of determining that point" (p. 154).

It is obvious that Breton's statement raises a number of questions without answering even one of them. The effect might be described as follows. The writer begins one step into his argument, asserting that everything leads to a belief without first asking if anything leads in that direction. Apparently, instead of heading off objections, he seeks to circumvent them. The precariousness of his argumentation when it is set on a rational plane cannot escape notice. We observe that he has come full circle: from belief to belief, instead of from hypothesis to reasonable deduction and defensible conclusion. Moreover, the pattern is consistent with the one laid down in the 1924 *Manifeste du surréalisme*, which opens assertively with the statement that man is a dreamer once and for all.

In other theoretical texts, as much as in his manifestoes, André Breton's method was to bypass conflict, ignore controversy, and move directly to an implied appeal for complicity. Seeking some explanation for that pattern, we can begin by reminding ourselves that to the surrealists for whom Breton spoke, the mind was not an instrument of measured evaluation or judgment. Nor was it the place where evidence is to be weighed dispassionately while its merits and demerits are subjected to detached scrutiny.

The mind was not the seat of reason to the surrealists. So they favored art that was anti-intellectual in nature. For this reason, Breton spoke of an intellectual crisis of consciousness. His outlook was profoundly influenced by the fact that art took on meaning in surrealism to the extent that, created in defiance of intellectual demands, upon completion, being antireasonable, it lent itself to scrutiny for which intellectual evaluation was untrained. Yet all surrealists were aware that the mind of modern Western man, living in a post-Cartesian world, has been invaded by reason. And they agreed that the effect upon twentieth-century man has been quite baleful. Of necessity, they were launched—as Breton described them—on the reconquest of the original powers of the mind, of faculties uncontaminated by rationality. They were eager to see the rational sequence in thought disrupted. They showed themselves particularly receptive to modes of expression that severed or seemed likely to break contact with rational thought processes.

Viewed from a rational perspective, therefore, the surrealist mind appeared committed to adamant nonacceptance. Meanwhile, seen from the perspective peculiar to surrealism, it was devoted to emancipation, treating nonacceptance as no less necessary than positive in effect. This is to say that the surrealist mind did not conceive of its responsibilities as reflecting standards set by reason but as disposing of the limitations prescribed by those standards.

To contend that in his comments on the certain point of the mind Breton failed to act responsibly betrays an inability to recognize where he felt sure his responsibility lay. It was not that he wished to conduct his presentation in a manner defiant of reason. Rather his approach was posited, as usual, on a denial of the relevance of reason to the belief from which his assumptions stemmed. He cannot be said to have used his objections to reasonable argument as an excuse for being unreasonable, for he regarded reason as impertinent to the human predicament and to its solution.

The thought process reflected in Breton's remarks about the liberative point of the mind was nondeductive, intuitive. It neither rose out of rational premises nor was erected rationally. The key elements were belief and desire, both antagonistic to rationality. The *Second manifeste* mentions on the very same page the "certain point of the mind" and a particular "mental place." On the succeeding page occurs an allusion to "the desire to proceed beyond insufficiency, the absurd distinction between beautiful and ugly, true and false, good and evil." The fact is of course that there is nothing absurd about a distinction generally accepted as incontestable, except that it separates where André Breton wished to see separation suppressed.

The early part of the second surrealist manifesto bears witness to "the frame of mind that we call surrealist and that one sees in this way concerned with itself" (p. 156). Breton's line of thought is governed throughout the passage in question less by reasoned argument than by desire, the supreme motivation for human action, according to surrealist doctrine. Thus the benefits of reaching the point of the mind are listed (though not exhaustively identified) in the subordinate clause of a sentence that directs attention forward, beyond the main clause, "Tout porte à croire que. . . ." The reader is enticed by desire—the possibility of wish fulfillment extending ahead of him—beyond protest or even hesitation into the realm of desire where the foundation of belief is laid. Or, to phrase things a little differently, nothing disposes us to agree with Breton unless we already share the belief he claims to be well-founded.

The *Second manifeste* represents surrealism as undertaking to "try the notions of reality and unreality, of reason and unreason, of reflection and impulse, of knowledge and 'fatal' ignorance, of the useful and the useless, etc" (pp. 170–71). It is apparent that the trial will take place in the court of "thought once and for all broken in to negation and to the negation of negation" (p. 171). What does this mean, precisely? Things begin to fall into place when we acknowledge that, despite the surrealists' preference for the word *irrational*, the surrealist mind functioned antirationally rather than irrationally. Its activity expressed the deep-seated conviction that thought must be freed from the impediments of reason, of the restrictions laid by reason on imaginative development. Meanwhile surealists were convinced that imagination had to be permitted complete freedom of operation so as to establish between man and ambient reality a relationship expressive of his desires.

Naturally, there was no possibility of reconciliation between people content with a perspective on reality provided and, they felt confident, assured by reason and, on the other side, those who in the name of the surrealist quest located in fulfillment of desire a harmony between man and his world which the others neither required nor saw cause to seek. The one group were content to accept the world as interpreted rationally. The other started out in the name of surrealism from the presupposition that reason places unwarranted limits on reality, more particularly on the relationship of reality to man's needs. The surrealists' objection to reason was from the first that it resisted full satisfaction of those needs. Hence seeking grounds for agreement with anyone placing trust in reason was pointless. Instead, the surrealists regarded radical departure from commonly accepted evaluative norms as not only permissible but mandatory, if their dearest aspirations were to be realized. Reaching the goals they proposed for themselves was not simply preferable to resigning themselves to the status quo carrying reason's approval. Participating in surrealism meant looking upon the pursuit of those goals as an inescapable obligation.

This was a distinguishing feature of the surrealist mind that, far from being cast adrift without purpose or direction in irrationality, it found both pleasure and stimulation in investigative techniques deliberately chosen or developed expressly for the purpose of defeating rationality. The surrealist mind's revolt against the narrow confinement of rational sequential thinking was a purposeful one. Within the surrealist camp, its consequences were not deemed haphazard, even when a technique commanding respect had been discovered quite by accident. This was because the surrealists ascribed to chance a beneficent role in the affairs of man whenever they saw it bringing into focus the capacity of the human mind to resist the limitations of rationalism. They judged it essential to the efficient and productive operation of the surrealist mind that it be cognizant at all times of the necessity to oppose rationality, fully aware of the degree of success it had attained at any given moment by implementing a favored creative technique in overthrowing rationalism and undermining man's confidence in reason as a responsible and reliable arbiter, capable of making sense in a way that all of us can and must accept.

Attaining the certain point of mind is not beyond human capability, surrealism taught. It simply marks progress that held meaning for the surrealist as long as he remained assured that the mind is not the seat of reason. Because therefore in modern Occidental culture the mind is generally identified with a rationalist point of view on man and his world, the surrealists had to acknowledge their task as embracing, from first to last, the liberation of the mind's activity from the confinement placed on it by reason. They realized that surrealism would not come fully into its own until that frustrating stage had been surpassed at which our rationalist education requires us to respect a number of contradictions. All the latter, we notice when reading the second surrealist manifesto, are constrictive. They impose on past experience and on our projections for the future boundaries which reason demands that we tolerate, however regretfully, and which desire prompts us to wish to see cast down.

As they perceived it, the surrealists were not preaching distortion of the mind. They were not bending it out of shape, either, in a foolhardy and inadmissible attempt to render it serviceable in an unprecedented way. They were convinced that their dominant ambitions were bringing them to a more adequate realization of the potentiality of the human mind, to better appreciation of its capabilities than is possible so long as the mind is regarded as fulfilling its prescribed function by meeting the demands of rationalism. In furthering the cause of surrealism, its defenders never doubted for an instant that they were aspiring to reach, after identifying it, the point at which the mind works with maximum efficiency. And efficiency in the context of surrealism meant for the mind operating outside the retarding influence of reason.

An essential feature of the announcement about the point of the mind in which the surrealists placed trust is that Breton's presentation was consistent with his view of the mind and reason as elements so dissociated that the productive activity of the former is impaired the moment the latter is allowed to influence imaginative play. In the opinion of the surrealists, the mind fills its emancipative role when it ventures outside the limits prescribed by reason in its interpretation of man's relations with himself and with his environment, penetrating a zone where imaginative play sets up relationships beyond the scope of rational association. At this stage, reason is not merely to be ignored; it is superseded, no longer serving as the instrument by which man tries to come to terms with the world around him. In spite of this, however, we arrive at an incomplete impression of the range of the surrealist mind as long as we go no further than recognizing its antagonism to rationality. Examination of the text of the *Second manifeste* makes clear that we miss the full import of the concept of the point of the mind, as well as of the manner in which that concept is brought before the reader, if we see here nothing beyond additional proof of the incompatibility of rationality and the surrealist outlook.

We come closer to appreciating the import of the concept if we consider just how it is formulated. Doing so requires attention to two features of Breton's text in particular: the argumentation, so to speak, and the language utilized for the conveyance of ideas.

With someone other than André Breton, attempting to analyze how his manifesto is put together would surely bring us up against a discernible strategy consciously used to conduct an argument. In the case of Breton's text, contempt for reason and for reasoned discourse is not the only complicating factor. Of course, the distinction between argumentation and language is somewhat false, possessing no virtue but that of convenience. Language takes its function from argument, after all. Nevertheless, this distinction is useful in this instance, given that one cannot speak of Breton's strategy with all the confidence one normally would enjoy when reviewing a manifesto composed and presented for public consumption.

No sooner do we concentrate on argumentation than it be-

comes plain that the word argument does not apply to the passage in the *Second manifeste du surréalisme* about the special
point of the mind. The opening phrase, "Tout porte à croire,"
suffices to indicate that the term is of questionable applicability.
Everything leads to a belief, we are informed. All the evidence
points in one direction, we are assured, even though we are
given no idea of the nature of the evidence. We are not permitted
to judge its persuasiveness for ourselves. Affirmation, not argumentation, serves to deny us the opportunity to test hypotheses
or even be convinced of their validity.

Reviewing Breton's declaration from the beginning, we notice
how the opening phrase, "Everything leads to the belief that . . ."
avoids personal reference. If we were to supply a pronoun absent
from the French, it would most likely be, "me" or "us." Two
versions then result. In the first, remaining modestly personal,
Breton would be speaking solely for himself. In the second (the
choice of Richard Searver and Helen R. Lane in a published
American translation) we could not be sure whether he was
speaking for the surrealist group only, or for mankind in general.
As it stands, Breton's initial assertion is intriguingly ambiguous.
It lends itself to three interpretations, potentially broad enough
to affirm general agreement and to invite the complicity of all
readers.

Looking back to the first surrealist manifesto, we discover
that a similarly structured phrase, "Cela donnerait à croire
que . . ." (p. 49) may be read as supposing total agreement on
the part of Breton's audience. It is followed closely by the very
construction isolated above in the *Second manifeste*. Now, referring to surrealism, Breton asserts, "Everything leads to the belief
that it acts on the mind the way narcotics do" (p. 51). There
is a major difference, all the same. In his original manifesto
Breton cannot be denied the right to make authoritative declarations about the effect of surrealism. In his second, generalization
presents as authoritative a statement asserting universal agreement without having demonstrated it. Are we to conclude that
the *Second manifeste* brings before us a stylistic device, used
to rhetorical effect? One might reply unhesitatingly in the affirm-
ative, sure of having caught Breton in the act of manipulating
reader response. Yet we are dealing with a writer already convinced of certain presuppositions even before he ascribes them
to anyone else. To attribute Breton's use of language to the requirements of rhetorical play simplifies the mental state in
which he wrote about the point of the mind.

Pausing over Breton's declaration, one might choose to look at it exclusively in the context of rhetoric. Examined this way, it is of passing interest only. Furthermore, its significance is obscured by considerations that divert attention from essentials. True, André Breton was a stylist whose language never betrayed negligence or insensitivity, and certainly never mental confusion. All the same, one can think of no occasion, in his writings, when concern for rhetoric takes precedence over conviction. Where rhetorical devices are plainly visible—and Breton made no effort to conceal them—they are always placed at the service of truth as he saw it and wished to share it with others. Treating "Tout porte à croire" as empty phrase, used for effect but without conviction, misleads us thoroughly.

To see the situation without bias, we have to notice that rhetoric in the *Second manifeste* as much as anywhere else in Breton's theoretical writings testifies to a mental attitude typical of the writer and representative of the surrealists. His theoretical works offer valuable indications of his outlook, linking aspiration, desire, and extrarational assertion in a projection from which the possibility of failure and disappointment is precluded. To hold Breton blameworthy for the claims he made when discussing the point of the mind leads to an inaccurate assessment of the significance of the language he employed. It impedes understanding his statements as testimony to the frame of mind in which he wrote.

The things we read at the beginning of the second surrealist manifesto would be less enlightening if we had in front of us nothing more significant than an attempt to draw readers onto ground where only a surrealist could keep his footing. We miss the most revealing aspect of Breton's text if we suppose him to have been practicing a manipulative verbal technique designed to trick his audience into accepting a viewpoint which, left to themselves, they would never share. Even so, the phrasing of the declaration about the point of the mind is such that objection to Breton's ideas places in a minority position anyone disagreeing with them. Having claimed that all the evidence supported his belief, André Breton left it up to the dissenters to present their case in defiance to the evidence. All the same, he did not begin to hint at the nature of that evidence. He did not even indicate which kind of evidence was 100 percent supportive of his belief. He simply declined to dignify dissent by taking issue with it. If all the evidence favors his belief, we infer, then seeking counterevidence is fruitless, just as it is foolish to contend that some actually exists.

Instead of hunting for signs of dialectical strategy in the Bretonian text, we ought to recognize the value of the short passage about the liberative point of the mind. The important factor is that Breton wrote not as an outsider speculating on the properties and potential of the surrealist mind, but as an insider whose ideas and their formulation came directly from that mind. The author of the surrealist manifestoes adopted the surrealist attitude without either reservation or hesitation. Doing so left no room for discussion, for positing objections or taking account of and dealing with any of them. This is the truly striking thing about Breton's statement with reference to the point of the mind: it pushed dispute aside, proceeding beyond argument to the level at which debatable hypotheses became incontrovertible truths.

Was plausibility André Breton's goal? Did he merely hope to get away with saying things that would impress his readers because he had the knack of turning a felicitous phrase? No sooner do we attempt to ward off the beguiling effects of such turns of phrase than we find the central issue has nothing to do, finally, with Breton's prose style or his sense of rhythm in the phrase. Here is the important discovery brought on by perusal of his second manifesto: he did not resort to blandishments, seeing no reason to persuade his audience to share his viewpoint in preference to any conflicting one. Breton was sure he was stating truths beyond debate. His impatience with opponents and contempt for former allies who had fallen by the wayside were less signs of an irritable temperament than indications of one central feature of the operation of the surrealist mind. That mind was so sure of itself that to engage in discussion—foreseeing and attempting to forestall objections—appeared quite superfluous. Being convinced of the truth of the ideas engendered by surrealist thinking left Breton not only without sympathy for anyone unreceptive to them but also of the opinion that dialogue was a waste of time. One does not weigh the pros and cons of truth. One subscribes to it and seeks to build upon it, without seriously entertaining the notion that anybody reacting responsibly could possibly raise skeptical questions or have reservations. Breton's reputation for intransigence, from which many have inferred that he was uncontrollably arrogant, owes much to an outlook that drew upon faith in surrealism as distilling truths beyond challenge.

If we must dismiss the idea that Breton aimed at plausibility, it is largely because he did not try to sway those whose thought processes diverged from his own—not merely because their thinking was governed by rationalism but because they accepted life as it appeared to be and therefore were guilty, as he put it, of resignation. Breton's own confidence in the emancipative point of the mind was nourished by his refusal to resign himself to an existence marked by anguish resulting from the necessity to take one choice (reality, shall we say) to the exclusion of another (dream, for instance). The *Second manifeste* reveals that the surrealists claimed the right and privilege to use the mind in a way not commonly acceptable to all. In their revolt against established customs in mental activity, the element most easily perceptible to outsiders was their rejection of rationalism. Just as important, though, as defeating reason and refuting the assertions it inspired was, in the surrealists' estimation, availing themselves of the benefits of the analogical principle. In this connection, perceptions enjoyed at the illuminating point of the mind facilitated detection of enlightening parallels and analogies. These cast down the barriers within which, in its reasoning mode, the mind is accustomed to propose hard and fast categories.

Surrealist thinking was dissident thinking, fired not by compromise or resignation but by rejection of the idea that the outer world, termed reality, exists separately from the inner world of consciousness.

All we learn about the surrealist mind appears distorted if we fail to keep one fact in sight. The surrealists did not pride themselves on having a mind different from anyone else. From their standpoint, the critical difference was that of the level of perception. Breton referred to this when he posited a certain point of the mind. In the final analysis—and yet this was the surrealists' starting point—the surrealist mind was the mind of man coming to profitable terms with objective reality at a certain point of perception. As that was the point where antinomies and contradictions disappeared, it was the one where the surreal eliminated altogether the negative effects of the real—transcending, then, a sense of frustration in the resolution of contradictions and the neutralization of negative forces under pressure from positive ones the surrealists regarded as within man's reach, as within the operative capacity of the human mind.

The long-term optimism of the surrealist outlook—unaffected by lack of success in the short term—was the result of the sur-

realists' conviction that the mind is capable of coming to terms
with reality beneficiently. And this conclusion seemed valid
for all men, not simply for a few. Despite the fear that surrealist doctrine would become contaminated (displayed by André
Breton especially), the long-term view involved all mankind
in release from limitations to which, to the surrealists' dismay,
so many people appeared entirely acquiescent.

André Breton did not claim in his second manifesto that things
truly are different once one has reached a certain point of the
mind. He stressed perception, the surrealist grasp on things.
As he did so, he intimated that the point of the mind so important to him and his associates was one to which the individual
accedes from the moment when fundamental antinomies no
longer appear as they did before, in contradiction. The things
themselves have not changed. What had come under modification is the individual's ability to respond or react to them. Things
might still remain contradictory, Breton's text allows us to infer
without actually telling us this. No matter, their contradiction
has been effaced from the mind that manages to perceive them
in reconciliation. The contradiction subsists but has lost its capacity to impress itself upon the mind in which perception
has resolved the conflict or contrast between them.
    The surrealist mind reconciled man and the world about
him, but in its own way. And since the mind belongs to man,
this meant that the world was meaningful, to the surrealist,
insofar as it coexists harmoniously with man. When Breton
talked of resolving certain antimonies, therefore, he was looking
forward to the day when the outer world would exist in a relationship acceptable to the mind of man. He never promised
to dispose of contradictions and antinomies. Nor did he hope
to do so. He felt that a great enough victory would have been
won the day nobody was aware of them any more, no longer
bound to take them into account. That day the outer world
would be adjusted to the inner world instead of the inner being
submissive to the outer.
    The optimism of surrealism (which, noticeably, outlasted its
defenders' faith in political solutions to the problems of human
existence) rested on the surrealists' faith in man's ability to
improve his perception of the world even when he cannot amel-
iorate the social conditions of human existence. Dwelling on
the failure of surrealism to effect a balance between idealistic
ambition and political activism, commentators seemed not to
have noticed that this failure was an object lesson to the sur-

realists. French surrealists learned enough from their foray into politics, during the years immediately preceding appearance of the 1929 manifesto, to satisfy themselves that solutions reached in the mind were more valuable and longer lasting than solutions of a sociopolitical nature. Failure, then, is an inappropriate term. The abandonment of hope in a political solution more accurately describes the step taken by the surrealists when turning away from material solutions.

The images found worthy of praise in the surrealist circle are anticipative, even annunciatory. They arise in the mind of the reader or spectator when "two realities" are brought together, as Breton described their operation in his first manifesto. It is evident from the effect of their conjunction upon the mind— which, the *Manifeste du surréalisme* insists, "has, to begin with, grasped nothing consciously" (p. 52)—that surrealist images make their initial impression at a point of consciousness other than the point of the mind mentioned in the *Second manifeste*. Surrealist verbal and pictorial images mark stages along the path to the point Breton confidently discussed.

There are, in consequence, two directions from which surrealist imagery may be examined and its quality judged. We may estimate the distance from familiar reality that our imagination is invited to travel by an image challenging to conventional views and commonplace assumptions. Alternatively, we may calculate the success of the image in revolting against familiar perspectives, estimating how far our response still needs to advance before it will demonstrate that perception that Breton took to be the signal benefit enjoyed by everyone who has gained access to a very special point of the mind. For an image in surrealism demonstrates its creator's achievement, not merely his will to achieve, in the area of mental enfranchisement. It indicates how far he or she still needed to travel, as much as it proved how far he or she had come already. At worst, the surrealist's image is proof of the limitations of his mind. At best, it offers glimpses of his capacity for self-liberation.

Surrealist imagery was a promise of what was to come, yet no more than a promise. The perspective in which it took on value, for the surrealists themselves, was influenced by current conditions of conception and understanding. In other words, the surrealists judged their own images by reference to a sense of loss, of deprivation, in relation to their consciousness of what was depressingly lacking in life. For this reason Breton spoke in his first manifesto of "a miraculous compensation" in which he placed the fullest confidence: "It is up to a marvelous com-

pensation to intervene—and it does intervene," he assured his
readers (p. 48). This is to say that the surrealists gauged the
success of their imagery from their departure point in dissatisfaction with the conditions of human life. Had they been able
to measure, instead, from the point of the mind mentioned in
the *Second manifeste*, the word "compensation" would have
had no meaning. It would have been inapplicable to a situation
in which perception surmounted all sense of incompleteness,
shortage, and failure. Thus although in harmony with desire,
projecting the world in greater accord with aspiration, the surrealist image remained compensatory. Yet it still could not be
said to exist as proof of the final transcendence of inner conflict,
attained at an advanced level of consciousness where no opposition would be perceptible any longer.

Breton did not pretend that surrealism was capable of disposing of contradictions that weigh on human experience. He spoke
of surmounting these in a manner, he implied, that renders
depressing antinomies powerless to restrain the imagination.
His train of thought was consistent with the following view:
"Perception and representation . . . are to be taken for the *products of dissociation of one, original faculty.* . . ." Making this
assertion in his *Point du jour* (1934), Breton added, "This state
of grace, all those who are concerned to define the true condition
of man aspire more or less confusedly to *find again.*"[1] He returned to the same topic in his lecture at Yale University on
10 December 1942: "For surrealism—and it is my opinion that
one day this will be its pride—everything will have served
to reduce those oppositions wrongly presented as insurmountable, deplorably dug over the ages, and the real alembics of
suffering: the opposition of madness and so-called reason that
refuses to take account of the irrational, the opposition of dream
to the "action" that believes it can mark dream with futility,
the opposition of mental representation to physical perception. . . ."[2] Breton, we notice, spoke consistently of a point of
the mind determinable by its effects.

What we have observed already—that Breton's assertions
about the point of the mind in which he placed faith grew out of
belief and ended in the motivating hope of determining—makes
it clear that those for whom he spoke did not start out with
the comforting assurance of having already attained that point.
They took encouragement and found motivation in their trust
in the determinability of a point from which phenomena commonly thought to oppose one another are perceived in harmony.
But that trust could scarcely be described as imperturbable.

In his essay "Limites non frontières du surréalisme" (based on a lecture delivered in London on the occasion of the 1936 International Exhibition of Surrealism), Breton betrayed the need to believe that had already made him a believer. After referring to "all the antinomies which, having existed before the form of social regime under which we live, are very likely not to disappear with it," he continued, "These antinomies require us to exert ourselves to remove them because they are felt cruelly . . . and because this suffering must not find man, any more than the other one, resigned. These antinomies are those of waking and sleeping (of reality and dream), of reason and madness, of objective and subjective, of perception and representation, of past and future, of the collective sense and of love, of life and death even."[3] Expansion of a list of contradictions familiar to us only brings out more clearly the essential question to which Breton's various statements all direct attention: where is the liberative point of the mind located?

It is evident that André Breton spoke of the emancipative point of the mind not as an excuse or to justify surrealist activity on the creative plane, but as granting significance to that activity and to its products, as rendering their evaluation possible. The curious thing is that in his *Second manifeste,* we encounter a contrast between the precision of the assertive phrase about the existence of the point of the mind (it is a certain point) and the uncertainty in which readers find themselves as soon as they ask where, exactly, they can expect to come upon that point. Is it located higher than intelligence, for instance? Or does it command our attention at a level below that occupied by reason?

It goes without saying that, to the surrealists, the point of the mind to which Breton drew attention was desirable. But was it attainable? Breton appears to have been inclined to skirt the question. All we can deduce from his writings is that the location of the point from which contradictions and antinomies ceased to be perceptible lay between the current inharmony and the harmony after which all surrealists yearned and of which they hoped for glimpses. It was situated, in other words, somewhere along a line connecting present dissatisfaction with ultimate full satisfaction. So far so good. But the important element, lending the surrealist perspective its distinctive features, was the value surrealists accorded harmony and satisfaction, as they distinguished between perception confirming rational prejudice and that which eliminated reason, denying its perti-

nence to man's relationship with the world around him and
with his desires. As neither harmony nor satisfaction of desire,
nor even desire itself, was closely defined in surrealist pronouncements, the special feature of the point in which all surrealists placed their faith was its elusiveness.

The assured manner in which André Breton referred to the
existence of the reconciliative point of the mind is not to be
taken as having reduced other surrealists' task to moving forward, with greater or lesser speed, from the present, point A,
to the future, a definite point B. The complexity of the surrealist
venture and the variety of artistic manifestations surviving from
it cannot be interpreted as proof that Breton and his companions
were seeking a fixed point from which each and every creative
artist in the surrealist group might estimate his distance the
moment he started out, subsequently checking his progress quite
accurately as he went along. The location of the illuminating
point varied from individual to individual, and even from moment to moment. At one time, its attainment might seem imminent, while at another it appeared no better than a remote
possibility. Never could a surrealist boast of being able to reach
it at will, when wishing to do so.

How to locate the point of the mind and attain it? This was,
in essence, the program the surrealists laid out for themselves.
The progression ascribed in the *Second manifeste* to those working for the surrealist cause called for advance from belief in
the existence of the liberative point of the mind to attainment
of that same point—from belief to its validation by proof, out
of trust into certainty, from promise to its fulfillment. However,
when we examine Breton's text, we perceive that the substantive
he employs, *determination*, lends itself to two interpretations.
First, it refers to the act of fixing the point in question. Second,
it alludes to bringing about a certain point of the mind so that
ultimately it exists because the individual has brought it into
existence. Thus our confidence in the surrealist undertaking
depends on our willingness to grant its participants the privilege
of searching for a point, of moving toward its establishment
more or less haphazardly, and more or less successfully.

Throughout its history, surrealist experimental endeavor was
sustained by hope of finding and reaching the liberative point
of the mind. The vitality of surrealist experimentation found
stimulus in the artist's awareness that the point was elusive,
to be sought again and again with every new experiment. Thus

struggle, not serenity, was the condition of surrealist creative action. A noteworthy feature of Breton's pronouncement on the subject of the point of the mind was that it offered surrealists no guarantees. Instead, it placed squarely on the individual's shoulders the onus of attaining the desired point and of proving he had done so by way of perceptions reflected in his creations.

In the postface to his *Aube à l'antipode* (published in 1966), Alain Jouffroy recalled an early moment of illumination he had experienced, representing his later poetic effort as directed a recapturing a privileged moment of revelation. Breton's attitude, in contrast, was far more typical of the surrealists'. Looking foward to discovery, not back. André Breton demonstrated faith in the future and in man's future place in the world. Nevertheless, he agreed with Jouffroy in locating salvation within man. Both had confidence in the individual's capacity, on a certain plane of response, to resolve in ways acceptable to himself conflicts apparent in the universe and in the human situation.

Consistently, from his first surrealist manifesto onward, Breton related progress to man's ability to advance under his own power, to find for himself. Thus because they related salvatory action of man's imagination to the powers of the mind, surrealists found the impetus to move forward in the direction where they were sure perception would be the agent of transformation. This explains Breton's allusion in his second manifesto to "that mental place from which one can no longer undertake except for oneself a perilous but, we think, a supreme reconnaissance . . ." (p. 154). The obligation to push forward toward the point of the mind rested with each individual surrealist, to be accepted for himself alone. Pursuit of the reconciliative point of the mind never reduced surrealist creative activity to stereotypy (condemned by André Breton as earlty as the *Manifeste du surréalisme*). Instead, it authenticated a variety of endeavor while still assuring variety well-defined unity of purpose. In the surrealist artist, responsibility to seek the point of the mind that could free perception was an obligation to the self, not to a tenet of doctrine. Yet it bore witness to needs that, although personal, were also experienced in common with those of other participants in the surrealists movement.

The surrealist did not follow Breton in accepting the notion of the point of the mind just because they thought doing so would allow them to pretend that no oppositions, conflicts, or antinomies existed in human affairs. Nor for that matter did they expect attainment of that point to remove these. For them, salvation lay in surmounting obstacles to happiness through perception. The only obligation to which the artist had to submit was self-imposed, born of self-interest in the cause of self-fulfillment. Having cited the example of surrealist verbal imagery in his original manifesto, André Breton commented, "But the mind that savors them derives from them the certainty of finding itself on *the right road*" (p. 55).

The idea of being on the right road bears out the surrealists' trust in perception as a projection of consciousness extending beyond either memory or rational proposition. Thus, for example, speaking of the automatic texts called *Poisson soluble*, Breton spoke in his 1924 manifesto, to which they were appended, of the "gains" that the contribution of surrealism is likely to make the reader's consciousness realize (p. 57). Perception was for Breton from the start of his life as a surrealist an educative procedure, restricted by nothing more than the limits of its own capabilities. Surrealist creative action would never cease to be tentative, its results neither entirely foreseeable nor demonstrably proportionate to effort. In this respect the notion of the point of the mind was in perfect accord with the surrealist perspective on art as revelation and, furthermore, on the creative gesture as introducing the artist to himself. In the context of surrealism, revelation lay beyond predictability and anticipation, outside the range of calculated inquiry in a field circumscribed by prior knowledge. In short, revelation was never censored or restricted by expectation.

Locating the point of the mind within the frame of the already known, the already experienced, would not merely have been contradictory. It would have violated the spirit of surrealism, so undermining the activity to which surrealist values and aspirations lent the significance of precious testimony. Meanwhile the elusiveness of the point of the mind provided safeguards against monotony in investigative methodology. For it discouraged the enervating thought that the investigator's chances of success were enhanced (or ever could be), in proportion as his command of a given technique increased with practice.

In the years following publication of his 1929 manifesto, André Breton never had occasion to repudiate or modify in any way a statement from that document: "I say that surrealism is still in its preparatory period and I hasten to add that this period may last as long as I do . . ." (p. 209). Although placed at a later stage in the *Second manifeste* than the allusion to the certain point of the mind, this statement complements the earlier declaration. Neither Breton nor any other surrealist ever claimed to have gained or earned ready access to the point of the mind preoccupying them all, even though at times their work afforded momentary glimpses of the perspectives it opened up. Jouffroy has confided in the postface to *Aube à l'antipode*, "In a letter, at that time (1947–48), Breton said to me that they [the poems in that collection, written when their author was not yet twenty years old] took their place 'on the plane of objective revelation itself,' that they 'contributed to rendering *true life* less absent!' This encouragement, as you can imagine, has had such an effect on my life that I have been able for a long time, despite extreme misery, to face poetry without despairing of it too much."[4] Even though by the time he wrote these words Jouffroy had not counted himself a surrealist for many years, he remained proudly true to the spirit of surrealism.

We should not wonder, by the way, at Breton's phrase "less absent." He was not patronizing a young disciple. Nor was he intending to damn Jouffroy with faint praise. So long as surrealism remained at its preparatory stage, Breton could not expect full enjoyment, by himself or anyone else, of the true life identified by a nineteenth-century poet, Arthur Rimbaud ("True Life is absent. We are not in the world . . .") in whom the surrealists perceived a forerunner. The validity of Breton's claim regarding the point of the mind to which he aspired could never be fully tested against his own experience or against that of any of his contemporaries. He and the others in the surrealist movement could counter an objection or complaint with the riposte that any estimate of their achievement, as of the viability of the idea of the point of the mind, was premature.

All the same, Breton's warning that surrealism in his lifetime was still in its initial stages was not provided as a safeguard against adverse criticism. It showed that he was alert to the obstacles standing between surrealist man and attainment of the emancipative point of the mind—not only social and moral obstacles but mental ones also. And it was the latter, he realized, that most urgently needed to be overthrown if the surrealists were not to be condemned by their own deficiencies and inadequacies to falling short of their goal.

The strength of Breton's claims for the liberative perception assured by attainment of the desirable point of the mind is really not open to discussion. One either agrees with the surrealists on this matter, or one does not, neither persuasion nor browbeating nor even cajolery being able to change one's posi-

tion. Passing value judgments entails subjectivization of the review process in a fashion that, satisfying though it may be,
negatively affects any appraisal of the significance of Breton's
statement. The result is acclamation or condemnation, as evaluation is obscured by one's inclination to share the viewpoint
adopted in the *Second manifeste* or to shy away from it. Thus
the interesting thing is neither Breton's confidence in the success
of the surrealist venture nor the risk of failure that the surrealists
nonetheless incurred. It is the orientation of thought of which
Breton's declaration is expressive. Hence we should examine
the notion of the point of the mind as a manifestation of the
surrealist mentality rather than as proof that one ought to be
taking surrealism any more or any less seriously.

Should the surrealist mind be assessed on the basis of its
achievements or according to its aspirations? The concrete evidence at our disposal is supplied by the former, in works produced in a wide range of media. However, the scope of the
surrealist venture, opening onto a broadening horizon, cannot
be gauged unless the latter receives attention as well. And granting attention in this instance does not mean invoking aspiration
so as to denigrate accomplishment. It is to André Breton's credit
that he insisted that surrealism be judged by the distance it
has traveled and also by the distance it still has to go to bring
its goals within reach.

Even after taking note of Breton's invitation to place surrealist
effort in perspective, some people are of the opinion that he
had no adequate defense against the charge of voluntary self-
delusion. This charge seems valid and pertinent as long as
Breton and his associates are not permitted the right to aspire
to live, by choice, on the plane of awareness where contradictions surmounted in thought no longer demand attention.
The surrealist's was a life of the mind, situating fulfillment
at a level of perception corresponding to a sensitivity deriving
vitality from inner demand, not from surrender or even compromise. Hence the accomplishments of the surrealist mind are
to be appraised against the criterion of perfect harmony, in
which perception disposes of all sense of contradiction and
mental conflict. Surrealism drew vitality less from celebrating
and boasting of its achievements than from emphasizing the
need to achieve even more, to progress further, to witness the
collapse of more and more of the antinomies plaguing mankind.
To the surrealists, transforming the world meant transforming
their perception of it. For this reason, only infidelity to the

fundamental principles they had embraced could have persuaded any of them to indulge knowingly in self-deception on a scale broad enough to convince them they need not consider themselves guilty of and accountable for it.

The surrealist mind drew strength of purpose from belief, from faith, from the myths sustained by surrealist aspirations. And it worked to bolster all of these. It found energy in intimations of the existence of an order situated beyond the reach of reason and unfettered by past experience. It generalized on the basis of desire, not objective evidence. Opposition from rational thinking only confirmed the surrealist mind in the decision it had made and the ambitions it sought to realize.

The surrealist mind was assertive, not argumentative. This is why surrealists never resorted to dispute as a means to test the strength of their convictions. A major consequence, which has done more to swell the ranks of surrealism's enemies than to win it recruits, has been the widespread impression that being a surrealist meant being obtuse, incapable of seeing another's point of view and granting it serious, courteous attention. Greater inclination to compromise might have won the surrealists more sympathy. Yet it would have conflicted with their conviction that resistance to surrealist theory, departure from its principles, and failure to adopt the perspectives to which it attributed value were all violations of the truth, unworthy of discussion because, by definition they were indefensible. However gentlemanly it might have appeared, a "meeting of the minds" would have seemed pointless. Surrealists would have found themselves wrestling with phantoms. They would have granted a semblance of vitality to something which, from their standpoint, was lifeless and must remain so. In order to continue to be true to surrealism, in persistent pursuit of a certain point of the mind, they had to remain firmly intransigent, whatever means society might employ to effect a reconciliation that participants in the surrealist venture regarded with unyielding mistrust.

Taking our cue from André Breton, we understood now better the force of an analogy presented in his second manifesto: "I ask people to kindly observe that surrealist research presents with alchemical research a noteworthy analogy of aim: the philosopher's stone is nothing but that which was to allow the imagination of man to take striking revenge upon everything and here we are again, after centuries of domestication of the mind and crazy resignation, trying to free that imagination once and for all by "*the long, immense, reasoned disordering of the sense*" [the phrase is, once more, Arthur Rimbaud's] and the rest. . . . And let it be fully understood that this is not a matter of simply regrouping words or of capriciously redistributing verbal images, but of recreating a state which no longer has any need to envy mental derangement . . ." (pp. 207–209). The effort to determine the point of the mind fascinating to Breton was not merely comparable to the alchemists' search for the philosopher's stone. Pressing further than comparison, Breton represented the *Grand oeuvre* as liberating the imagination from domestication and resignation. He went so far as to speak of the philosopher's stone as though the ambitions keeping alchemy live for so long had been the very ambitions of surrealism in his lifetime. He did not present a case convincing enough to induce many individuals outside surrealism to follow him in treating alchemy in this fashion. Even so, his attempt to establish a close parallel between alchemy and surrealism confirms that no understanding of the surrealist mentality is possible before we have weighed the importance the *Second manifeste* places on determining a certain point of the mind.

Conclusion

In the *Second manifeste du surréalism* three declarations all
point in the same direction. The first is assertive, announcing, "We combat poetic indifference, the misappropriation of
art, erudite research, pure speculation in all their forms . . ."
(p. 159). The second is explicative: "This is because unflinch-
ing fidelity to the commitments of surrealism presupposes dis-
interestedness, contempt for risk, refusal to compromise, of
which very few men show themselves, in the long run, capable"
(p. 160). Recapitulative, the third confirms the surrealists' dissident attitude: "We say that the surrealist process has a chance
of being carried through only if it is effected in conditions of
asépsie morale [mental and moral asepsis] about which there
are still very few men willing to hear" (p. 221).

Nothing surprises us here. Instead, Breton's manifesto reaf-
firms what half a decade of surrealist productivity had demonstrated before 1929. Surrealism, we are being reminded,
developed out of aspirations set in perspective by revulsion
and resistance, both directed against common assumptions on
subjects ranging as wide as the nature of reality and the role
of the artist in society. The surrealist mind was formed by the
interplay, in thought, of negative and positive demands.

In surrealism, it was not just a matter of gradually replacing
a negative approach with a positive one as the surrealist movement's momentum increased. From the first, in a number of
respects the surrealists adopted a negative stance to further a
positive program. Meanwhile, the surrealist mind could never
be accused of posturing, of adopting this or that position just
for effect. Indeed, the fascination it offers in retrospect lies in
the consistency of the program it laid out, in the purposeful
manner in which surrealist thinking worked to defend and promote that program. Arbitrariness was not a characteristic of
the surrealist mind. All the same, we should be in error, if
we believe that mind to have been rigidly following a rigorous
plan of campaign, fully detailed from the start.

The surrealists began with a few glimpses of promising possi-

207

bilities. Responding eagerly to these, they undertook to explore certain avenues of inquiry. Some of the latter were selected speculatively, on a theoretical footing. Others, though, were discovered during the exploratory process itself, sometimes by accident. It is a measure of the suppleness of the surrealist mind that taking advantage of unanticipated revelations and drawing them into the surrealist scheme of things was an effortless feature of surrealism's advance out of doubt and dissatisfaction into hope and self-confidence.

The surrealist mind asserted its presence and influence as the unifying element connecting a variety of activities in diverse media, as the unifying evaluative force accepting or rejecting, approving or disapproving efforts and approaches endorsed or rejected in the name of surrealism. To unify without restricting, to give and acknowledge direction without inhibiting forward movement—that was its role.

The deductions we have made from a few pronouncements scattered throughout Breton's *Second manifeste* highlight the centrality of a controlling mind. The latter gave a common sense of purpose and orientation to the diversified activities in which surrealists engaged: a few of them—Breton, Peret, and Nora Mitrani (who died young), for instance—throughout their adult lives; others for a period of time brief enough, in some cases, to be measured in months. As we notice this however, we should also take note of something tending to cloud a picture we have just seemed to have outlined fairly clearly.

When referring to the surrealist mind, we open the door on the false supposition that all surrealists were of one mind at all times. Inevitably, it appears, one cannot expect to approve the concept of such a mind without risk of supporting a view of surrealism that narrows the surrealists' field of action. One is the danger of confining it within a frame from which independent thought and individualistic examination of the potential of art are precluded, their sacrifice seeming a fair price to pay for clear definition.

The benefits of studying the surrealist mind have nothing to do with limiting our field of inquiry. On the contrary, they contribute directly to broadening our awareness of certain interrelationships. These, in turn, deepen our understanding of the manner in which the surrealists came to terms with their world, by reacting on a level of response that they deemed warranted attachment of the adjective "poetic." Indeed, a fitting description of the operation of the surrealist mind would identify the accurate definition of poetry as its main goal. It is fair to characterize the surrealist mind as having aimed to devise and implement methods worthy to be designated poetic.

Is such an interpretation disappointingly bathetic, its introduction at this late stage quite simply anticlimactic? The surrealists would not have considered it in this manner. Nor would they have conceded that when they supported such a view they were capitulating ignominiously or else seeking an uneasy truce with their enemies or again trying to reassure persons in whom surrealism appeared fully capable of releasing misgivings, if not quite alarm. It is less the familiarity of the term *poetry* that counts, now, than the value with which surrealists invested it and the singular vitality contributed to their creative endeavors by their idea of the poetic.

At the beginning of his *La poésie moderne et le sacré*, Jules Monnerot links modern poetry and surrealist poetry,[1] announcing in a note that his book aspires to shed light on "the conjunction of these two qualities [sic]" (p. 184). Actually, though, Bédouin, Péret, and other surrealists went further to equate surrealism with poetry in general. Knowing the following is therefore essential to better appreciation of how the surrealist mind worked. Surrealists never supposed their own interpretation of poetry to be innovative, as departing perceptibly from universal standards, openly defiant of acceptable norms. Their attitude and conduct reflected firm assurance that their fidelity to the eternal ideals of poetry was above question and beyond reproach. Their confidence laid the foundation for a recurrent theme in published commentary on the nature of poetry by the most original surrealist poet in the French language or any other, Benjamin Péret.

As a theoretician of surrealism, Péret is less well known by far than André Breton. All the same, he contributed significantly to the maturation of surrealist poetic theory. Someone who turns to Peret's remarks about poetry only after becoming acquainted with a few of his poetic texts is likely to be taken off guard, though. Péret's observations on the poetic give no forewarning of the boldness typified in his verbal images. Far from it, Benjamin Péret seems at first glance to have had traditionalist leanings and persistently called upon poets to return to and draw upon the purest sources of the poetic. Stressing the need for poetry to be revolutionary, this most revolutionary of surrealist poets claimed that poetry has always been revolutionary by nature. His outlook was representative of those sharing his dedication to the cause of surrealism. It lent itself to convenient summary in Jean-Louis Bédouin's *La poésie surréaliste:* "In truth, surrealist poetry is not of a different essence from that of all authentic poetry. It is, in the full sense of the term, poetry. . . ."[2]

In Bédouin's statement the salient word is, of course, "authentic." Its prominence in surrealist discussions of the poetic explains the surrealists' behavior toward anyone skeptical about their concept of poetry or opposed to it. In their estimation, such an individual obviously deserves nothing better than relegation to the status of false prophet or—perhaps even lower—of false poet, practitioner of the inauthentic. Surrealists regarded his assumptions as patently inapplicable and as leading him, when he doubts surrealism, to doubt the viability of poetry at the same time.

This is not the place to continue an analysis of surrealist poetics begun elsewhere.[3] It is enough to notice that we face a contradiction at this point. If surrealism and poetry in fact were one, then why have surrealism's detractors not been able to acknowledge this or even to recognize it? Taking up the same question from another perspective, we may ask who enjoys the right of arbitration with respect to the authentic in poetry. We discover that the surrealist group invariably reserved that right to themselves. Meanwhile nothing published by any participant in the surrealist movement at any time in its history, offers guidance on how to deal with our question. If we look to the surrealist group for assistance, we are left with nothing more convincing than the judgment that anybody challenging the equation of surrealism with poetry stands as condemned by his own obtuseness. Impatience with their critics and even with people inclined to be sympathetic but nevertheless unconvinced did not serve to win acceptance for surrealism or tolerance of the expressive modes through which the surrealist mind made its presence felt. As for the posture typical of surrealists vis-à-vis those in disagreement with them it offered little encouragement and less enlightenment. Opponents were dismissed as ignorant, foolish, or patently stupid, apparently as unintelligent as they were unimaginative. The surrealists treated them as mendacious philistines or criminals whose misdeeds, being no more likely to suffer correction than to earn excuse, need not be detailed.

It was not simply that a surrealist's wholehearted reliance on poetry made him hostile to anyone who did not share and—as he saw it—never could share his sense of the poetic. Our grasp on his motivation still remains unsure, unless we have detected

in surrealist conduct more logic than the majority of its enemies have glimpsed. Initially Péret sounds inconsistent, alluding
often to the marvelous "heart and nervous system of all poetry")
without ever going on to define it for the benefit of an uninformed audience. Placed against the background of surrealist
thought, however, his refusal to furnish a definition is comprehensible. It indicates that he judged the linguistic mode in which
theoretical principles are outlined too far removed from poetry
to circumscribe the poetic in terms communicable prosaically.
Péret and his fellow surrealists felt certain that poetry as discovery, illumination, and revelation could not be encompassed
within the mundane language of prose.

In clarification of the issues involved when we are contemplating the operation of the surrealist mind, one may say that it
centered on poetic exchange. Something else ought to be added,
also. The exchange surrealists relied on poetry to bring about
endowed the poetic with a character that despite their belief
that poetry has always had but one function allows us to speak
after all of a surrealist form of poetic communication. And so,
under the rubric of surrealist poetry it is crucial to respect
the broad range of forms assumed by the poetic in a variety
of media and to recognize these forms as manifesting a persistent
fundamental unity of purpose. Free of aesthetic constraints and
more than simply expressive, they were all investigative.

In surrealism, the connection was close and abiding between
rejection of aesthetic demands and acceptance of imperatives
directing poetic action into investigative channels. The surrealists did not invoke those imperatives merely in order to rationa-
lize their rejection of aestheticism, as a way of passing off
weaknesses that an aesthetician surely would detect and condemn. It was scarcely by sensitivity to embarrassing inadequacies in one area that a surrealist was inspired to emphasize
preferential concern with another area, where those same inadequacies could not be held against him. Someone suspicious
of the surrealists' motives here betrays his or her acknowledgment of priorities that no surrealist took seriously and had been
pushed aside by other priorities, combining to grant surrealist
poetry investigative significance. As the surrealists saw it, poetry
was valorized by its ability to effect revelation of the unknown
in place of celebration of the familiar presented in aesthetically
defensible terms.

To the surrealist mind poetic viability appeared to have nothing to do with aesthetic values. It had everything to do, however,

with use of investigative instruments, and not verbal ones exclusively. Surrealist instrumentation qualified for the designation
"poetic" to the degree that it succeeded in transforming the
previously unknown, first into the knowable and ultimately into
the known. The scale of measurement may be said to have
ceased to bear any relationship to the pursuit of the beautiful.
More accurately, it can be identified as ignoring beauty judged
by aesthetic criteria and replacing it with beauty of a radically
different sort, prized in surrealist circles for shedding light
where darkness had reigned before.

An outsider might view as part obstinacy, part snobbery something that was among surrealists a natural response to mental
attitudes in their estimation not worth taking seriously. There
were indeed no grounds for communication between the surrealist mind and anyone, dubious of its significance, who kept his
distance from surrealism or in the spirit of healthy skepticism
wished merely to probe surrealist ideas by pushing exponents
of those ideas onto the defensive. Refusing to engage in persuasive exposition, André Breton set an example for which, one
of his disciples was to observe in 1977, he paid a high price.
In Gérard Legrand's Breton we read, "For not having wished
to set himself up as a professor or a 'guru,' for having even
disclaimed to join in the game of the 'successful' or 'cursed'
writer, one of the most powerful inspirers of the first half of
this century (a 'half' of which May 68 would suffice to show
that its projected shadow has not stopped spreading) is in danger
of undergoing a particularly unjust posthumous 'purgatory.'"[4]
In a uniformly laudatory evaluation of Breton's accomplishments, colored by his close association with him in the Paris
surrealist group, Legrand goes on to remark, "It is in the final
analysis by the incompatible movement peculiar to his thought
that Breton found himself led . . . to embrace in his glance
human destiny as a whole and especially the nodal problem
of cognition."[5]

The surrealist mind was doggedly isolationist. It wanted nothing to do with minds entertaining predispositions, presuppositions, and ambitions divergent from its own. This explains
Breton's announcement during an interview concentrating on
a former surrealist, Antonin Artaud, that there could be, for
poetry, no other "reefs" than banality and "universal consent."[6]
Thinking as a surrealist was neither a convenience nor a privilege to be enjoyed from time to time—momentarily or for a

longer period—when mood or whim dictated. The surrealist
mind could not be shed like a topcoat whenever the intellectual
climate discouraged its use. Nor could it be resumed the moment
the weather changed. Anyone who knew from inside the surrealist circle what it meant to share in the surrealist mind knew
too that surrealism could not be summoned to occupy the artist's
mind for a while, then dismissed the instant surrealist perspectives ceased to be welcome or looked inappropriate, only to
be subsequently called back into service, if need be. Cohabitation
with any other was impossible. The surrealist mind's essential
features, after all, were the intransigent pursuit of its own goals,
unwavering preoccupation with its own aspirations, and total
commitment to a line of conduct and to the application of methods it judged appropriate. Cooperation and even peaceful coexis-
tence with the nonsurrealist mind were seen by the surrealists
as compromising, as contaminating acceptable standards too
dangerous to be tolerated and in any case of no real advantage
to surrealism. Consenting to be less than totally independent
would have entailed repudiation of a "Declaration" dated 27
January 1925 that had described surrealism as "a means for
the total liberation of the mind [esprit]." It would have meant
at the same time failure to promote, in Jean-Louis Bedouin's
phrase, "a new regime of the mind" (p. 17).

Central to the surrealist venture was poetry, described by
Bédouin as taking on again its true meaning of "activity of the
mind" (p. 19). Small wonder that Bédouin went on to quote
Péret's definition of poetry as "the source of all knowledge and
that knowledge [connaissance] itself in its most immaculate aspect." In surrealist thought, the balance of two meanings of
esprit (mind and spirit) was the counterpart of the balance
achieved by cognition and knowledge, both rendered in French
by one word, connaissance. To protest that mind and spirit
are not really interchangeable or to question whether knowledge
and cognition are indeed the same things would have made
little impression on Breton and his friends. The surrealist mind
was self-sufficient, for this reason both independent of outside
support and invulnerable by outsiders.

The important factor is that surrealists were united in placing
trust in the cognitive capacity of the poetic, seeing it as truly
the distinguishing feature of poetry. But they all declined to
accept an obligation to specify precisely what they hoped to
learn from poetic investigation. In fact, they would have seemed
bent on avoiding the question, when responding honestly that

their hope was to learn through poetry things they did not know already. And yet in doing so they would have continued to be faithful to the spirit of surrealism. Dissatisfied with most of what was known to them, as to the people around them, they pinned their faith on the still unknown. Resorting to art as a means of bringing the latter into their experience, they considered it mandatory to refrain from projecting the outcome of poetic inquiry. Furthermore, they regarded reasoned mental projection as inconsistent with successful pursuit and full attainment of surrealist ambitions. They were convinced that the latter could be realized only when and where anticipation had been outpaced after betraying damaging weaknesses—the result of reason's intrusion—limiting any imagination betraying respect for the boundaries prescribed by the already known.

The surrealist mind turned away from the known because it located fulfillment in the yet to be known. Disappointment with the present and alarm at the confinement to which speculative thought appeared committed while remaining attentive to it induced the surrealists to situate knowledge beyond the horizon of the familiar. Meanwhile they elevated poetry to a rank beyond compare when they ascribed to it the irreplaceable role of carrying thought past the familiar, once imaginative release had opened a pathway to increased knowledge.

All in all, if we had to point to a single word as the focal point of surrealist thinking as it guided surrealist creative activity, that word would be Legrand's: *cognition*. The surrealist mind evolved its distinguishing characteristics from the necessity to establish and practice modes of inquiry for which meaningful vindication came through enhanced knowledge in keeping with desire. Apparently permitted the utmost freedom of operation— because it was conducted in defiance of norms and regulations widely approved in Western literature and painting, for example—the surrealist mind's search for increased knowledge was more precisely oriented than might appear. Certainly, it had a sharper focus than contemporary opponents of surrealism appreciated. It displayed more discipline than mistrustful critics have ever associated with surrealist endeavor. The principle of accountability takes on much clearer outline as soon as we become sensitive to the surrealists' devotion to cognition.

The surrealist mind was poised expectantly between the present and the future. This is to say that surrealists looked optimistically to the future, secure in the belief that poetry would bring about an improvement upon current conditions of life and thought. Thus the norm by which life was to be judged was not provided by the mundane, fixing experience and its potential entirely by reference to the known. It was, more excitingly, the still unknown or, as the surrealists preferred to regard it, the yet to be known. The fascination of participating in surrealism lay not in tilting at windmills, then, but in watching barriers topple, awareness expand, and reality become enriched as more and more obstacles collapsed before the progress of a sensibility advancing under propulsion from desire into the rarefied atmosphere of poetic consciousness. There imagination would not be weighed down by the ballast of reason, habit, routine, and nostalgia for the familiar.

Two statements in the *Second manifeste* complement one another, as they testify to the nature of the surrealist quest. The first clearly isolates an obligation: "It is up to us, I was saying then, to seek to perceive more and more clearly what is being hatched without man's knowledge in the depths of his mind [*esprit*], even if he were to begin by blaming us for his own whirlwind" (p. 191). The second provides a description, as Breton reminds his audience that the idea of surrealism tends simply toward "total recuperation" of our psychic strength by a means that is nothing other, he asserts, than "a vertiginous descent into ourselves," otherwise characterized in his test as "systematic illumination of the hidden places and progressive obscuration of the other places," in short, "a perpetual walk in the forbidden zone" (pp. 167–68). Wondering why exactly Breton invited readers of his first surrealist manifesto to "spit in passing" on Edgar Allan Poe, we witness here a revival of the image dominating Poe's story, *Descent into the Maelstrom*. In the 1929 *Manifeste*, it relates to discovery through a loss of control that is welcomed—or ought to be—even when not deliberately sought or its vertiginous effects distress the conscious mind habitually trustful of reason.

Eulogizing the poetry of André Breton, Alain Jouffroy borrows remarkably similar language, describing automatic writing as "the invention of a writing of life, of a life of writing, which knocks down the water-tight bulkheads that one raises against the whirlpools in a ship that *must* sink."[7] With the idea of the poetically oriented mind as one that is, from reason's standpoint, in danger of foundering, and that, in order for surrealism's aspirations to be fully realized, "*must* sink," goes another, underlined by Jouffroy: "'The white graph on a black background that we call thought' belongs to no one, not even to the person formulating it."[8] In surrealism, therefore, thought "throws itself into a possibility the end of which will never be determined in advance." As Jouffroy puts it, "A great poet does not express himself, he speaks, he writes, and his word, his writing are liberty become a lioness, the world become a lion, history slamming all doors and reducing the bars of the cage to powder."[9] Interestingly, the former surrealist Jouffroy presents his opinions as applying to any poet who has reached greatness. Yet he states a position to which neither Breton nor Péret nor any other surrealist would have objected.

When the rational mind founders, surrealists were convinced, loss becomes the path to gain and furthermore has a general, not private significance of unforeseeable potential. Surrealist theory left no room for discussion on this subject. In the surrealists' eyes, the opinion to which we have heard Breton subscribe was beyond dispute. This does not mean, thought, that it has gone undisputed or that surrealist theory has escaped censure.

No one has voiced reservations more intelligently and in more measured tones than Robert Champigny, whose discussion of the 1924 *Manifeste du surréalisme* permits us to estimate the distance between surrealism and its critics.[10] Champigny's comments do not deserve attention as adducing proof in support of the hypothesis that Breton was right and those who contradicted him were wrong (or of the reverse, for that matter). They are noteworthy for another reason altogether.

Champigny advances part way to tracking down the central question raised by the first surrealist manifesto when, having outlined several objections, he concludes, "The difficulty that has just been analyzed resembles the one raised by certain theological texts about mystical experience. The theologian tries to win over the prestige of this type of experience to the advantage of a certain sect or a certain dogma. Hence the confusion between the definition of a certain type of experience and the definition of a dogma."[11] But just like everything else he wrote about surrealism on a theoretical level, Breton's original manifesto was really only an outgrowth of the definition of a certain kind of experience.

Summarizing the theoretical bases of surrealism during a speech delivered in Havana on 11 August 1967, Jean Schuster coincidentally dismissed Champigny's judgment of theoretical surrealism as dogmatic. "Surrealism is not a doctrine," Schuster declared, "or a philosophy, or a school. It does not claim to hold any absolute truth. Its fundamental principles are brought from day to day face to face with reality, life, the evolution of the world and the progress of knowledge. This is why its principles are not dogmas: they fix a body of constants and variables which protect it from any sclerosis."[12] Thus, had Robert Champigny fully understood the essentials, he would not have embarked on dissecting the phrase "the real functioning of thought," borrowed from the famous definition of surrealism. He would have appreciated that protesting Breton's claim to be talking about the *real* functioning of thought was futile.

As Champigny should have appreciated, his reservations would have made no impression on the French surrealist leader. The author of the surrealist manifestoes could have lent no credence to strictures denying him the right to define the real by reference to what he believed to be real because he found it so. Champigny stops short of acknowledging this when he writes, "In the definition of surrealism, the adjective 'real' qualifies the functioning of thought as it is expressed in surrealist language. . . . Interpreted ontologically, the adjective 'real' therefore appears to qualify exclusively the logic of surrealist language. . . ."[13] But where did the logic of surrealist language lie, if not in the mode of thought expressing the surrealist mind?

Champigny chooses to approach surrealist language as though it were an independent organism, functioning on its own and for its own purposes. He fails to trace it to its source. Yet that source deserves acknowledgment, surrealist language being no more than its expression, even when we are considering the utterances of Robert Desnos during periods of hypnotic trance. True, Breton praised Desnos for "speaking Surrealist," but one does not have to be adept in a new language ("Surrealist") in order to recognize that the logic of surrealist language originates in surrealism as experienced and projected through the surrealist mind. If Champigny has any inkling of this, he nevertheless prefers to take no account of it. Instead, he remarks, "Breton wishes to ruin the ontological prestige attaching to what one may call the logic of the real, that is to say, to the spatio-temporal and causal logic used by historical practical language."[14] Clearly, when he sets up one kind of logic in opposition to another, Champigny is trying to claim the real for one side and deny the surrealist side access to it. So we can follow his example and speak of "the logic of the real" only after discounting the logic of surrealist language and with it the autonomy of the surrealist mind.

Champigny is scarcely alone in seeing nothing reprehensible in making an implicit plea for denying the autonomy of the surrealist mind. Nor can he be singled out for condemning the surrealists' flagrant disregard for a form of logic to which not even one of them granted validity. The radical difference between the viewpoint adopted and defended in Champigny's *Pour une esthétique de l'essai* and the one expressed in surrealism lay in the surrealists' unwillingness to espouse the idea of the real to which Champigny subscribed, an idea against which surrealism had risen in revolt and with which it scorned reconciliation. Champigny and the surrealists are separated not so much by conflict over the meaning of logic but, far more significantly, at the very foundations of thought on which their conflicting interpretations of logic stand. Saying this, however, we still have not represented the situation with full accuracy. We are following Champigny's lead with too much docility, neglecting to question his assumption that "the logic of the real" antedated "the logic of surrealist language." Thus we find ourselves agreeing with him in attributing the former precedence over the latter, concurrently ascribing "the logic of the real" an authority which, it now would appear, the surrealists were quite presumptuous in daring to challenge.

Of course, permitting Champigny to lead us does keep us alert to the outlaw status of surrealism, which no surrealist ever denied or regretted. But at the same time it inclines us to infer that right is, and should always remain, on the side of the law against which the surrealists rebelled. In consequence the surrealist mind is disadvantaged, not to say handicapped. It is thrown into a situation demanding self-justification such as is not required in Champigny's critical frame of a mind content to assert and demonstrate "the logic of the real." This concept draws strength from the links implied in Champigny's phrase: that the logical is real and furthermore, the real is logical. Anyone accepting these links as firm and resistant to argument has come more than halfway to the belief that only reality supports logic, which is therefore properly to be considered its expression. If this is indeed true, then what room can there be for a logic that, departing from the real, as Champigny speaks of reality, stands outside and opposes it?

The surrealists refused to be enticed onto the slippery ground where one is led by the inferences Champigny incites us to draw. They never forgot that, in the surrealist mind, the real was not an objectively verifiable phenomenon to which one and all must submit; it was rather a subjective perception colored by desire. There, in consequence, logic was granted independence of rationality and might even operate anti-reasonably. It was transformed into the expression of a deductive principle functioning in contradistinction to reason but, despite Champigny's argument, not impertinently after all.

Champigny's references to ontology reveal that he is no less prejudiced than Breton and hence no less selective when ontology claims his attention. It might even be argued that a verification procedure such as he would consider objective is, ultimately no less subjective than was the surrealists', which was posited on wholehearted trust in "the logic of the real." As for the surrealists, one ought to concede at the very least that they were quite conscious of having made a choice when they followed Breton in favoring what "could be" over what "manifestly is."

Unflaggingly the surrealist mind sought the hidden in preference to the manifest and the possible over the present, just as it pursued the knowable instead of meditating on the known. This is why the future, not the past, was the true measure of its accomplishments, the polestar by which it steered its exploratory course. Breton's injunction that we judge surrealism by what it still had to do in order to achieve its ultimate goals clearly reflected the orientation of surrealist thought. At the risk of seeming to leave himself and his companions open to adverse criticism, he emphasized the optimism of surrealism, rejecting a pessimistic interpretation of the role of the surrealist mind as he turned his back on those inclined or eager to propose one.

Champigny's remarks on the *Manifeste du surréalisme* present one more interesting feature, representative of critical evaluations of surrealism, including commentary far less fair-minded than his own. Whether sympathetic to surrealism or aggressively antagonistic to it, critics have shared with Champigny an inclination to discuss features of the surrealist mind without naming it, without openly acknowledging that it existed and functioned purposefully.

It would be unjust to hint at a ploy designed to bring discredit on the surrealist mind by scrupulous avoidance of overt references to it. In fact, no sign of prevarication can be detected on the part of those who have passed judgment on surrealism.

We cannot honestly speak of voluntary blindness in the critics. However, we observe in their published assessments ample proof of marked astigmatism. This weakness has prevented commentators from recognizing something of fundamental importance. In their discussions of surrealist painting, shall we say, they are not dealing with pictorial phenomena in a medium completely isolated from all others through which the surrealists had occasion to express themselves. They are facing no more than one expression of the surrealist mind, complemented by its expressions in other media. Furthermore, all manifestations of the surrealist mind are mutually enlightening. For this reason they all shed light on the source from which they emanate and to which they owe the meaning they held for surrealists. To identify an interrelationship between surrealist modes of creative communication without concurrently admitting that they found their unity in the surrealist mind, where they all originated, means failure to grant that mind its due. And ignoring or misunderstanding the surrealist mind can only impair our comprehension of surrealism.

Study of the surrealist mind allows the objective witness to perceive in surrealism greater seriousness of purpose and significance than it has been generally granted. However, something more than confirmation of surrealism's claim to respectability awaits at the end of our inquiry, as deeper respect helps give direction to further investigations.

Beginning by entertaining the hypothesis that a surrealist mind might indeed have existed and might even have functioned productively has enabled us to circumvent a major obstacle to progress: the prejudiced notion that in the absence of a concerted plan drawn up by its defenders, surrealism found no better than haphazard expression, wihtout consistency, because there was really—so we are encouraged to believe—no sustained purpose behind surrealist experimentation in a broad variety of creative modes. Even so, searching for evidence of a surrealist mind and of its effects can be interpreted, in retrospect as an act of confidence in a far-ranging movement that ever since the 1920s has enjoyed the confidence of relatively few people—least of all, it seems at times, the critics. In the final analysis, proof of the vitality and active influence of the surrealist mind vindicates surrealism, not an individual who with some degree of perseverance has sought and gathered pertinent evidence of representative value. Hence the satisfaction afforded by his undertaking is not egocentric, rewarding a commentator who believes he can congratulate himself at last on having made a point. It is the pleasure of having learned to comprehend surrealism a little better and, in addition, the hope of having shared with his readers a measure of increased understanding.

Notes

Chapter 1. A Surrealist Mind?

1. André Breton, *Manifestes du surréalisme* (Paris: Jean-Jacques Pauvert, [1962]), p. 22. In addition to Breton's manifestos, this volume contains, among other texts, his "Du surréalisme en ses oeuvres vives," "Prolégomènes à un troisième manifeste du surréalisme ou non," and "Situation surréaliste de l'objet." Subsequent references to this volume will be cited parenthetically in the text.
2. Lucy R. Lippard, ed., *Surrealists on Art* (Englewood Cliffs, N.J.: Prentice-Hall, 1970), p. 1.
3. Ibid., p. 2.
4. Charles Edward Gauss, *The Aesthetic Theories of French Artists from Realism to Surrealism* (Baltimore: Johns Hopkins University Press, 1966), p. 85.
5. Ibid., p. 92.
6. Anna Balakian, *Surrealism: The Road to the Absolute* (New York: Dutton, 1970), p. 124.
7. Ibid., p. 138.
8. Roger Caillois, "Divergences et complicités," *La nouvelle revue française* 172 (1 April 1967): 698.
9. André Breton, interview by Guy Dumur, in *Le nouvel observateur* (10 December 1964).
10. André Breton, *Les pas perdus* (Paris: Editions de la Nouvelle Revue Franç aise, 1924), p. 189. Subsequent references to this volume will be cited parenthetically, in the text.
11. Philippe Soupault, *Profils perdus* (Paris: Mercure de France, 1963), p. 166.

Chapter 2. The Automatic Principle: Why Write?

1. Colette Gaudin, "Tours et détours négatifs dans 'La confession dédaigneuse' de Breton," *Romanic Review* 71, no. 4 (November 1980): 394–412.
2. André Breton and Jean Schuster, "Art poétique," *BIEF: jonction surréaliste* 7 (1 June 1959), no pagination.
3. The catalogue of the International Surrealist Exhibition held at the D'Arcy Galleries, New York in 1960–61 bore the title *Surrealist Intrusion in the Enchanters' Domain*.
4. André Breton, *Anthologie de l'humour noir* (Paris: Jean-Jacques Pauvert, 1966), p. 260.
5. Noam Chomsky, "Mental Representations," *Syracuse Scholar* 4, no. 2 (Fall 1983): 6.
6. André Breton, *Arcane 17 ente d'Ajours* (Paris: Sagittaire, 1947), p. 148.

Chapter 3. The Critical Reception: What Is Poetry?

1. Vratislav Effenberger, "La parole et l'état," in *La civilisation surréaliste*, ed. Vincent Bounoure (Paris: Payot, 1976), p. 227.

2. Vincent Bounoure, "Du surréalisme restreint au surréalisme généralisé," in Bounoure, *Civilisation surréaliste*, p. 256.

3. Ibid., p. 257.

4. Jean-Louis Bédouin, "Cycle de l'objet," in Bounoure, *Civilisation surréaliste*, p. 295.

5. Vincent Bounoure and Vratislav Effenberger, "L'invention du monde," in Bounoure, *Civilisation surréaliste*, p. 30.

6. Ibid., p. 31.

7. André Breton, "Du surréalisme et ses oeuvres vives," p. 355.

8. André Breton, "Prolégomènes à un troisième manifeste du surréalisme ou non" (1942), p. 344.

9. André Breton, "Du surréalisme en ses oeuvres vives," p. 363.

10. Nicolas Calas, *Art in the Age of Risk* (New York: Dutton, 1968), p. 15.

Chapter 4. Surrealist Poetry in Writing and Painting

1. André Breton, *Le surréalisme et la peinture* (Paris: Gallimard, 1965). Subsequent references to this volume will be cited parenthetically in the text.

2. Christopher Robinson, *French Literature in the Twentieth Century* (Newton Abbot: David & Charles; Totowa, N.J.: Barnes & Noble, 1980), p. 135.

3. André Breton, "Le merveilleux contre le mystère" (1936), in his *La clé des champs* (Paris: Sagittaire, 1953), p. 8. Subsequent references to this volume will be cited parenthetically in the text.

4. Benjamin Péret, "La pensée est UNE et indivisible," *VVV* 4 (February 1944): 10.

5. Pierre Mabille, *Le merveilleux* (Paris: Editions des Quatre Vents, 1946), p. 17.

6. Ibid., p. 68.

7. Ibid., p. 69.

8. André Breton, *Yves Tanguy* (New York: Pierre Matisse Editions, 1946), p. 11. Subsequent references to this volume will be cited parenthetically in the text.

9. See the artist's statement in the catalogue, *Marcel Mariën: retrospective et nouveautés 1937–67* (Brussels: Galerie Defacqz, 1967), p. 20.

10. Jean Schuster, "A l'ordre de la nuit, au désordre du jour," *L'Archibras* 1 (1 April 1967): 9.

11. See Jean Schuster, *Développements sur l'infra-réalisme de Matta* (Paris: Eric Losfeld, 1970), pp. 10–11.

12. Ibid., p. 19.

13. Ibid., p. 16.

14. Ibid., p. 17.

15. André Breton, *Le surréalisme et la peinture* (Paris: Gallimard, 1965), p. 46. Subsequent references to this volume will be cited parenthetically in the text.

Chapter 5. Painting in the Surrealist Mind

1. An interesting and revealing feature of the surrealist lexicon is that it granted prominence to words of which *desire* is the most striking. *Desire* draws attention to the anti-intellectual frame of mind characteristic of the surrealists, eluding confinement within the framework of rational discourse. It turns discussion toward the ineffable, where close definition is less pertinent to surrealism's ambitions than to opening up perspectives of inexhaustible promise. One looks in vain for a definition of desire in the *Dictionnaire abrégé du surréalisme* assembled by André Breton and Paul Eluard for the 1938 International Surrealist Exhibition. However, an extensive note on the meaning of painting appears in that volume over Breton's initials. See *Dictionnaire abrégé du surréalisme* (1938, reprint, Paris: José Corti, 1969), p. 20.

2. William S. Rubin, *Dada and Surrealist Art* (New York: Harry N. Abrams, n.d.).

3. Ibid., p. 7.

4. See José Pierre, "Dada, le surréalisme et le ketchup," *La quinzaine littéraire*, 16–30 September 1975. The author's own comments on Rubin's book are found in *Surrealist TransformaCtion* 6 (1973): 38–43. A personal attack on Rubin is not intended here. The motive for citing writings readily accessible to an American audience is to contrast the critical mind with the surrealist mind.

5. Rubin, *Dada*, p. 7.

Chapter 6. Creativity and Criticism

1. Quoted in James Thrall Soby, *Yves Tanguy* (New York: Museum of Modern Art, 1955), p. 17.

2. Jean Schuster, "A l'ordre de la nuit," 4.

3. During an interview granted Yvonne Baby for *Le monde*, 1 June 1961.

4. André Tinel, "Format écolier," *Cahiers Dada surréalisme* 1 (1966): 83.

5. André Breton, "Braise au trépied de Kéridwen," foreword to Jean Markale, *Les grands bardes gallois* (1956), reprinted in *Perspective cavalière* (Paris: Gallimard, 1970), p. 130.

6. Roger Cardinal, "Breton–'Au beau demi-jour de 1934,'," in Peter H. Nurse, ed., *The Art of Criticism: Essays in French Literary Analysis* (Edinburgh: Edinburgh University Press, 1969), p. 258. Subsequent references to this essay will be cited parenthetically in the text. Cardinal takes no account of the fact that Eluard acknowledged the purity with which automatism found expression in Péret's writing when openly admitting that Péret was a greater poet than he. See Jehan Mayoux, "Benjamin Péret: la fourchette coupante," *Le surréalisme, même* 2 (Spring 1967): 156.

7. See the letter from André Breton to Jean Gaulmier, quoted by the latter in the introduction to his *édition commentée* of Breton's *Ode à Charles Fourier* (Paris: Klincksieck, 1947), pp. 7–8.

8. Bernard Weinberg, *The Limits of Symbolism* (Chicago: University of Chicago Press, 1966), pp. 1, 2.

9. André Breton, "Au beau demi-jour," in L'air del'eau (Cahiers d'Art, [1934], n.p.); also published in Poèmes (Paris: Gallimard, 1948), p. 116.

10. Breton and Schuster, Art poétique, no pagination.

11. Isidore Ducasse, comte de Lautréamont, Poésies, première édition commentée (Paris: Le Terrain Vague, 1960), p. 11. Subsequent references to this volume will be cited parenthetically in the text.

12. Frederick Brown, "Creation versus Literature: Breton and the Surrealist Movement," in John K. Simon, ed., Modern French Criticism from Proust and Valéry to Structuralism (Chicago: University of Chicago Press, 1972), pp. 123–46.

13. Schuster, "A l'ordre de la nuit."

14. Ibid., p. 7.

15. Jean-Louis Bédouin, Benjamin Péret (Paris: Seghers, 1961), pp. 45–46.

16. Antonin Artaud, Correspondance avec Jacques Rivière, in Oeuvres complètes, vol. 1 (Paris: Gallimard, 1956). p. 21.

17. Ibid., p. 21.

18. Benjamin Péret, "Le déshonneur des poètes" précédé de "La parole est à Péret" (Paris: Jean-Jacques Pauvert, [1965]), p. 75.

19. Pierre Mabille, Le Merveilleux, p. 81.

20. Mayoux, "Benjamin Péret," p. 154–55.

21. Jean-Louis Bédouin, La poésie surréaliste (Paris: Seghers, 1964), p. 12.

22. Ibid., p. 69.

23. Benjamin Péret, "Le déshonneur des poètes" précédé de "La parole est à Péret" (Paris: Jean Jacques Pauvert, [1965]), p. 71.

24. Péret, Déshonneur, p. 75.

25. Breton explained his position in an important preface, "La nuit du Rose-Hôtel et la collection 'Révélation' qu'elle inaugure," to Maurice Fourré's novel, La nuit du Rose-Hôtel (Paris: Gallimard, 1950), where he stressed "the share I intend to give to spiritual adventure and the limitless field I assign it" (p. 9).

26. Nora Mitrani, "Le congrès s'amuse," Médium: communication surréaliste, n.s. 1 (November 1953): 16.

27. Ado Kyrou, Le surréalisme au cinéma, rev. ed. (Paris: Le Terrain Vague, 1963), p. 271.

28. Ibid., p. 279.

29. Gherasim Luca, Gellu Naum, Virgil Teodorescu, and Trost, Eloge de "Malombra," Bucharest: 1947; L'Age du Cinéma 4–5 (August–November 1951), special issue devoted to surrealism.

30. Paul Hammond, "Off at a Tangent" (introduction to The Shadow and its Shadow: Surrealist Writings on Cinema [London: British Film Institute, 1978]), p. 6.

31. Ibid., p. 8.

32. Breton's statement is borrowed from the notice on Péret in his Anthologie de l'humour noir, p. 505.

33. André Breton, "Fronton virage," preface to Jean Ferry, Une étude sur Raymond Roussel (Paris: Arcanes, 1953), p. 14.

34. Paul Eluard, preface to Benjamin Péret, De derrière les fagots (Paris: Pléiade, Gallimard, 1968), vd. II, p. 846.

35. Vincent Bounoure, "Surrealism and the Savage Heart," in the catalogue, Surrealist Intrusion in the Enchanters' Domain (New York: D'Arcy Galleries, 1960), p. 27.

Chapter 7. The Critical Example: André Breton on Painting

1. Rubin, *Dada*, p. 123.

Chapter 8. Perspectives on the Avant-Garde

1. John Weightman, *The Concept of the Avant-Garde: Explorations in Modernism* (LaSalle, Ill.: Library Press, 1973), p. 208.
2. André Breton, "La Nuit du Rose-Hôtel et la Collection 'Révélation' qu'elle inaugure," p. 9.
3. José Pierre, *Le surréalisme* (Lausanne: Editions Rencontre, 1966), p. 9.
4. Gilles Ehrmann, *Les inspirés et leurs demeures* (Paris: Le Temps, [1962]).
5. José Pierre, *Le surréalisme: dictionnaire de poche* (Paris: Fernand Hazan, 1973), p. 54.
6. From a letter quoted by Breton in an appendix to his *Second manifeste*, p. 229.
7. André Breton, "Jean-Pierre Brisset," in *Anthologie de l'humour noir* (Paris: Sagittaire, [1940]), p. 145.
8. Robinson, *French Literature*, p. 6.
9. Both photographs are reproduced in André Breton, *Poésie et autre* (Paris: Le Club du meilleur livre, 1960), p. 114.
10. In *Album Eluard* (Paris: Bibliothèque de la Pléiade, 1968), p. 139, Ségalat accompanies a photograph of Breton and Eluard, lying side by side like figures on a medieval tomb, with the words, "On the sand, they play dead. Eluard, artless, is a recumbent figure in good faith, but André Breton has his eyes half open." So eager is Ségalat to contrast Breton's behavior with Eluard's "artlessness" that he does not entertain the possibility that the fault—if fault there were—might have been the photographer's. In the long run, it was Breton who displayed artlessness. When the anti-Stalinist Zavis Kalandra was condemned to death in his native Czechoslovakia, Breton demanded that Eluard, who had abandoned surrealism for communism, intercede in his behalf. Eluard refused. Kalandra was executed in 1950. Visiting Prague in April of that year and Moscow for the May Day celebrations, Eluard showed that he still knew when to keep his eyes closed.
11. Breton and Eluard, eds., *Dictionnaire abrégé du surréalisme*, p. 733.
12. See Breton, "Fronton virage," p. 12.
13. Quoted by Pierre Lazareff in *Paris-Midi*, 3 August 1933.
14. André Breton, "Belvédere," in Gilles Ehrmann, *Les inspirés et leurs demeures*, p. xvii. Breton's text is dated October 1962.
15. Breton, "Fronton virage," p. 18.
16. Ibid., p. 20.
17. André Breton, *Nadja* (Paris: Gallimard, 1928), pp. 63–64.

Chapter 9. "A Certain Point of the Mind"

1. André Breton, *Point du jour* (Paris: Gallimard, 1934), p. 250.
2. Breton delivered his lecture at Conway Hall on 16 June. It was published in English in Herbert Read's symposium, *Surrealism* (London: Black Sun Press,

1936). The French text was offered in *La nouvelle revue Française* in February 1937.

3. André Breton, in Read, *Surrealism*, p. 105.

4. Letter to the author. See J. H. Matthews, ed., *French Surrealist Poetry* (London: University of London Press, 1966; Minneapolis: University of Minnesota Press, 1967), p. 108.

Conclusion

1. Jules Monnerot, *La poésie moderne et le sacré* (Paris: Gallimard, 1945), p. 15.

2. Bédouin, *Poésie surréaliste*, p. 11.

3. See J. H. Matthews, *Toward the Poetics of Surrealism* (Syracuse, N.Y.: Syracuse University Press, 1976).

4. Gérard Legrand, *Breton* (Paris: Pierre Belfond, 1977), p. 7.

5. Ibid., p. 13.

6. André Breton, interview published in *La tour de feu* 63–64 (December 1959), reprinted in *Perpective cavalière* under the title, "Sur Antonin Artaud." See p. 171.

7. Alain Jouffroy, introduction to André Breton, *Clair de terre* (Paris: Gallimard, 1966), p. 13.

8. Ibid., p. 15.

9. Ibid., p. 16.

10. In Robert Champigny, *Pour une esthétique de l'essai* (Paris: Lettres Modernes, 1967).

11. Ibid., p. 14.

12. Jean Schuster, "Les bases théoriques du surréalisme," in *Archives 57/68: batailles pour le surréalisme* (Paris: Eric Losfeld, 1969), p. 153.

13. Champigny, *Pour une esthétique de l'essai*, pp. 15–16.

14. Ibid., p. 17.

Bibliography

Artaud, Antonin. *Oeuvres complètes*. Vol. 1. Paris: Gallimard, 1956.

Balakian, Anna. *Surrealism: The Road to the Absolute*. New York: Dutton, 1970.

Bédoin, Jean-Louis. *Benjamin Péret*. Paris: Seghers, 1961.

———. *La Poésie surréaliste*. Paris: Seghers, 1964.

Bounoure, Vincent, ed. *Civilisation surréaliste*. Paris: Payot, 1976.

Breton, André. *Anthologie de l'humoir noir*. 1940. Rev. ed. Paris: Jean-Jacques Pauvert, 1966.

———. *Arcane 17 ente d'Adjours*. Paris: Sagittaire, 1947.

———. "La mise sons whisky marin se fait en crème kaki l'en cinq anatomies—vive le sport—Max Ernst." From exhibition catalog. *An sans pareil—Exposition Dada—Max Ernst*. 1921.

———. *Clair de terre*. Paris: Gallimard, 1966.

———. *La clé des champs*. Paris: Sagittaire, 1953.

———. *Légitime Défense*. Le Revolution Surrealiste, no. 8 (December 1926).

———. *Nadja*. Paris: Gallimard, 1928.

———. "La nuit du Rose-Hôtel et la collection 'Révélation' qu'elle inaugure." Preface to Maurice Fourre's novel, *La nuit du Rose-Hôtel*. Paris: Gallimard, 1950.

———. *Manifestes du surréalisme, Poisson soluble*. Paris: Jean-Jacques Pauvert, n.d. [1962].

———. *Ode à Charles Fourier*. Edition commentée by Jean Gaulmier. Paris: Klincksieck, 1961.

———. *Les pas perdus*. Paris: Editions de la Nouvelle Revue Française, 1924.

———. *Perspective cavalière*. Paris: Gallimard, 1970.

———. *Poésie et autre*. Paris: Le Club du Meilleur Livre, 1960.

———. *Point du jour*. Paris: Gallimard, 1934.

———. *Le surréalisme et la peinture*. Paris: Gallimard, 1965.

———. *Les Vases Communicants*. Paris: Gallimard, [1955].

———. *Yves Tanguy*. New York: Pierre Matisse Editions, 1946.

Breton, André, and Jean Schuster. "Art poetique." *BIEF: jonction surréaliste* 7 (1 June 1959): no pagination.

Breton, André and Paul Eluard, eds. *Dictionnaire abrégé du surréalisme*. 1938. Reprint. Paris: José Corti, 1969.

Caillois, Roger. "Divergences et complicités." *La nouvelle revue française* 172 (1 April 1967): 686–98.

Calas, Nicholas. *Art in the Age of Risk*. New York: Dutton, 1968.

Champigny, Robert. *Pour une esthétique de l'essai*. Paris: Lettres Modernes, 1967.

Chomsky, Noam. "Mental Representations." *Syracuse Scholar* 4, 2 (Fall 1983).

Ducasse, Isidore, Comte de Lautréamont. *Poésies, première édition commentée*. Paris: Le Terrain Vague, 1960 [actually not published until 1962].

Ehrmann, Gilles. *Les inspirés et leurs demeures*. Paris: Le Temps, [1962].

Eluard, Paul. "Prière d'insérer pour 'se derrière les fagots' de Benjamin Péret." In *Jeures Complètes*. Paris: Pléiade, Gallimard, 1968.

Ernst, Max. "Au delà de la peinture." *Cahiers d'Art*, no. 6–7 (1936).

Ferry, Jean. *Une étude sur Raymond Roussel*. Paris: Arcane, 1953.

Gaudin, Colette. "Tours et detours négatifs dans 'La confession dédaigneuse' de Breton." *Romanic Review* 71, no. 4 (November 1980): 394–412.

Gauss, Charles Edward. *The Aesthetic Theories of French Artists from Realism to Surrealism*. Baltimore: Johns Hopkins University Press, 1966.

Hammond, Paul. *The Shadow and Its Shadow: Surrealist Writings on Cinema*. London: British Film Institute, 1978.

Kyrou, Adonis. *Le surréalisme au cinéma*. Rev. ed. Paris: Le Terrain Vague, 1963.

Lazareff, Pierre. [Article]. *Paris-Midi*. 3 August 1933.

Legrand, Gérard. *Breton*. Paris: Pierre Belfond, 1977.

Lippard, Lucy R., ed. *Surrealists on Art*. Englewood Cliffs, N.J.: Prentice-Hall, 1970.

Luca, Gherasim, Gellu Naum, Virgil Teodorescu, and Trost. *Eloge de "Malombra."* Bucharest: 1947; *L'age du cinéma* 4–5 (August–November 1951).

Mabille, Pierre. *Le Merveilleux*. Paris: Editions des Quatres Vents, 1946.

Mariën, Marcel. *Marcel Mariën: rétrospective et nouveautés, 1937–67*. Brussels: Galerie Defacqz, 1967.

Matthews, J. H., ed. *An Anthology of French Surrealist Poetry*. London: University of London Press, 1966; Minneapolis: University of Minnesota Press, 1967.

———. Review of William S. Rubin, *Dada and Surrealist Art*. In *Surrealist Transformations* 6 (1973): 38–43.

———. *Toward the Poetics of Surrealism*. Syracuse, N.Y.: Syracuse University Press, 1976.

Mayoux, Jehan. "Benjamin Péret: la fourchette coupant." *Le Surréalisme, même* 2 (Spring 1957): 150–58.

Mitrani, Nora. "Le Congrès s'amuse." *Médium: communication surréaliste*, n.s. (November 1953).

Monnerot, Jules. *La poésie moderne et le sacré*. Paris: Gallimard, 1945.

Nurse, Peter H., ed. *The Art of Criticism: Essays in French Literary Analysis*. Edinburgh: Edinburgh University Press, 1969.

Péret, Benjamin. *"Le déshonneur des poètes" précédé de "La parole est à Péret."* Paris: Jean-Jacques Pauvert, n.d. [1965].

———. "La Pensée est UNE et indivisible." *VVV* 4 (February 1944): 9–13.

Pierre, José. "Dada, le surréalisme et le ketchup." *La Quinzaine littéraire*,

16–30 September 1975.

———. *Le surréalisme*. Lausanne: Editions Rencontre, 1966; Paris: Fernand Hazen, 1973.

Read, Herbert., ed. *Surrealism*. London: Black Sun Press, 1963.

Robinson, Christopher. *French Literature in the Twentieth Century*. Totowa, N.J.: Barnes and Noble, 1980.

Rubin, William S. *Dada and Surrealist Art*. New York: Harry N. Abrams, n.d. [1968].

Schuster, Jean. *Archives 57/68: batailles pour le surréalisme*. Paris: Eric Losfeld, 1969.

———. *Développements sur "l'infra-réalisme" de Matta*. Paris: Eric Losfeld, 1970.

———. "A l'ordre de la nuit, au désordre du jour." *L'Archibras* (1 April 1967): 4–9.

Ségalat, Roger J., ed. *Album Eluard*. Paris: Bibliothèque de la Pléiade, 1968.

Simon, John K., ed. *Modern French Criticism from Proust and Valéry to Structuralism*. Chicago: University of Chicago Press, 1972.

Soby, James Thrall., ed. *Yves Tanguy*. New York: Museum of Modern Art, 1955.

Soupault, Philippe. *Profils perdus*. Paris: Mercure de France, 1963.

Surrealist Intrusion in the Enchanter's Domain. New York: D'Arcy Galleries, 1960.

Tinel, André. "Format écolier." *Cahiers Dada surréalisme* 1 (1967): 76–91.

Weightman, John. *The Concept of Avant-Garde: Explorations in Modernism*. LaSalle, Ill.: Library Press, 1973.

Weinberg, Bernard. *The Limits of Symbolism*. Chicago: University of Chicago Press, 1966.

Index

Alquié, Ferdinand, 20
Apollinaire, Guillaume, 32
Aragon, Louis, 31, 52, 62, 96, 135, 173
Arp, Jean (Hans), 120, 157, 164
Arrabal, Fernando, 177
Artaud, Antonin, 131, 132, 134, 177, 212

Balakian, Anna, 19, 20
Baudelaire, Charles, 165
Beckett, Samuel, 167
Bédouin, Jean-Louis, 68, 131–33, 137, 209–10, 213
Borges, Jose-Luis, 166
Bounoure, Vincent, 67–68, 71, 143
Braque, Georges, 151–52, 155
Braun, Sidney D., 19
Breton, André, 15–19, 21–23, 25, 27–35, 37–40, 42–57, 59–62, 66–67, 69–72, 76–83, 85, 87, 90–98, 100–102, 105–6, 112–14, 121–28, 130–40, 146–64, 167, 172–84, 186–89, 191–208, 212, 215–17
Brisset, Jean-Pierre, 177
Brown, Frederick, 130
Brunius, Jacques B., 179, 180
Buñel, Luis, 123, 179

Calas, Nicolas, 77
Callois, Roger, 21
Camus, Albert, 172
Cardinal, Roger, 124–25, 128
Céline, 10
Champigny, Robert, 216–18
Char, René, 96
Cheval, Ferdinand (Le Facteur), 164, 174, 178–84
Chomsky, Noam, 55
Corbière, Tristan, 50
Corcuff, Leon, 174
Cortazar, 166
Crastre, Victor, 20

Cravan, Arthur, 131
Crevel, René, 57, 62

Dada, 19, 29, 60, 108, 116–17
Dali, Salvador, 30, 96, 107, 121–22, 177
De Chazal, Malcolm, 164
De Chirico, Giorgio, 146, 155–56, 176
Derain, André, 151, 155–56
De Saint-Pierre, Bernardin, 165
Descartes, René, 134, 139
Desnos, Robert, 217
Dostoievsky, Fyodor, 61
Ducasse, Isadore. See Lautréamont, compte de
Duchamp, Marcel, 95, 146, 174
Dufy, Raoul, 120
Dujardin, Edouard, 165
Dumur, Guy, 23

Effenberger, Vratislav, 67–68, 71
Ehrmann, Gilles, 174, 179, 181
Elléouët, Aube (Breton), 181
Eluard, Paul, 62, 81, 96, 132–35, 139
Ernst, Max, 81, 88–89, 91, 96, 101–3, 120, 122, 146, 152–53, 156, 158, 177

Fauvism, 84, 165, 168
Ferry, Jean, 138, 180, 182
Foucault, Michel, 167
Fourier, Charles, 124
Fourré, Maurice, 167, 169, 171–72, 174
Frances, Esteban, 121
Freud, Sigmund, 19, 27, 39, 43, 52
Futurism, 165

Gallimard, Gaston, 134, 172
Gauss, Charles Edward, 19
Gide, André, 32, 131
Giorgione, 177
Glahn, Lt., 31

Goldfayn, Georges, 129, 137
Gracq, Julian, 130, 134
Granell, E. F. (Eugenio Fernandez), 11

Hamsun, Knud, 31
Hegel, 19
Hooreman, Paul, 150

Ingres, 179
Ionesco, Eugène, 177

Jarry, Alfred, 177
Jezek, Jaroslav, 150
John XXIII (pope), 123
Jouffroy, Alain, 201, 215–16
Joyce, James, 166

Kandinsky, Wassily, 175–76
Kyrou, Ado, 134–35, 137, 179

Lane, Helen R., 192
Lautréamont, compte de (Isadore Ducasse), 121, 129–30, 137, 167, 177
Lawrence, D. H. (David Herbert), 166
Lebel, Jean-Jacques, 169
Legrand, Gérard, 129, 137, 212, 214
Limbour, Georges, 177
Lippard, Lucy R., 18–19
Loti, Pierre, 167, 177

Mabille, Pierre, 92–93, 131–32
Maddox, Conroy, 121
Magritte, René, 120, 170
Mallarmé, Stéphane, 32, 87–88
Man Ray, 156
Mansour, Joyce, 10, 97
Mariën, Marcel, 95
Masson, André, 152–53
Matta (Roberto Antonio Sebastian Matta Echaurrén), 97, 107, 121
Maupassant, Guy de, 10
Mayoux, Jehan, 10, 132
Miró, Joan, 81, 122, 137, 152–53, 156, 160
Mitrani, Nora, 208
Monnerot, Jules, 209
Moreau, Gustave, 146
Murnau, F. W., 156

Naville, Pierre, 81, 105, 150–52, 154
Nougé, Paul, 120

Onslow-Ford, Gordon Max, 121

Perceval, 134, 139
Péret, Benjamin, 10–11, 52, 62, 66, 81, 90, 92, 121–22, 130–34, 137–39, 150, 208–9, 211, 213, 216
Picabia, Francis, 155
Picasso, Pablo, 151–52, 154–55, 167, 171
Pierre, José, 18, 110, 113, 150, 173, 176
Poe, Edgar Allen, 153, 215
Prassinos, Gisèle, 177

Queneau, Raymond, 166

Ragghianti, Carlo Ludovico, 170
Read, Herbert, 53
Redon, Odilon, 146
Reverdy, Pierre, 113
Rimbaud, Arthur, 130, 203, 206
Riviére, Jacques, 131
Robbe-Grillet, Alain, 167
Robinson, Christopher, 85, 177
Rousseau, Henri (Le Douanier), 171, 175–76
Roussel, Raymond, 131, 138, 167, 175, 177, 180, 182–84
Royère, Jean, 32
Rubin, William Stanley, 109–10, 112, 115, 154

Saint-Pol-Roux, 126
Sampson, George, 166
Sartre, Jean-Paul, 165–66
Schuster, Jean, 39, 76, 96–97, 127, 129–30, 135, 138, 216
Searver, Richard, 192
Siqueiros, David Alfaro, 97
Soldati, Mario, 135
Soupault, Philippe, 27–29, 31, 37–38, 135, 182
Souris, André, 150
Stendhal, 32, 94
Symbolism, 74

Tanguy, Yves, 81, 93–96, 112, 120, 135–37, 146–49, 152, 157–59
Tintel, André, 124
Titian, 177
Trevelyan, Julien, 98

Trouille, Clovis, 171, 176–77

Vaché, Jacques, 32, 131
Valéry, Paul, 32, 132
Verlaine, Paul, 86
Verne, Jules, 177
Viélé-Griffin, Francis, 32
Vinci, Leonardo da, 123

Von Sternberg, Joseph, 135
Vorticism, 165

Weightman, John, 171
Weinberg, Bernard, 125–28

Zola, Emile, 10